BORN-DIGITAL
DESIGN RECORDS

TRENDS IN
ARCHIVES
PRACTICE

Trends in Archives Practice is an open-ended series by the Society of American Archivists featuring brief, authoritative treatments—written and edited by top-level professionals—that fill significant gaps in archival literature. Modules treat discrete topics relating to the practical management of archives and manuscript collections in the digital age. They are essential reading for students and practicing archivists, as well as for anyone applying archival practices to information management challenges.

Modules are clustered together by topic and can be purchased in print or digital format (Adobe Digital Editions PDF, EPUB, or Amazon Kindle). Modules are also available individually in digital format so that readers can mix and match modules that best satisfy their needs and interests. All are available at archivists.org/bookstore.

ARCHIVAL ARRANGEMENT AND DESCRIPTION
Module 1: *Standards for Archival Description*
Module 2: *Processing Digital Records and Manuscripts*
Module 3: *Designing Descriptive and Access Systems*

RIGHTS IN THE DIGITAL ERA
Module 4: *Understanding Copyright Law*
Module 5: *Balancing Privacy and Restrictions: Personal and Family Papers*
Module 6: *Balancing Privacy and Restrictions: Organizational, Business, and Government Records*
Module 7: *Managing Rights and Permissions*

BECOMING A TRUSTED DIGITAL REPOSITORY (*Module 8*)

TEACHING WITH PRIMARY SOURCES
Module 9: *Contextualizing Archival Literacy*
Module 10: *Teaching with Archives: A Guide for Archivists, Librarians, and Educators*
Module 11: *Connecting Students and Primary Sources: Cases and Examples*

DIGITAL PRESERVATION
Module 12: *Preserving Digital Objects*
Module 13: *Digital Preservation Storage and Retrieval*

APPRAISAL AND ACQUISITION STRATEGIES
Module 14: *Appraising Digital Records*
Module 15: *Collecting Digital Manuscripts and Archives*
Module 16: *Accessioning Digital Archives*

PUTTING DESCRIPTIVE STANDARDS TO WORK
Module 17: *Implementing DACS: A Guide to the Archival Content Standard*
Module 18: *Using EAD3*
Module 19: *Introducing EAC-CPF*
Module 20: *Sharing Archival Metadata*

ENGAGEMENT IN THE DIGITAL ERA
Module 21: *Lights, Camera, Archives!*
Module 22: *Engaging Users with Archives: Programs That Get Results*
Module 23: *Establishing Archival Connections through Online Engagement*

BORN-DIGITAL DESIGN RECORDS
Module 24: *Navigating the Technical Landscape of Born-Digital Design Records*
Module 25: *Emerging Best Practices in the Accession, Preservation, and Emulation of Born-Digital Design Records*
Module 26: *Case Studies in Born-Digital Design Records*

TRENDS IN
ARCHIVES
PRACTICE

BORN-DIGITAL DESIGN RECORDS

Edited by Samantha Winn

SOCIETY OF
American
Archivists

CHICAGO

Society of American Archivists
www.archivists.org

© 2022 by the Society of American Archivists.

All rights reserved. No part of this publication may be reproduced, stored in a retrieval system, or transmitted in any form or by any means without prior permission from the publisher.

Library of Congress Control Number: 2022940339

Printed in the United States of America.

ISBN-978-1-945246-87-6 (paperback)
ISBN-978-1-945246-85-2 (pdf)
ISBN-978-1-945246-86-9 (ePub)

Graphic design by Sweeney Design, kasween@sbcglobal.net.

Table *of* Contents

INTRODUCTION
ABOUT BORN-DIGITAL DESIGN RECORDS • 1
SAMANTHA WINN

MODULE 24
NAVIGATING THE TECHNICAL LANDSCAPE OF BORN-DIGITAL DESIGN RECORDS • 11
KRISTINE FALLON, ALIZA LEVENTHAL, AND ZACH VOWELL

MODULE 25
EMERGING BEST PRACTICES IN THE ACCESSION, PRESERVATION, AND EMULATION OF BORN-DIGITAL DESIGN MATERIALS • 87
JODY THOMPSON, EUAN COCHRANE, ALIZA LEVENTHAL, LAURA SCHROFFEL, AND EMILY VIGOR

MODULE 26
CASE STUDIES IN BORN-DIGITAL DESIGN RECORDS • 165
ALIZA LEVENTHAL, STEFANA BREITWIESER, ALEXANDRA JOKINEN, MIREILLE NAPPERT, AND ZACH VOWELL

INTRODUCTION

About *Born-Digital Design Records*

SAMANTHA WINN

The Society of American Archivists' (SAA) Architectural Records Roundtable (ARR), renamed Design Records Section (DRS) in 2017, first mobilized in 1985 to build on the momentum of the Cooperative Preservation of Architectural Records project (CoPAR). Aiming to foster camaraderie, provide a community of practice, and support scholarship among archival workers caring for design records, the DRS celebrated its twenty-fifth anniversary at the 2015 SAA Annual Meeting in Cleveland. Founding member Tawny Ryan Nelb recounted milestones in the section's history and called for a new wave of scholarship to document the advancements in archival practice regarding records of the built environment.

This call resonated strongly with the Design Records Section leaders. In 2015, Aliza Leventhal began her first term as section co-chair. I joined her in 2016 as junior co-chair, and we began working on various publication proposals with the 2016–2017 steering committee. The following modules represent the culmination of one such initiative. Like many section members, I first encountered born-digital design records in the field. In 2014, I began as a collections archivist for Virginia Tech's International Archives of Women in Architecture (IAWA). The management of born-digital design records from ingest to access was among the stickiest challenges of my tenure. It also guided the future of Virginia Tech University Library's approach to digital assets management and data preservation. For every successful project and program, I remain indebted to the cutting-edge research of Design Records Section members, critical insights from the IAWA board and other industry leaders, and a bevy of interdisciplinary troubleshooters from within and beyond the university.

Written and informed by some of the leading voices in the management of born-digital design records, these modules represent the collaborative output of many current and former DRS steering committee members and taskforce leaders, industry partners, and pioneers in the application of computer-aided design. The modules deal with the unique technical landscape of born-digital design records; emerging best practices in the accession, preservation, and emulation of these materials; and functional case studies from a variety of academic, corporate, and museum-based archives. With historical overviews, use cases, practical tool registries, sample workflows, and robust glossaries of terms, these modules are designed to appeal to archival workers in a variety of institutional contexts, including business archives, architectural firms, museums, universities, and government offices. The modules provide archival workers of all experience levels with an accessible introduction to the management of digital design records.

The authors of these modules constitute a deep roster of theoretical and practical expertise across multiple industries and institution types. In Module 24, "Navigating the Technical Landscape of Born-Digital Design Records," architect Kristine Fallon partners with Aliza Leventhal, former DRS leader and former corporate archivist with Sasaki Associates, and Zach Vowell, principle investigator for Software Preservation Network, to document technical concepts and dependencies for the successful management of born-digital design records. Laura Schroffel of the Getty Research Institute, Jody Thompson of Georgia Tech, Emily Vigor of the University of California Berkeley's Environmental Design Archives, Euan Cochrane of Yale University, and Aliza Leventhal capture the state of practice in Module 25, "Emerging Best Practices in the Accession, Preservation, and

Emulation of Born-Digital Design Records." Finally, Aliza Leventhal and Zach Vowell partner with Stefana Breitwieser of the Icahn School of Medicine's Arthur H. Aufses, Jr., MD Archives; Alex Jokinen of the Canadian Center for Architecture; and Mireille Nappert of HEC Montréal in Module 26, "Case Studies in Born-Digital Design Records," to present a series of explanatory case studies which tie together recommendations of the prior two modules.

Milestones in the Management of Born-Digital Design Records

Custodians of traditionally analog design records can refer to guidelines and best practices which emerged directly from or alongside the early work of CoPAR and the DRS, including Schrock and Cooper's *Records for Architectural Offices: Suggestions for the Organization, Storage, and Conservation of Architectural Office Archives* (1992), Porter and Thornes's *A Guide to the Description of Architectural Drawings* (1994), the International Council on Archives' *A Guide to the Archival Care of Architectural Records: 19th–20th Centuries* (2000), and Waverly B. Lowell and Tawny Ryan Nelb's landmark 2006 book, *Architectural Records: Managing Design and Construction Records*.

Meanwhile, design professions have operated in digital environments for decades, with early computer-aided design (CAD) explorations dating back to the early 1960s.[1] By the turn of the twenty-first century, the vast majority of design records were born digital. In her 1998 review of computing in design, Kristine Fallon reported that "more than 85 percent of design firms" had licenses for Autodesk's CAD systems by the mid-1990s, representing both the broad adoption of CAD technology in design and the dominance of Autodesk's proprietary software. Similarly, in their 2015 thesis, "Preservation and Access of Born-Digital Architectural Design Records in an OAIS-Type Archive," Tessa Walsh reported that building information modeling

---

[1] Kristine Fallon, "Early Computer Graphics Developments in the Architecture, Engineering and Construction Industry," *IEEE Annals of the History of Computing* 20, no. 2 (1998): 21–23, https://doi.org/10.1109/85.667293.

(BIM) systems were employed by more than 70 percent of North American architects and contractors in 2012.[2]

Archival workers have discussed the management of born-digital design records for nearly as long as firms have produced them, anticipating the challenges such records would bring when the pioneering generations of CAD/BIM users retired.[3] In 1994, the Canadian Centre for Architecture partnered with the Joint Committee on Canadian Architectural Records and Research (JCCARR) and SAA's Architectural Records Roundtable to host a Working Conference on Establishing Principles for the Appraisal and Selection of Architectural Records.[4] *American Archivist* dedicated its Spring 1996 special issue to architectural, engineering, and construction records, featuring significant coverage of the 1994 Working Conference and its sponsoring entities.

In his comprehensive history of the conference proceedings, Nicholas Olsberg, ARR chair from 1992 to 1994, warned that "only a fraction of the world's archives have electronic records programs or expertise" and expressed concern that archivists were particularly unprepared to address the logistical and legal challenges of providing access to born-digital design records.[5] Olsberg called on archivists to develop case studies "to evaluate the effect of electronic techniques on the nature, permanence, and accessibility of essential documentation of the design process."[6] In "Architectural Archives in the Digital Era," architecture professor and scholar, William J. Mitchell reported on the

---

[2] Tessa Walsh, "Preservation and Access of Born-Digital Architectural Design Records in an OAIS-Type Archive," Monograph. Simmons College, 2015, 6–7, https://spectrum.library.concordia.ca/985426.

[3] This history has been documented most extensively by Ann R. E. Armstrong, "Architectural Archives/Archiving Architecture: The Digital ERA," *Art Documentation: Journal of the Art Libraries Society of North America* 25, no. 2 (2006): 12–17, https://doi.org/10.1086/adx.25.2.27949434; Kathryn Pierce, "Collaborative Efforts to Preserve Born-Digital Architectural Records: A Case Study Documenting Present-Day Practice," *Art Documentation: Journal of the Art Libraries Society of North America* 30, no. 2 (2011): 43–48, https://doi.org/10.1086/adx.30.2.41244064; Anne Barrett, "Born-Digital Architectural Records: Defining the Archivable Record," University of North Carolina at Chapel Hill, 2012, https://doi.org/10.17615/m3x3-mg52; Laura Tatum, "Documenting Design: A Survey of State-of-the-Art Practice for Archiving Architectural Records," *Art Documentation: Journal of the Art Libraries Society of North America* 21, no. 2 (2002): 25–31, https://doi.org/10.1086/adx.21.2.27949204; and Walsh, "Preservation and Access of Born-Digital Architectural Design Records."

[4] For a comprehensive discussion of the Working Conference behind the scenes, see Nicholas Olsberg, "Documenting Twentieth-Century Architecture: Crisis and Opportunity," *American Archivist* 59, no. 2 (1996): 128–135, https://doi.org/10.17723/aarc.59.2.987g764618231248.

[5] Olsberg, "Documenting Twentieth-Century Architecture," 132–133.

[6] Olsberg, "Documenting Twentieth-Century Architecture," 133–135.

rapid adoption of digital records in architectural practice.[7] Mitchell warned that "the combined problems of immense volume, unstable storage media, and obsolete software and hardware add up to some very tough problems for the archivist to deal with," noting further challenges with conflicting intellectual property interests.[8]

Despite these early insights, practitioners struggled to implement scalable solutions or standard practices. In a 2002 survey published in *Art Documentation*, Laura Tatum argued that American archivists were so focused on providing electronic access to digitized materials that they were simply "not yet dealing with the issue of digitally-born information."[9] Although Tatum lauded individual efforts by archival consultant Tawny Ryan Nelb, her analysis found that most advancements came out of architectural and archaeological practice. She cited the long-term contributions of William J. Mitchell and presentations by architects and architectural technologists at the 2000 *Architectural Records Conference by the Conservation Center for Art and Historic Artifacts*.[10] John Burns, Bradley Hörst, and Tony Aeck spoke from their experiences in architectural firms and historical preservation offices.[11] Recognizing that born-digital design records meet different needs throughout their lifecycle, Aeck called for a "strategic alliance" between design professionals and preservation fields.[12]

Moving Toward Solutions

The first decade of the twenty-first century saw a renaissance of cross-disciplinary collaborations. In 2004, the Department of Architecture

---

7   William Mitchell, "Architectural Archives in the Digital Era," edited by Nicholas Olsberg. *American Archivist* 59, no. 2 (1996): 201–202, https://doi.org/10.17723/aarc.59.2.506h724783065016.
8   Mitchell, "Architectural Archives in the Digital Era," 203–204.
9   Tatum, "Documenting Design," 25.
10 Tatum, "Documenting Design," 27–28.
11 John A. Burns, "The Digital Revolution and Architectural Records: HABS/HAER at the Threshold of the Twenty-First Century," Philadelphia, PA, 2000, https://web.archive.org/web/20050427171201/http://www.ccaha.org/arch_rec/lecture.php?lec_id=burns_digital; Bradly Hörst, "Guidelines for Managing and Preserving Electronic Files in an Architectural Firm," Philadelphia, PA, 2000, https://web.archive.org/web/20050501082606/http://www.ccaha.org/arch_rec/lecture.php?lec_num=22; Tony Aeck, "Current and Emerging Documentation and Archiving Methods in Architectural Practice," Philadelphia, PA, 2000, https://web.archive.org/web/20050427170812/http://www.ccaha.org/arch_rec/lecture.php?lec_id=aeck_current.
12 Aeck, "Current and Emerging Documentation and Archiving Methods."

of the Art Institute of Chicago published *Collecting, Archiving and Exhibiting Digital Design Data*, a landmark study conducted by Kristine Fallon Associates that established some of the first concrete and scalable recommendations for cultural heritage organizations.[13] ISO 82045-5:2005, "Application of metadata for the construction and facility management sector," was adopted in July 2005.[14]

In 2007, several implementation teams met in Paris to showcase their progress toward preserving born-digital design records. Highlighted projects included the AIC's Digital Archive for Architecture System (DAArch), which sought to implement the recommendations of the 2004 Art Institute/Fallon Associates study.[15] Other projects which gained traction in this decade included the European Union's SHAMAN project (Sustaining Heritage Access Through Multivalent Archiving) and MIT's FAÇADE (Future-proofing Architectural Computer-Aided Design) project, funded in part by Institute of Museum and Library Services (IMLS) and conducted from 2006 to 2009.[16] These were followed by FAÇADE2, a joint collaboration between MIT and Harvard, and DURAARK (Durable Architectural Knowledge) in Europe.[17] Although these initiatives laid significant groundwork for future solutions by examining essential functions, building workflows, and testing technical requirements, no single system emerged as a transferrable, sustainable, and scalable platform for the preservation of born-digital design records.[18]

In August 2012, SAA's DRS established a dedicated taskforce—the Digital Design Records Taskforce, originally named the CAD/BIM Taskforce—to investigate the future of born-digital design records. Recognizing the progression of architectural practice and the growing adoption of digital design records as contractual documents, the taskforce aimed to identify research and advocacy needs, build relationships with experts in adjacent fields, and establish best practices

---

13 Kristine Fallon Associates, Inc., "Digital Design Data: Project Update, October 2007." As of this publication, the full report is available at https://web.archive.org/web/20180926091355/http://www.artic.edu/collections/digital-design-data.
14 It was withdrawn in January 2016. 14:00-17:00, "ISO 82045-5."
15 David Peyceré and Florence Wierre, eds., *Architecture and Digital Archives, Architecture in the Digital Age: A Question of Memory* (Gollion: Infolio, 2008).
16 Alex Ball, "Preserving Computer-Aided Design (CAD)," 1st ed. Digital Preservation Coalition, April 1, 2013, 21–22, https://doi.org/10.7207/twr13-02.
17 Harvard Library Lab, "FACADE2," https://osc.hul.harvard.edu/liblab/projects/facade2; "DURAARK – Durable Architectural Knowledge, http://duraark.eu.
18 Walsh, "Preservation and Access of Born-Digital Architectural Design Records," 12–14.

for preservation and emulation of born-digital design records.[19] One of the group's first initiatives was an ambitious bibliography of born-digital design record history.[20] Subsequent projects included international surveys of digital design holdings in the United States, Canada, and United Kingdom; an updated bibliography of foundational, interdisciplinary resources; panel presentations at SAA Annual Meetings and Research Forums; and special publications through SAA, including these modules.

Expanding and Developing Resources

In recent years, many conversations and resources have evolved within individual institutions, like the Canadian Centre for Architecture (CCA), as well as through collaborations such as the ones facilitated by the Software Preservation Network (SPN) and Digital Design Records Taskforce (DDRTF). The CCA has demonstrated significant capacity for developing transferable tools and workflows,[21] and has made many of its in-house digital preservation tools free and open-source.[22] The SPN, which maintains significant ties with the DDRTF, has hosted research forums, exploratory grants, and communities of practice for the preservation and emulation of software in cultural heritage institutions.

Three additional forums have provided significant platforms for advancement and collaboration in recent years. "Designing the Future Landscape: Digital Architecture, Design and Engineering Assets," a meeting that took place in November 2017, reflected the most significant gathering of design professionals and cultural heritage

---

19   Society of American Archivists, "Digital Design Records Taskforce," https://www2
     .archivists.org/groups/design-records-section/digital-design-records-taskforce, captured at
     https://perma.cc/7G95-34T7.
20   Aliza Leventhal and Ines Zalduendo, "Draft Bibliography on Studies Dealing with Legal,
     Technical, and Curatorial Issues Related to Born-Digital Architectural Records," Digital
     Design Records Task Force, Society of American Archivists, 2013, https://www2.archivists
     .org/sites/all/files/AR%20Taskforce_Born%20Digital%20StudiesBibliography_AL+IZ
     _FinalDraft_revised.pdf, captured at https://perma.cc/X748-EH5M.
21   Canadian Centre of Architecture (CCA), "Coping with Complex Digital Objects"
     documents CCA's innovations in digital preservation and archaeology between 2013 and
     2016. For further discussion of tools developed for digital design records, see Tessa Walsh,
     "Data-Driven Reporting and Processing of Digital Archives with Brunnhilde," *Practical
     Technology for Archives* 1, no. 8 (2017), https://digitalcommons.ilr.cornell.edu/pta/vol1
     /iss8/1.
22   The majority are available from https://github.com/CCA-Public.

professionals on the question of born-digital design records since the 2000 *Architectural Records Conference by the Conservation Center for Art and Historic Artifacts*.[23] In April 2018, Harvard University hosted the IMLS-funded forum, *Building for Tomorrow: Collaborative Development of Sustainable Infrastructure for Architectural and Design Documentation*.[24] In April 2020, the Digital Preservation Coalition hosted the United Kingdom-based virtual briefing day, *Building a Digital Future: Challenges & Solutions for Preserving 3D Models*, during which speakers from a range of backgrounds and experiences described preservation challenges and solutions developed in a variety of digital contexts.[25]

The first two of these historic gatherings provided fuel for the writing of these modules in 2018, which aim to capture the state of archival practice at the beginning of a new decade. The authors of these modules have outlined the norms of record production in design professions, explained fundamental technical challenges for the transfer and preservation of these records, and demonstrated adaptable workflows from a variety of institutional contexts. Other recent publications of note include

- reports from the multi-institution emulation research cohort, Fostering a Community of Practice (FCOP), hosted by SPN from 2018 to 2020, which covers a variety of topics, including the University of Virginia's work with born-digital design records;[26]
- the article "An Archive of Interfaces: Exploring the Potential of Emulation for Software Research, Pedagogy, and Design" by Daniel Cardoso-Llach, Eric Kaltman, Emek Erdolu, and Zachary Furste, who facilitated a cross-discipline exploratory course leveraging EaaSI as a potential pedagogical tool for

---

23 Aliza Leventhal, *Designing the Future Landscape: Digital Architecture, Design & Engineering Assets,* Washington, DC: Library of Congress, 2018, https://loc.gov/preservation/digital/meetings/DesigningTheFutureLandscapeReport.pdf, captured at https://perma.cc/GC8Y-LLVF.
24 Ann Whiteside, "Building for Tomorrow Forum Report," September 2018, https://projects.iq.harvard.edu/files/buildingtomorrow/files/building_for_tomorrow_-_forum_report.pdf, captured at https://perma.cc/7E4Q-LN4C.
25 Digital Preservation Coalition, "Building a Digital Future: Challenges & Solutions for Preserving 3D Models," April 2020, https://www.dpconline.org/events/past-events/preserving-3d-digital-engineering-models-a-briefing-day.
26 Fostering a Community of Practice, https://www.softwarepreservationnetwork.org/fcop.

teaching architecture, architectural history, and technology history;[27]
- the Fall/Winter 2021 issue of *American Archivist* (volume 84, issue 2), which features a special section on architecture and design records, including born-digital design records;[28]
- the 2021 Digital Preservation Coalition Technology Watch Report *Preserving Born-Digital Design and Construction Records* by Aliza Leventhal and Jody Thompson, which provides archival professionals, active designers, and facilities managers with context to consider preservation approaches that account for both the technical and cultural components of the broad range of complex digital objects created throughout the course of designing, implementing, and maintaining a built space.[29]

Significant opportunity remains for future research, however. The community still needs viable preservation frameworks that can be implemented at scale, particularly for records and data produced in cloud-based environments. We also need a better understanding of how researchers will use these materials in the future. It is our hope that this publication will mark progress toward standardization and best practices that can be implemented by a broad spectrum of archival workers.

---

27 Daniel Cardoso-Llach, Eric Kaltman, Emek Erdolu, and Zachary Furste, "An Archive of Interfaces: Exploring the Potential of Emulation for Software Research, Pedagogy, and Design," *Proceedings of the ACM on Human-Computer Interaction* 5, no. 2 (2021): 1–22, https://dl.acm.org/doi/10.1145/3476035.

28 Special Section: Design Records, guest editor Karen Trivette, *American Archivist* 84, no. 2 (2021), https://meridian.allenpress.com/american-archivist/issue/84/2.

29 *Preserving Born-Digital Design and Construction Records*, Digital Preservation Coalition Technology Watch Report, 2021, http://doi.org/10.7207/twr21-01.

Samantha Winn *managed the International Archives of Women in Architecture at Virginia Tech from 2014 to 2020. She co-chaired the Society of American Archivists' Design Records Section from 2016 to 2018 and served on the Digital Design Records Taskforce. In 2020, she joined the University of Arizona's School of Information as a PhD student, where she focuses on comparative archival practice, information ethics, and climate change.*

MODULE 24

NAVIGATING THE TECHNICAL LANDSCAPE OF BORN-DIGITAL DESIGN RECORDS

Kristine Fallon, Aliza Leventhal, and Zach Vowell

Module 24 Contents

Introduction • 15

Digital Design Record Creators and Custodians • 15
    Design Firms • 16
    Facility Management Groups • 17
    Records Management Groups • 18
    Archives and Museum Collections • 19

Design Phases, Workflows, and Products • 19
    Design Phases • 20
    Design Outputs • 21
        Pre-Contract Work • 21
        Pre-Design • 23
        Schematic Design • 23
        Design Development • 24
        Construction Documents • 25
        Procurement • 26
        Construction • 26

Digital Workflows and Archival Assumptions • 28

Case Studies • 29
    Ross Barney Architects • 30
    Valerio Dewalt Train Associates, Inc. • 34

The Nature of Computer Graphic Design Data • 38

Common File Types and Software • 44

Information Forms and Formats • 49
    Unstructured Form • 49
    Structured Form • 50
    Proprietary Format • 50
    Standard Format • 50

Baseline Competencies for Archivists • 51
  Design Data Production Standards • 51
  Format Standards • 55
    Data Type: Drawings, Documents, and Presentations (Without Audio or Video) • 56
    Data Type: Raster Graphics • 57
    Data Type: Vector Graphics • 58
    Data Type: Born-Digital Video • 59
    Data Type: Geospatial • 61
    Data Type: Building Information Modeling (BIM) • 61

Basic Considerations for Archivists • 63
  Common Challenges in Establishing File Integrity • 63
  Navigating Software Dependencies • 68
  Cloud-Based Applications • 70
  Free Readers • 71

Recommendations • 72
  Archival Approaches • 72
  Recommendations for the Design Office • 75

Conclusion • 77

Appendix Glossary of Terminology • 78

Bibliography • 83

14 BORN-DIGITAL DESIGN RECORDS

ABOUT THE AUTHORS

Kristine K. Fallon, FAIA, has been a pioneer in the application of computer technology in the design and construction industries since the 1970s. Her career in the industry as a licensed architect spans forty years, leading technology implementation at major design firms, starting at SOM, as well as twenty-five years in her own firm. In the 1990s, she developed curricula and taught "Computers in Architecture," graduate and undergraduate levels, at the University of Illinois at Chicago. From 2007 to 2016, she again developed curriculum and taught "Computer-Integrated Project Delivery" in the master of project management program at Northwestern University's McCormick School of Engineering. She has been a consultant to software companies, including Autodesk and Revit Technology Corporation; design firms; corporate facilities groups; federal, state and local agencies; and contractors. She has led award-winning technology implementations for capital program management. She has spoken at design and construction technology conferences worldwide, written a number of articles and two books, and conducted federally-funded research on BIM-related topics. She was also the principal consultant and author of the Art Institute of Chicago's 2004 *Collecting, Archiving, and Exhibiting Design Data* study.

Aliza Leventhal contributed to this module in her previous role as the corporate archivist and librarian for Sasaki, a Boston-based interdisciplinary design firm (2014–2019). She currently is the head of the Prints and Photographs Division's Technical Services Section at the Library of Congress. Leventhal is the co-founder and co-chair of the Society of American Archivists' (SAA) Design Records Section's Digital Design Records Task Force, and has written and presented extensively in a variety of forums including SAA, the Visual Resources Association, International Confederation of Architectural Museums, and the Library of Congress. She is the co-author of the Digital Preservation Coalition *Preserving Born-Digital Design and Construction Records* Technology Watch Report. She holds an MLIS and an MA in history from Simmons University's Archives Management Program.

Zach Vowell is a digital archivist at California Polytechnic State University's Robert E. Kennedy Library, where his responsibilities include preserving, describing, and providing access to born-digital design records. He also cofounded the Software Preservation Network (SPN) and co-led two SPN-affiliated IMLS-funded grant projects during his time at Cal Poly. Prior to moving to San Luis Obispo in 2013, Vowell worked as a digital archivist at the Briscoe Center for American History, University of Texas (UT) at Austin, as an archivist for the UT Videogame Archive, and as a digitization project archivist. Vowell also received his MS in information studies from UT–Austin in 2006.

Introduction

This module introduces the production of digital design records, with an overview of workflows, software, and data types commonly used in design for the built environment. In addition, this module reviews essential tools and resources for archivists and offers two case studies of digital practice. The collection policies of museums and archival organizations dictate different treatment of born-digital computer graphic design data. The final third of this module describes technical challenges that archival organizations and museums may encounter, issues that are explored in greater depth in *Module 25: Emerging Best Practices in the Accession, Preservation, and Emulation of Born-Digital Design Materials* and *Module 26: Case Studies in Born-Digital Design Records*. Finally, the module includes a bibliography and a glossary of both design/construction and digital design terminology.

Digital Design Record Creators and Custodians

For many organizations, a digital design file may not, in and of itself, be an object of interest. Often, the focus is the actual building, park, or urban development. Any digital design data are secondary sources that provide insights into the design process and the decisions taken and may also document options explored and rejected. In addition, the design data may document the exact location of "hidden" building or site systems, such as plumbing and electrical runs in walls and buried site infrastructure, and may contain descriptive information about building equipment, such as manufacturer, model number, and performance requirements. This latter information is of particular interest to facility managers and design firms that are renovating or updating a built space or structure.

Where the archive's goal is documentation of a person's or firm's body of work, the born-digital computer graphic design data assume greatest importance when archivists examine unbuilt work or the work product of a designer who uses **algorithmic generation of form**.[1] The data may be the only source of information about unbuilt projects and unsuccessful competition entries. Here are key questions archivists

---

1 Throughout this module, design/construction and digital design terminology are in bold type. Definitions for these terms are compiled in a glossary in the appendix.

must ask themselves when developing an archival approach for born-digital design data:

1. Do you want to be able to modify or manipulate the design file in the future or just view and print it?
2. How long do you want to be able to access or reuse the data? Buildings have long lives compared to software products, and archives are presumably interested in preserving collections in perpetuity.

Each type of organization discussed in this section has some key business and/or regulatory issues to address relating to the preservation of digital design data. All organizations have resource constraints that must be taken into consideration when developing their archiving approach. Museums and institutional archives balance their current and long-term resources with their collection policies to ensure that they are able to continue to build their collections over time. This requires institutions to have appraisal guidelines to prevent having to store and provide access to unwanted or out-of-scope material, as determined by the content (e.g., a project's financial documents) or the format (e.g., physical models).

Design Firms

The design and construction industry is involved in producing high-value, one-off products with a significant impact on public health and safety. Project execution takes place over an extended period of time, often several years. From a business perspective, design firms need to maintain documentation of their work at various project milestones to support invoicing and demonstrate contract compliance. In addition, due to the public health and safety impacts, the final design must be approved by the local zoning and building authority and constructed based on the approved documents. Any deviations during construction must be approved by the designer and shown on **record drawings**, as the designer is professionally liable for the adequacy of the design.

Every design firm needs to safeguard its project documentation accordingly, ideally through its records management program. Since building permits are still issued based on paper or e-paper documents, it is this documentation that must be preserved, and it should never be modified or updated. Adobe's[2] Portable Document Format (PDF) is typically used for this type of documentation. Fortunately, there are legal limits to the period of time after construction when a defect that appears can be considered the architect's fault (statute of repose) and also to the period of time after discovering a defect that a claimant must file suit (statute of limitations). These time periods are established by state law. Thus, the duration for which this portion of the firm's archive must be preserved is limited.

However, every design firm, no matter its size, needs to be able to access and reuse data from former projects. These projects contain proven design elements and technical details that are frequently incorporated into subsequent projects. This creates another use for the archive. Maintaining archives in the format in which the data were produced—a proprietary format—makes the most sense for this use. In the event that the authoring software is discontinued, either by the software vendor or by the firm's decision to move to another product, the firm will need to plan to move this resource data to the new system.

Finally, a former client or new owner may request an addition or alteration to one of the firm's projects. This means that it must be possible to modify the data. However, such a request may not be received until the building has been in operation for twenty-five years. So, there is a need not only for reusability but also for longevity. To address this use, firms should maintain archives also in a standard format appropriate to the original data. Standard formats are discussed later in this module.

Facility Management Groups

The term *facility management* covers a broad range of uses, from space planning and leasing to building equipment operation and maintenance. Many facility management groups use specialized software systems to support these activities. Major components of these systems typically include a graphic capability that displays facility floor plans or their 3D equivalent and a database that contains information about the contents of the facility, including spaces, building systems, equipment, furniture, and so forth. These system components are often linked so that, using a database search, a user can locate a specific room on the

---

2 All brand names, product names, or trademarks belong to their respective holders.

floor plan, or, by selecting a piece of equipment from the floor plan, the user can display its manufacturer, model, size, capacity, installation date, and so on. Significant planning is required to repurpose design data for ingest into such a facility management system. As long as the facility management system is operational, however, the data is accessible and reusable.

Facility management groups are often the caretakers of project-specific documentation beyond that required by the facility management system. To this extent, their role includes responsibilities of a records management group. The documentation in question would include the complete set of project drawings and specifications; the record drawings; and with increasing frequency, the **Building Information Model (BIM)**. BIM is an emerging method of documenting buildings, which contains a nearly complete simulacrum of the building's physical features as well as the information describing the individual components, such as structural member sizes and **properties** and the sustainability properties of the building products and materials. A project's record drawings should not be changed. However, copies of these record drawings (which may be replaced by record building information models in future projects) will be modified when designing updates, additions, and reconfigurations of the facility. Because the life of a building project significantly exceeds that of a software product, this information should be maintained in standard format as well as its original format.

Records Management Groups

Government agencies and large corporations and institutions may have designated records managers, in addition to internal design groups and facility managers. These records managers are responsible for maintaining good documentation of the facilities as they exist and records of previous projects, as well as capturing records from new projects as they close out, and facilitating records destruction based on the organization's records retention schedule.[3] Depending on the type of the facility, there may be regulatory requirements dictating the types of documentation to be maintained. This is particularly the case in the process and pharmaceuticals industry. Typically, records managers are responsible for maintaining static information—data that

---

[3] American Institute of Architects, *The Architect's Handbook for Professional Practice*, 14th ed. (New York: John Wiley & Sons, 2008), 445–453.

will not be altered. Where this is the case, the documentation should be archived in standard formats. Suitable formats are discussed later in this module.

Archives and Museum Collections

Archives and museum repositories have varying purposes, resulting in different uses of born-digital design data. These are covered in Modules 25 and 26.

Design Phases, Workflows, and Products

Whether embedded in design and facility management offices or in more traditional archival and museum repositories, anyone working with **born-digital design records** benefits from a better understanding of how design records are produced.[4] According to Waverly Lowell and Tawny Ryan Nelb, design records, both paper-based and born-digital, "have their language and visual lexicon" to express design intent and specific construction guidance or instructions.[5] A certain level of visual literacy enables design records users to identify core elements of the drawings and appreciate the nuanced information being expressed.[6] However, being visually literate of born-digital design records can be especially challenging, as contextual information is often lacking and a collective aesthetic or nostalgic appreciation has not yet been developed for the born-digital the way it has been developed for blueprints or original drawings on trace or linen. Perhaps the greatest challenge with computer graphic design data is that, when one first approaches the data, there is nothing to "see" but folder structures populated with hundreds or thousands of files, most cryptically named. Therefore, before any visual literacy can be exercised, it is necessary to determine

---

[4] Much of the information in this section discusses workflows and features of design data from an architecture lens. The majority of this discussion is applicable to the other design disciplines that address the built environment. Product design, which involves strict liability that creates unique requirements for the maintenance of information and traceability, is not discussed here.

[5] Waverly Lowell and Tawny Ryan Nelb, *Architectural Records: Managing Design and Construction Records* (Chicago: Society of American Archivists, 2006), xiii.

[6] Association of College & Research Libraries, "ACRL Visual Literacy Competency Standards for Higher Education," October 27, 2011, www.ala.org/acrl/standards/visualliteracy, captured at https://perma.cc/TJ4N-BRX2.

which files hold the design data being sought and how to open and view those files.

In 2004, the Department of Architecture of the Art Institute of Chicago published *Collecting, Archiving and Exhibiting Digital Design Data*, a landmark study conducted by Kristine Fallon Associates that established some of the first concrete and scalable recommendations for cultural heritage organizations. A key finding of the study was that, in design projects for the built environment, it is possible to identify **outputs**—images or other digital artifacts that the designer chose to communicate to their team or client.[7] These outputs often document design options, a major design decision, or the deliverable at the conclusion of a specific design phase. The study also found that, although content may have been created using dozens of software tools, outputs could be completely described in a handful of standard data formats, which are readily viewable. This provides a starting point for exploration of the born-digital design data.

Design Phases

In a building project, the phases of design are defined in the contract between the owner and designer. This is typically a standard legal contract produced by an industry organization, but owners may make modifications. Perhaps the best known standard contract is the American Institute of Architects' (AIA) Standard Form of Agreement Between Owner and Architect. This document is updated approximately every ten years; as of this writing, the current version is B101™-2017.[8]

Not all projects have all phases, and some projects incorporate additional phases. For example, the initial design team may take the project through the Design Development phase and then turn it over to a construction manager or a local architect (especially in the case of international projects) for the Construction Documents, Procurement, and Construction phases. The contract, if available, will identify such anomalies. Sometimes, a great design idea never gets beyond the competition or proposal stage. Alternatively, a project may go all the way through the Construction Documents phase but never be built.

---

7   Kristine Fallon Associates, Inc., *Collecting, Archiving and Exhibiting Digital Design Data* (Chicago: Art Institute of Chicago, 2004)
8   American Institute of Architects, *AIA Document B101™-2017: Standard Agreement Between Owner and Architect* (Washington, DC: American Institute of Architects, 2017).

Very few design projects are undertaken by a single designer or even a single design firm. There are critical inputs from the project owner or developer, who may have their own consultants. The lead design firm will typically use a number of specialty consultants; for example, a project led by an architectural firm may have sub-consulting structural, electrical, and mechanical engineering firms. In fact, the trend appears to be toward an increasing number of specialty consultants. It is important for an archivist documenting an entire project to understand which design aspects were the responsibility of each team member. There are some firms that have developed long-term relationships and worked together on numerous projects over decades. It is important to acknowledge the collaborative nature of such a design process and resist the urge to attribute the entire design to the lead designer or even the lead design firm. The design contract will list the consultants engaged by both the owner and the architect.

Design Outputs

The specific outputs required from the design team are also spelled out in the contract with the project owner. These are frequently referred to as **deliverables**. If the archivist has access to the contract, it provides a listing of deliverables—outputs—that should be present in the design data. This is an excellent starting point for evaluating the scope of the digital content. *AIA Document B101™-2017* lists specific deliverables for each project phase as it describes the scope of design services (see Figure 1). These may be modified based on the specific project. The AIA's description of these deliverables is based on non-digital practice. The form of these deliverables may vary considerably with digital design techniques. Following is a larger discussion of the phases and their associated outputs, including other phases that may occur in any given project.

Pre-Contract Work. Some of the most stunning computer graphic design data are created in pursuit of a project. This may be either a proposal presentation or a competition entry. The design team will often develop a design concept and present it in high-quality images, either static renderings or video animations. These are important design records because they often demonstrate design thinking freed from the constraints of practicality and budget; they are also important

Schematic Design phase

- Evaluation of owner-provided requirements
- Preliminary design illustrating the scale and relationship of project components
- Drawings, including site plan and preliminary building plans, sections, and elevations
- Possibly: study models (physical or digital), perspective sketches, digital representations
- Sustainable design alternatives (materials, building orientation, etc.)
- Cost estimate

Design Development phase

- Drawings: plans, sections, elevations, typical construction details
- Diagrammatic layouts of building systems (mechanical, electrical, etc.)
- Outline specifications identifying major materials and systems and establishing their quality

Construction Documents phase

- Detailed drawings (see list above)
- Specifications detailing the quality level and performance of materials and systems
- Updated cost estimate
- Project manual
    - Conditions of the contract for construction
    - Specifications
    - Possibly bidding requirements and sample forms

Procurement phase

- Responses to questions from bidders
- Addenda
    - Clarifications/interpretations of bidding documents
    - Approved alternates and/or substitutions
- Bid results

Construction phase

- Evaluations of contractor's work
- Certificates of Payment to Contractor
- Approved contractor submittals
- Change Orders and Change Directives
- Equipment manuals, warranties, waivers of lien and other documents required of the contractor
- Certificate of Substantial Completion
- Final Certificate for Payment

Figure 1: Summary of design outputs from building projects, based on American Institute of Architects, *AIA Document B101™-2017: Standard Agreement Between Owner and Architect* (Washington, DC: American Institute of Architects, 2017).

because not all of these projects will have been executed, so there may be no other record. What the design team will not have taken into consideration is the longevity of such data. Designers may use personal rather than office software to develop complex forms or render an image, leaving a trail of file formats that are unfamiliar even to their team members. If the presentation is exclusively electronic, images may be in low resolution. Marketing materials, including proposal and competition entries, may be stored separately from project data, so the archivist may need to search for them. Because of the primacy of the images, both image resolution and color accuracy will be key considerations with this material.

Pre-Design. Some projects, especially large ones, have a Pre-Design phase.[9] The designer may or may not be involved during this phase. Activities such as planning, site selection, and financial projections/project budgeting occur. The decision to pursue specific sustainability goals or certifications may be made at this time as well. The digital artifacts from this phase are primarily non-graphic—numbers, analyses, reports—but may include mapping, diagrams, very preliminary design visions, and **electronic flythroughs** of the potential project or site. If the project itself (rather than the designer or design firm) is the focus of the archival effort, the information from this phase will be of great interest.

The Pre-Design phase is particularly important in regional and urban planning projects, where the key activities would be data gathering (e.g., base mapping, historic resource inventory, environmental factors) and analysis (e.g., site utilization study, parking, circulation, and transportation analysis). **Geographic Information Systems (GIS)** are frequently used for these activities.

Schematic Design. The first major activity in Schematic Design is for the designer to understand and confirm the owner's assumptions, including the **program**, site limitations, zoning requirements, project budget, and consulting services required. The second activity is preliminary design. Typically, the designer will develop multiple options to address the program and site. These are usually quite simple,

---

9   The AIA does not consider the Pre-design phase to be a basic service, and it is not included in *B101™-2017*.

addressing the general arrangement and scale of the project elements. In this process, the designer is likely to use multiple media—physical models, hand sketches and three-dimensional (3D) digital models. This material is of interest because it illustrates the "what might have been" schemes that were not selected. Often, digital photography and photo montage techniques are used to integrate the site and to bring non-digital elements into a digital presentation to the client. Archiving this presentation, which may be in PPTX, DOCX, or PDF format or another electronic publishing format, is a good way to capture a record of the project's preliminary design.

Once the owner has selected a design option, the designer proceeds with Schematic Design. From the archivist's perspective, schematic design is important because it is probably the clearest indication of the initial design intent, especially the aesthetics of the project. It includes such information as the overall form, the placement on the site, the three-dimensional arrangement of the program spaces, the selection of building materials, **systems** and equipment, sustainability considerations, and cost estimate. There will be preliminary drawings, such as plans, sections, and elevations. This may well be the phase during which the broadest range of digital design tools is used to experiment with form, optimize site placement, make the project sustainable, and generate drawings. It is also the phase in which the "hand" of the lead designer is most likely to be present among the digital artifacts. Again, the output from several digital design tools may be brought into one or more digital presentations, including flythroughs and other animations for the client. These form an excellent starting point for the archivist.

Design Development. There can be noticeable differences between the Schematic Design and Design Development phases that reflect changes to program, form, systems, and/or materials in an effort to align the project with the client's budget. This means that design exploration and the generation of materials similar to the Schematic Design's files may continue into the Design Development phase. According to the AIA, the Design Development phase establishes and documents the size and character of the project "as to architectural, structural, mechanical and electrical systems, and other appropriate elements."[10] It is also

---

10   American Institute of Architects, *AIA Document B101™-2017*, Section 3.3.1.

the phase when the outline specification is produced. This is typically a text document that identifies the building's principal materials and systems and sets the overall project quality. Deliverables, as defined by *AIA Document B101™-2017*, include plans, sections, elevations, typical construction details, and diagrammatic layouts of building systems, as well as the outline specification.

In the Design Development phase, the firm's standard digital production tools come into prominence—software such as AutoCAD or Revit—and more individuals, including outside consultants, begin to participate in design decision-making. There may be multiple milestones at which the design is reviewed, and the outputs used during these reviews will assist the archivist in capturing the evolution of the design. The folder structure used by the design team will indicate these milestones.

Construction Documents. In the Construction Documents phase, the design team develops the detailed information that will be provided to local authorities for approvals, as well as to the contractor for the purposes of pricing, bidding on, and building the project. The major outputs of the Construction Documents phase are detailed drawings and specifications that define the quality levels and performance criteria of construction materials, building systems, and workmanship. This phase documents the final design intent and describes, in detail, all materials, systems, and equipment included in the project. It also sets out the business terms and contractor deliverables for bidding and project delivery. The construction drawings will contain architectural details and those of the various engineering systems, such as showing how an irregular geometric surface is structurally supported. Some decisions are delegated to the contractor, including the selection of the specific building product (e.g., chiller, water heater, light fixture, door) as long as it conforms to the quality levels and performance criteria documented. Such selections must be approved by the designer. For the archivist, the construction documents contain the most complete and detailed description of the project as designed.

During the Construction Documents phase, there are multiple design reviews, and the outputs used for these reviews should always be checkpointed by the designers. Again, these materials are useful to the archivist for tracking the design's evolution.

As of 2020, many project teams use BIM tools to produce most drawings, although standard details, such as roof flashing, may be inserted as two-dimensional (2D) drawings. Note that this powerful class of software is focused on building information, although it does have extensions for civil and landscape elements. BIM tools allow for different "views" of the building information: it may be viewed as a rendered perspective, a set of 2D drawings, an interactive 3D model, or a list of rooms, doors, windows, and so on (these formatted lists are included in the drawings as **schedules**). Toward the end of the Construction Documents phase, some firms extract the drawing set from the BIM software and transfer it into a format compatible with their 2D CAD (**computer-aided design**) system. They then review the 2D drawings and pick up revisions and corrections in the CAD files. Although some specification data may be embedded in the BIM, the specification produced as a text document almost always takes precedence when a conflict arises among project information sources. It also always contains more information than what is embedded in the BIM. For example, it documents which **submittals**—an important source of building information—are required from the contractor.

Procurement. The contractor is normally selected during the Procurement phase, although there are several alternative project delivery approaches whereby the contractor is involved during design. The architect provides important services during this phase, but there is little "design" activity *per se*. Exceptions include an instance in which a contractor bidding on the project asks a question that results in the architect's making a change to the drawings or specifications. This change will be issued as an **addendum** to all bidders. A contractor bidding on the project may also propose an alternate to a building material or system that may be accepted by the owner and incorporated into the project. Thus, the bidding phase may be the source of deviations between the project as designed and the project as constructed.

Construction. The contractor has the major responsibility during the Construction phase. Designers' Construction phase activities, often referred to as construction administration, or CA, include:

- Answering questions from the contractor. The designer will often issue a drawing—an **ASK** (Architect's Sketch)—to clarify the design intent.

- Observing the contractor's work to see that it conforms to the design intent incorporated in the construction documents and meets the quality level defined in the specifications
- Monitoring the contractor's progress and certifying payments requested by the contractor. Near the end of the project, the designer will prepare a **punchlist** of any outstanding issues that must be addressed by the contractor.
- Reviewing submittals, the product data and samples, and fabrication drawings submitted by the contractor to determine their conformance with the construction documents. Submittals contain a great deal of information about what is in the building and how it is installed, which is of particular interest to facility managers and future design teams engaged to add to or renovate the building. This information may also be of interest to future researchers. Other submittals are the operations and maintenance manuals, spare parts lists, and warranties for the building equipment—information that is also critical to facility managers. The architect plays a key role in requiring these submittals (in the specifications), tracking the receipt of the required submittals, approving the submittals, and delivering the approved submittals to the project owner at the end of construction. Submittals are increasingly routed electronically; however, they are frequently scans of printed materials.
- Resolving problems and owner requests for changes. Questions from the contractor, unavailability of construction products or materials, and field problems—issues that arise during construction that make it difficult, costly, or impossible to proceed as intended—may result in changes to the design. In addition, the owner frequently requests changes during construction, typically in response to changing business conditions. Such changes are documented as **Change Orders** or **Change Directives** and are the main source of deviations between the project as-designed and the project as-constructed.
- Documenting the construction progress through photographs from details to full site perspective.

During construction, the contractor is required to maintain a markup set of drawings and specifications showing any changes. In the age of BIM, this is accomplished quite differently on different projects. In some cases, a printed set of documents is redlined—deviations from the drawings are noted in red pencil. Sometimes the architect updates the construction documents to reflect the changes. Some owners now request that the BIM or CAD files be updated to reflect the physical changes. If they exist, these files are the most accurate representation of the building as constructed.

Digital Workflows and Archival Assumptions

Design firms have business reasons to maintain archives of their project work. They will typically organize that information by design phase, often creating separate folder trees for graphic and technical information versus administrative information (contract, correspondence, meeting minutes, memos, etc.). Figure 2 shows the Drawings folder structure used by the design firm Ross Barney Architects. The Archive folder will make it relatively easy to identify the final deliverables from the major design phases. The design options explored are gathered in the Concepts folder. The graphic information provided by the engineering consultants is organized in the Consultants folder. The Presentations folder is where PowerPoint presentations are stored, specifically those from the Schematic Design and Design Development phases. As mentioned above, what the designer chose to include in the presentations, the images selected, and the sequence of the presentation all provide valuable insight into the designer's thought process and design priorities—a useful roadmap for the archivist. There is a caveat, however: not all firms are quite so organized and, even if they are, they may organize the data differently.

Depending on the collection policy, an archival repository may be interested in this project and want to ensure that some or all of this material can be transported to the repository's computers and made accessible to researchers for a long, long time. This requires thoughtful and careful conversion of the data from proprietary formats to archival formats. The section Baseline Competencies for Archivists below discusses challenges and stumbling blocks in the accurate capture and conversion into archival formats and includes a list of file formats suitable for long-term archiving.

- **Archive:** Archive of project drawings at the completion of project phases
  - **Schematic Design**
  - **Design Development**
  - **Construction Documents**
  - **Borders:** Title blocks, borders, and so on, for the project. These are presentation and contract documents borders.
- **Concepts:** CAD files of design options
- **Consultants:** Files from consultants
  - **MEP**
  - **Structural**
  - **Civil**
  - **Misc.:** Landscaping, kitchen, and so on
- **Existing Building:** Existing building drawings provided by the client
- **Sheet Files:** Plot files for the project
- **ASK:** Architect's sketch files issued during the project
  - **Construction Documents**
  - **Bidding**
  - **Construction Administration**
- **Temp:** For study drawings
- **Presentation:** Final presentation drawings (PowerPoint files)
  - **Schematic Design**
  - **Design Development**

Figure 2: Drawings folder structure used by Ross Barney Architects; bold type indicates folder names

Case Studies

In 2004, the Art Institute of Chicago (AIC) Department of Architecture published *Collecting, Archiving, and Exhibiting Digital Design Data*. Section 1 of this publication contained nine in-depth case studies of design firms' use of digital design tools. The case studies documented each firm's responses to a survey on digital design tools and how they are applied, plus an in-depth look at a specific project that explored the steps in the design process; who participated in those steps; what design tools, electronic and other, were used; and the major outputs, digital and physical, from each step. The following are two case studies of firms that were used as illustrations in the AIC's study; each shows how these firms are working today, what tools they are now using, and what has changed over fifteen years.

Ross Barney Architects

Founded in 1981, Ross Barney Architects is an architecture, urban design, and landscape architecture firm currently led by Carol Ross Barney, FAIA. The firm's work is focused on the creation of civic architecture and public spaces. The practice is research-focused and has always been interested in incorporating digital design tools in its workflow.

After several firm members reviewed the case study published in 2004, their conclusion was that the process had not changed but the tools had, and the outputs had changed somewhat. The firm now uses 3D printing and laser cutting to produce models and mockups. Computer tools are frequently used during early interactions with clients, and there is more realism earlier in the project. Instead of producing rough cardboard models to study massing options, for example, those explorations are likely done on computers using SketchUp.

The firm used more digital design tools in 2019 than in 2004. Whereas the Autodesk products Architectural Desktop and Revit were used in 2004 for a broad range of design activities, including design exploration and presentation, in 2019, AutoCAD and Revit were used exclusively for documentation. SketchUp and Rhinoceros, or Rhino, had been added to the digital toolbox for design exploration and presentation. These software packages were also occasionally employed for documentation, making it easier to construct a specific feature or detail. These SketchUp or Rhino elements were then added to the Revit model. Paired with SketchUp and Rhino were Enscape and V-Ray for rendering. These visualization tools replaced AccuRender and Autodesk VIZ.

Similarly, the 2004 use of Adobe Photoshop had expanded to include Adobe Illustrator and InDesign for the production of 2D materials throughout the design process, starting in marketing and business development. The firm continued to use Microsoft PowerPoint for presentations.

Navigating the Technical Landscape of Born-Digital Design Records   31

Over the fifteen-year period, a major shift involved a move to online interaction with clients and other team members. The firm was using GoToMeeting for design exploration with, and presentations to, clients. It was also used for collaboration with consultants. During programming, paper survey forms collated in a Microsoft Access database had been replaced by online survey tools SurveyMonkey and Poll Everywhere.

The firm has a comprehensive folder structure for capturing project information and checkpointing the design at project milestones. The intricacies of that structure are shown in Figure 3.

Is there a good way to attribute a design file to a specific Ross Barney Architects team member? No. Although early in a project, while exploring and validating concepts, individuals might append their initials to a file name or even create a subfolder with their names, they may start with a file created by somebody else or, as the design evolves, others might contribute or edit. Their "personal" folder may contain image resources drawn from other projects or the web. Authorship in such an open, collaborative design environment is impossible to ascribe. The genesis of the final design concept may also be difficult to ascertain by opening the file, since much content in the file may have been discarded just by suppressing its visibility.

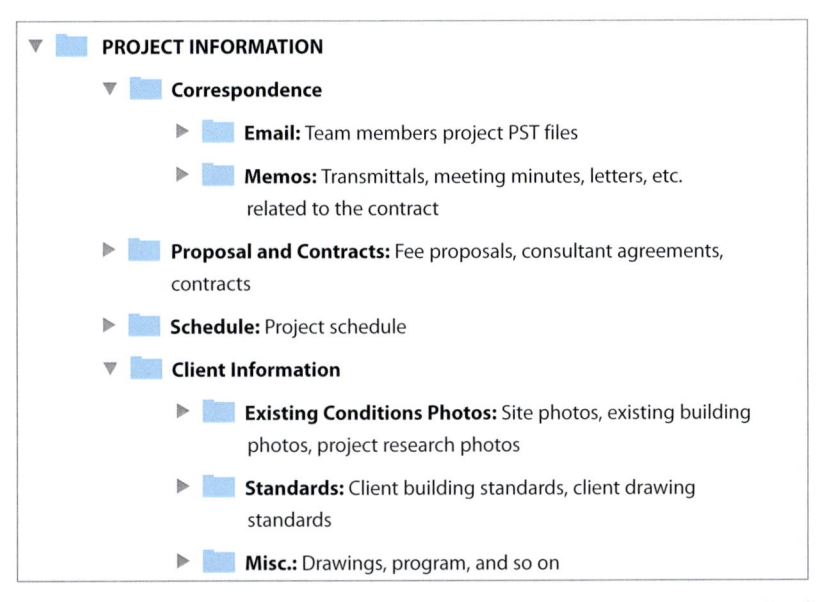

▼ 📁 **PROJECT INFORMATION**
  ▼ 📁 **Correspondence**
    ▶ 📁 **Email:** Team members project PST files
    ▶ 📁 **Memos:** Transmittals, meeting minutes, letters, etc. related to the contract
  ▶ 📁 **Proposal and Contracts:** Fee proposals, consultant agreements, contracts
  ▶ 📁 **Schedule:** Project schedule
  ▼ 📁 **Client Information**
    ▶ 📁 **Existing Conditions Photos:** Site photos, existing building photos, project research photos
    ▶ 📁 **Standards:** Client building standards, client drawing standards
    ▶ 📁 **Misc.:** Drawings, program, and so on

continued

- 📁 **PROGRAMMING:** Files and drawings prepared for programming of the project or for feasibility studies
- 📂 **CORRESPONDENCE**
    - 📁 **Programming:** Memos, letters, transmittal, meeting minutes for Programming or Studies phase of the project
    - 📁 **Schematic Design:** Memos, letters, transmittal, meeting minutes for Schematic Design phase of the project
    - 📁 **Design Development:** Memos, letters, transmittal, meeting minutes for Design Development phase of the project
    - 📁 **Construction Documents:** Memos, letters, transmittal, meeting minutes for Construction Document phase of the project
    - 📁 **Bidding:** Memos, letters, transmittal, meeting minutes, addenda for Bidding phase of the project
    - 📁 **Code:** Code search information
- 📂 **DRAWINGS**
    - 📂 **Archive:** Archive of project drawings at the completion of project phases
        - 📁 **Schematic Design**
        - 📁 **Design Development**
        - 📁 **Construction Documents**
    - 📁 **Borders:** Title blocks, borders, and so on, for the project; should be presentation and contract documents borders
    - 📁 **Concepts:** CAD files of design options
    - 📂 **Consultants:** Files from consultants
        - 📁 **MEP**
        - 📁 **Structural**
        - 📁 **Civil**
        - 📁 **Misc.:** Landscaping, kitchen, and so on
    - 📁 **Existing Building:** Existing building drawings provided by the client
    - 📁 **Sheet Files:** plot files for the project

- **DRAWINGS**
  - **ASK:** Architect's sketch files issued during the project
    - **Construction Documents**
    - **Bidding**
    - **Construction Administration**
  - **Temp:** For study drawings
  - **Presentation:** Final presentation drawings (PowerPoint files)
    - **Schematic Design**
    - **Design Development**
    - **Civil**
    - **Misc.:** Landscaping, kitchen, and so on
- **SPECIFICATIONS**
  - **Product Information:** Cut sheets, product data for items incorporated in the project.
  - **Specification Sections:** Project specifications
  - **Archive:** Archive project specs at completion of project phases
    - **Schematic Design**
    - **Design Development**
    - **Construction Documents**
- **COST ESTIMATE:** Construction cost estimate information
- **CONSTRUCTION ADMINISTRATION**
  - **Correspondence**
    - **RFI:** Request for information responses for the project
    - **Memos:** Memos for the project
    - **Transmittals:** Transmittals for the project
    - **Misc Douments.:** Landscaping, kitchen, and so on
  - **RFP and Change Orders:** Request for proposal and change orders, construction change directives for the project
  - **Submittals:** Electronic submittals for the project
  - **Field Reports:** Field reports for the project
  - **Closeout:** Punchlist for the project, certificates, and so on

Figure 3: Ross Barney Architects project folder structure; bold type indicates folder names

Valerio Dewalt Train Associates, Inc.

Valerio Dewalt Train Associates, Inc., is a Chicago-based firm with offices in Denver, San Francisco, and Palo Alto. According to the firm's website, "Curious by nature, our process is focused on discovery, leading to an understanding of the questions design should answer."[11] In addition, the firm says that "Our diverse practice leads to cross-pollinating of ideas laying fresh eyes on old issues, asking essential questions and finding out-of-the-box solutions."[12] The firm has avoided specialization and addresses a range of building types—residential, commercial, educational, and recreational. Principal Joe Valerio, FAIA, was a member of the Advisory Committee for the Art Institute of Chicago's *Collecting, Archiving, and Exhibiting Digital Design Data* study and contributed a case study.

In comparing the design process documented in 2004 to 2019 practices, the firm concluded that the design process had not changed but the digital tools had. Also, the computing environment had changed radically, with impacts on archival issues.

In 2019 as well as 2004, a design project always started with a hand sketch. This was scanned and brought into the computer environment, where it was used as the basis for design exploration and validation. There was variation among designers concerning how quickly they moved the design process to the computer. At that point, design became a collaborative effort, with multiple individuals contributing. In 2004, Valerio Dewalt Train's CAD tool was MicroStation, which the firm used for 2D and 3D work. By 2019, use of MicroStation was minimal and Revit had become the firm's primary design exploration, visualization, and documentation tool. The firm's architects had added Rhinoceros for early design exploration or when something was difficult to model in Revit. They also noted that the Autodesk software subscription for Revit included many other products and that these were sometimes used as well. At the end of the day, all final design elements were in the Revit model. They used Lumion for producing renderings. Lumion exports JPG images, and these images were considered important outputs. Since 2004, the use of Photoshop had expanded to

---

11 Valerio Dewalt Train Associates, "How We Work," https://www.buildordie.com/about, accessed August 28, 2019.
12 Valerio Dewalt Train Associates, "Our Clients," https://www.buildordie.com/about, accessed August 28, 2019.

the use of the other software products in the Adobe Creative Suite—Illustrator and InDesign, as well as Photoshop. This was in part due to the fact that the firm had added graphics and branding groups that made extensive use of these tools.

The firm has consistently used a standard folder structure for its projects. By 2019, there were often 500 GB of data associated with each project, leading to the need for a common organization system that would allow architects to quickly find the information they needed. That folder structure is shown in Figure 4. Note that there are subfolders in multiple locations named "YYYYMMDD-Description." The firm checkpointed their models constantly. They created an archive version every time there was a meeting, a review, or a deliverable and whenever they were beginning a major design change. The estimate was thirty to forty model versions archived per project. These folders, named with a date and a description, would be helpful for an archivist unfamiliar with the project.

The largest technology change was the firm's move to the cloud, running subscription software on virtual machines. Architects could access high-power computing and their desktop computers via the internet from any computer, anywhere. The firm stored its data on the Google cloud. Architects shared data with clients and consultants via DropBox and similar systems. Principal David Rasche speculated on some of the impacts of these moves on archival concerns:

- *Subscription software:* Moving from perpetual licensing to subscription means that the firm cannot keep copies of previous software versions. Autodesk allows subscription customers to access a limited number of previous versions. Unless the firm undertakes ongoing migrations of all their archives, there is concern that some data will become inaccessible.
- *Cloud storage:* The firm moved its data to Google Drive, which supports versioning. Each time anyone saves a file, a new version is created with metadata that indicates, among other things, who saved the file. Depending on how many previous versions are maintained, these versions, with their metadata, could be helpful to archivists, particularly in understanding authorship.

- ▼ 📁 **G**
  - ▼ 📁 **00-Distribution**
    - ▶ 📁 **Progress—Plots & Prints**
    - ▼ 📁 **Out**
      - ▶ 📁 **YYYYMMDD-Description**
    - ▼ 📁 **In**
      - ▶ 📁 **YYYYMMDD-Description**
    - ▼ 📁 **Contract Documents**
      - ▶ 📁 **ASK**
      - ▶ 📁 **Current Set**
      - ▶ 📁 **Issuances**
  - ▼ 📁 **10-Design**
    - ▶ 📁 **Render & Sketches**
    - ▶ 📁 **SD-DD**
    - ▶ 📁 **3D**
    - ▼ 📁 **Archive**
      - ▶ 📁 **YYYYMMDD-Description**
  - ▼ 📁 **20-BIM**
    - ▼ 📁 **Archive**
      - ▶ 📁 **YYYYMMDD-Description**
  - ▼ 📁 **30-ConsAdmin**
    - ▶ 📁 **Punch List**
    - ▶ 📁 **Addendum**
    - ▶ 📁 **Bulletin**
    - ▶ 📁 **Log**
    - ▼ 📁 **RFI**
      - ▶ 📁 **ANSWERED**
      - ▶ 📁 **PENDING**

Navigating the Technical Landscape of Born-Digital Design Records   37

- ▼ Submittals
  - ▼ REVIEWED
    - ▶ 27 00 00-Communications
    - ▶ 02 00 00-Existing Conditions
    - ▶ 03 00 00-Concrete
    - ▶ 04 00 00-Masonry
    - ▶ 05 00 00-Metals
    - ▶ 06 00 00-Wood_Plastics
    - ▶ 07 00 00-Thermal_Moisture Protection
    - ▶ 08 00 00-Openings
    - ▶ 09 00 00-Finishes
    - ▶ 10 00 00-Specialties
    - ▶ 11 00 00-Equipment
    - ▶ 12 00 00-Furnishings
    - ▶ 13 00 00-Special Construction
    - ▶ 14 00 00-Conveying Equipment
    - ▶ 21 00 00-Fire Suppression
    - ▶ 22 00 00-Plumbing
    - ▶ 23 00 00-HVAC (Heating, Ventilation, and Air Conditioning)
    - ▶ 25 00 00-Integrated Automation
    - ▶ 26 00 00-Electrial
    - ▶ 28 00 00-Electronic Safety & Security
    - ▶ 31 00 00-Earthwork
    - ▶ 32 00 00-Exterior Improvements
    - ▶ 33 00 00-Utilities
- ▼ 40-Information
  - ▼ Budget

continued

38 BORN-DIGITAL DESIGN RECORDS

```
                    ▶ 📁 Templates
                    ▶ 📁 Program
                    ▶ 📁 Minutes
                    ▶ 📁 Sustainability
        ▶ 📁 Contracts
        ▶ 📁 Presentations
        ▶ 📁 Permits
        ▼ 📁 Photos
              ▶ 📁 YYMMDD-Description
        ▼ 📁 Research
              ▶ 📁 Code Search
        ▶ 📁 Schedule
```

Figure 4: Valerio Dewalt Train project folder structure

The Nature of Computer Graphic Design Data

"Design data" can be almost anything—a list of the types of spaces required in an office building, the results of a structural analysis, detailed sustainability information about materials and products, cost estimates, and so on. But the type of design information that is the most engaging and typically of greatest interest is graphic information. The two major types of graphic information are raster and vector.

A large amount of computer graphic information is based on rasters (pixels, grid cells). This is a very basic form that encodes digital photographs, photo montages, video frames, renderings, and land cover/use maps. In all cases, the raster has a value and a location relative to some base point. In the case of a photograph, rendering, or video frame, the value is the color or gray tone. In the case of a map, that value may be elevation, rainfall, population density, average income, and so on. Most rasters also have a size, which in the worlds of photography and printing are known as *resolution*. In the case of map/GIS data, the size may be life-sized vs. to scale—a one-mile population density grid, for example.

Vector data describes an object using mathematical notation (x, y, and, sometimes, z coordinates). There are two major categories of vector data:[13]

- *Boundary representation (B-rep):* The building blocks of B-rep data are points, lines, and surfaces. Surfaces are closed, bounded areas. B-rep data can be 2D or 3D. In 3D, these models represent the surface, or the boundary, of the object, not its volume. The object is defined by a closed, oriented set of bounded surfaces.
- *Constructive Solid Geometry (CSG):* A CSG model defines the volumes of the objects. For CSG, the basic elements are polyhedral—cylinder, block, sphere, cone, and so on. These polyhedra can be combined and edited through Boolean operations (e.g., union, intersection, difference, and chamfer).

Early design software used one or the other vector data type. Architecturally oriented software tended toward B-rep. This was partly because line drawing was the major activity of the profession but also because B-rep required fewer computational resources than CSG and therefore allowed users to work faster on early generations of hardware, particularly with larger data sets. CSG was typically used in manufacturing software, where the objects being modeled created smaller data sets and the Boolean operations used on the data paralleled machining techniques. Today, most design software uses a combination of B-rep and CSG data and operations.

Different software companies implemented somewhat different geometric constructs in their products. A good example is NURBS—the non-uniform rational basis spline. This is a mathematical model used for generating smooth, flowing curves and curved surfaces. Initially, the NURBS element was incorporated into software that was directed at the automotive and aerospace industries but was not used in most architectural software. The assumption that architecture was inherently rectilinear prompted Canadian architect Douglas Cardinal to adopt mechanical rather than architectural software in the early 1980s to allow him to stake out and accurately dimension his curvilinear designs. Years later, Frank Gehry's office selected CATIA

---

13 Chuck Eastman, Paul Teicholz, Rafael Sacks and Kathleen Liston, *BIM Handbook (A Guide to Building Information Modeling for Owners, Managers, Designers, Engineers, and Contractors)*, 2nd ed. (Hoboken, NJ: John Wiley & Sons, 2011), 31–34.

(Computer-Aided Three-dimensional Interactive Application), known as an aerospace design software package. Today, NURBS is incorporated into many architecturally oriented software products.

For a long while, raster and vector were the only types of computer graphic data. In the twenty-first century, point clouds, created by laser scanning an existing object, emerged as a new graphic data type. Point clouds contain a series of *x, y,* and *z* coordinates that define positions in space. They are very large data sets. The typical use is to capture an accurate 3D image of existing conditions. This can be a site, the façade of an existing building, or the building's interior spaces and details. As such, point cloud data are not truly *design* data, as they are *not* a digital artifact directly produced by a designer; however, they may be valuable to certain archives. Although point clouds are huge, their data structure is simple.

Aside from point clouds, all computer graphic data generated from the 1970s to today are either raster or vector data. What has changed tremendously is the toolset—the software features—provided by the various products to create, edit, visualize, and give meaning to the graphic elements. This has changed the contents of the data files.

Very early B-rep data had a simple file structure, as little as a list of points, each with an ID (an integer) and *x, y* or *x, y, z* coordinates; then a list of lines, with the IDs of the two points they connected; then a list of surfaces, with the ordered IDs of the points they connected. The early software might provide a command to draw a circle, but, once generated, that circle would be stored as a series of short line segments. The files were often plain text so they could be read directly. Early computer graphics software and data structures were designed to function with extremely limited computer memory and computational power, and designed to allow the fastest possible display of the data on a computer graphics terminal. From the user's perspective, speed was the overriding issue in early computer graphics systems. As computer hardware became more powerful, it became possible to add special geometric constructs, such as circles, as data elements, and store just the center point and radius in the file. The circle would be re-created each time the file was read.

This was all what is now called unstructured data; looking at the contents of the file, there was no way to understand what any of the geometry represented. Early computer graphic systems dealt with geometric constructs, not with walls, doors, columns, or drafting symbols. As software products targeted to specific industries emerged, the elements available in the systems were named to correspond with the terminology familiar to the target market. A system might introduce a "column bubble" element. The underlying code and data structure, however, was the same as that for a generic circle. Similarly, the systems began to create commands that semi-automated certain repetitive drawing actions, such as inserting windows and doors in walls, resolving the intersection of two walls, or entering dimensions. As this occurred, computer graphic software began to be referred to as computer-aided design (CAD) software.

CAD systems introduced organizational structures to help users manage their CAD data. Constructs such as groups, layers, symbols ("blocks" in AutoCAD), and external reference files (X-refs) related graphic elements to each other, allowing them to be manipulated in a single operation and allowing designers to see progress and changes by other team members. Examples of capabilities provided by these organizational structures include:

- Group "Office Type A" could be copied and repeated
- Display could be turned off for layer "I-FURN"
- Symbol "NorthArrow" could be inserted on the drawing
- The mechanical engineers could underlay the architectural and structural CAD files as they routed their ductwork. If there was an architectural or structural design change, they would see it the next time they opened the file.

Many of these organizational structures were based on manual techniques. For example, symbols/blocks were a more flexible version of the physical templates that provided drafting symbols, such as door swings and bathroom fixtures at different scales so that they could be quickly traced onto manual drawings. Layers and external references were analogous to overlay drafting. In overlay drafting, multiple mylar drawings were registered and printed together. For example, a mechanical plan might be made up of the structural plan, showing columns; the architectural plan, showing walls; and the drawing of the mechanical equipment layout and ductwork. In the CAD environment, these three components of the mechanical plan could be stored in separate files and externally referenced (X-refs). Layers allowed selective display of different information in a single file. For example, furniture could be arranged on the architectural floor plan file but on a different layer. Display could be turned off for the furniture layer to produce the architectural plan drawing and then turned on to produce the furniture plan.

Some organizational structures allow data to exist in the file that do not appear on any drawings or other outputs created by the design firm. For example, a designer might begin a design by opening a CAD file from a previous project, creating a new layer, tracing over or copying certain elements of the previous project, and then turning off display of the previous project's layer(s). This creates a question for the archivist: What about the status and relevance of the non-displayed data? Another issue is that any vector drawing or image may require the registration of multiple files (X-refs). If the software cannot resolve the links to the reference files, typically because those files have been deleted or moved, the original drawing cannot be displayed. There is a second issue as to the ownership and copyright of data that may be present on the architect's hard drive and seen on the architectural drawings but was actually created by, say, an owner's consultant. Some systems stored symbol libraries and even color palettes in separate files. This allowed them to be maintained and updated centrally. However, if the original library or palette is no longer available at the time the archivist is viewing the file, some elements may be missing, or their representation may not reflect the original design.

Then there is **attribute**, or property, data. This is descriptive information about a specific graphic element, group, or symbol. A structural engineer might have a library of standard steel beams and columns. When they insert a "W16x36" into their drawing or model, it comes not only with a graphic representation but also all of the structural properties of that beam. This type of data is sometimes referred to as *metadata* but, since metadata has a different meaning for archivists (e.g., Dublin Core), the term *attribute* will be used here. It is attribute data that allows CAD and BIM files to be used for such activities as structural analysis, energy analysis, and cost estimating, among others. There is also a set of attributes that support visualization by defining, for example, a surface's color, roughness, and reflectance. For a line, these properties would include color, thickness, and line style (solid, dotted, dot-dash, etc.). CAD and BIM systems have multiple ways of relating attributes to their graphic elements, including using links to external files, websites, and databases.

Both GIS and BIM software work with structured data, which is immediately machine-interpretable. The data structure indicates what each graphic element represents in real-world terms.

GIS encompasses both spatial (graphic) and attribute information. It uses both B-rep vector data and raster data, referred to as *grid* data. This data is organized into map themes or overlays, such as roads, rivers, elevations, population, vegetation, and so on, and stored in a database system. GIS also stores related non-spatial information (attributes) in the database system and links them to the relevant spatial entities. For example, the spatial information about a real estate parcel boundary might be linked to a street address, an owner name, an assessed value, and a water utility account.[14]

A GIS data set may include many files. Queries are used to retrieve the relevant data and represent it correctly. Some of the data may be in public databases, such as the real estate parcel data discussed above, and accessed online rather than stored locally. A "map" may be just a graphical snapshot in the project files. Although some GIS software products support "packaging" the data that are included in a specific map, this may not have been done. In that case, it will be challenging to regenerate accurately a map produced ten years ago.

BIM is **object-based** and follows **parametric design**. This is a very different data structure. Object-based parametric modeling does not represent objects with fixed geometry. Rather, it defines parameters and rules that determine the geometry and some attributes. The parameters and rules can relate the object to other objects, allowing it to automatically update based on other changes in the model. This is referred to as the object's **behavior**. Object-based parametric modeling was originally developed for manufacturing, but the architecture-focused software products have developed somewhat differently. BIM software—architecturally oriented parametric object modeling—predefines the building object classes. These align with real-world design

---

14 Robert M. Itami and Robert J. Raulings, *SAGE Introductory Guidebook* (Melbourne, Australia: Digital Land Systems Research, 1993), excerpt available at https://www.cs.upc.edu/~lpv/general.dir/whatgis.html, captured at https://perma.cc/U54B-26B2.

elements, such as walls, roofs, columns, beams, slabs, and so on. An **object class** allows for the creation of any number of **object instances** that vary, based on their individual parameter values and relationships with other objects.[15] Because the object classes align with real-world elements and incorporate their behavior, this type of software is very domain specific. BIM software is therefore quite specific to buildings, although there are extensions for civil and landscape objects.

Object attributes are required for analyses. The BIM software products attempt to include a number of useful attributes in their object classes. However, because the number of potential analyses is open-ended and each analysis requires different information, the supplied attributes may be ignored by the user while additional attributes are added. Also, virtual objects such as furniture and equipment are often supplied by their manufacturers, complete with a set of attributes. Sometimes a designer will use such an object because of its appearance or function and be unaware of the attributes included. This leads to questions as to which of the attributes in a BIM file were really intended.

Object-based parametric software for manufacturing incorporates tools to create custom parametric objects that incorporate the company's knowledge and best practices. This capability is increasingly of interest to other design disciplines.

Common File Types and Software

Part of the complexity of addressing born-digital design records is the wide range of software and file types that fall in the category. From the earliest times of designers incorporating computers into their work, software designed for other disciplines has been adapted to perform a function in the design process.[16] The potential breadth of the options is further exacerbated by the small number of born-digital design files that have been accessioned by archives—meaning that the archival profession is not yet able to comprehensively define the scope of the problem of collecting, preserving, and providing access to born-digital

---

15 Eastman, Teicholz, Sacks, and Liston, *BIM Handbook*, 31–34.
16 Maya for Jurassic Park, *Designing the Future Landscape: Digital Architecture, Design & Engineering Assets* Morning Session, 2017. Video. Time stamp: 33:28, link: https://youtu.be/8XMko7E49E4?t=2008 .

2015 Firm-Oriented

8.1. What software does your firm currently support and/or use?

Response	Count	
→ Adobe Suite	9	90.0%
→ Autodesk – AutoCAD	9	90.0%
Autodesk – 3DsMax	5	50.0%
→ Autodesk – Revit	8	80.0%
Sketchup	4	40.0%
Rhino	5	50.0%
Piranesi	2	20.0%
form·Z	1	10.0%
V-Ray	3	30.0%
Maxwell	1	10.0%
Lumion	2	20.0%
Grasshopper	2	20.0%
→ GIS Software (ex. ESRI, Google Earth Pro, etc.)	4	40.0%
Autodesk – Ecotect	1	10.0%
Other, please specify	4	40.0%

Total respondents: 10

2016 Archives-Oriented

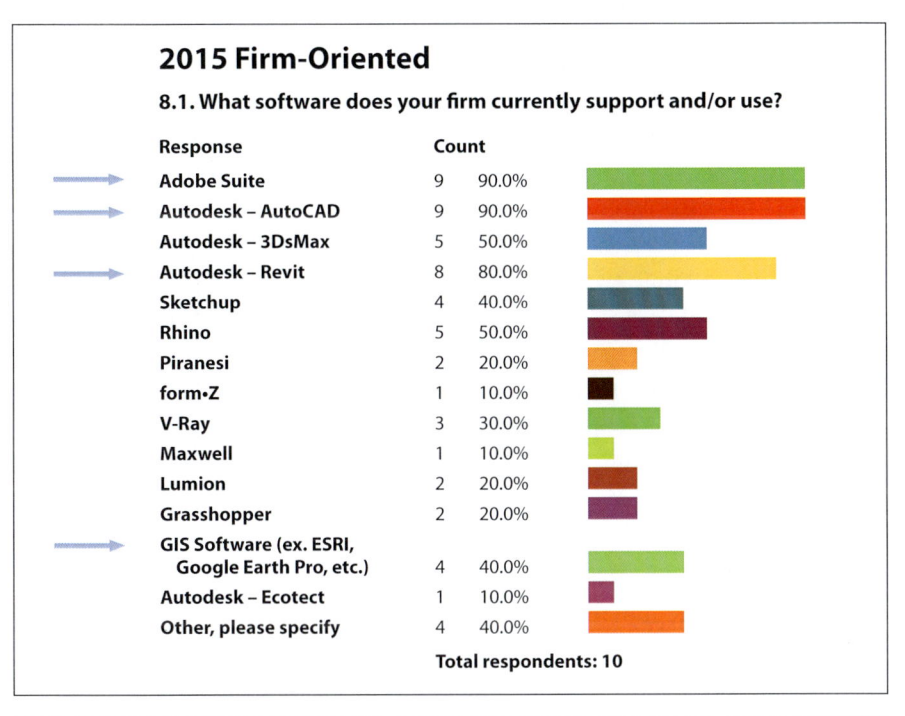

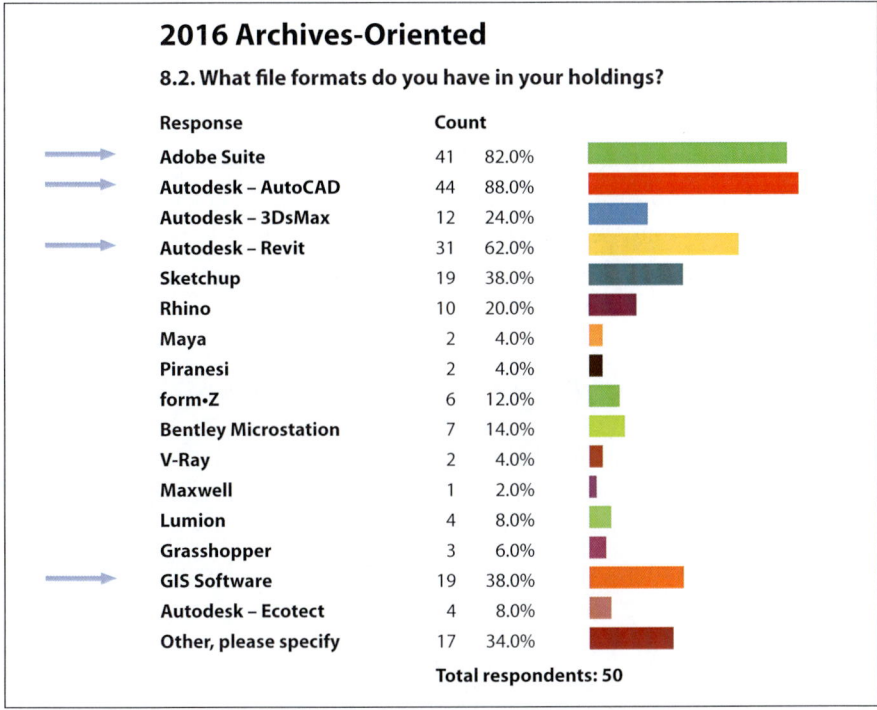

8.2. What file formats do you have in your holdings?

Response	Count	
→ Adobe Suite	41	82.0%
→ Autodesk – AutoCAD	44	88.0%
Autodesk – 3DsMax	12	24.0%
→ Autodesk – Revit	31	62.0%
Sketchup	19	38.0%
Rhino	10	20.0%
Maya	2	4.0%
Piranesi	2	4.0%
form·Z	6	12.0%
Bentley Microstation	7	14.0%
V-Ray	2	4.0%
Maxwell	1	2.0%
Lumion	4	8.0%
Grasshopper	3	6.0%
→ GIS Software	19	38.0%
Autodesk – Ecotect	4	8.0%
Other, please specify	17	34.0%

Total respondents: 50

Figure 5: Comparisons of software present in U.S.-based firms and archival institutions from the 2015 and 2016 surveys by the Society of American Archivists Design Records Section's CAD/BIM Taskforce (now Digital Design Records Taskforce)

design files. In an effort to glean an understanding of the software and file types that make up the universe of born-digital design records, five surveys have been conducted since 2004.

The first survey, conducted by Kristine Fallon Associates, on behalf of the Art Institute of Chicago's Department of Architecture in 2004, contextualized case studies about specific design firms' design activities with a broader sampling of software use by design firms. The next two surveys were conducted in 2015 and 2016 by Aliza Leventhal and the SAA Design Records Section (DRS) CAD/BIM Taskforce (known since 2019 as the Digital Design Records Taskforce). They were shared on the DRS's listserv to learn what software and file types had been included in already accessioned collections and what software and file types were present in active firms through corporate architectural archivists.[17] The fourth survey, conducted by Birgitte Sauge from the Norwegian National Museet, mirrored the 2016 survey's questions but solicited responses from the approximately 200 design firms in Norway.[18] The fifth survey, conducted by the authors of this module, solicited responses from the SAA DRS in an effort to provide a current supplement to the findings of the previous surveys. The trends and findings are presented here with cautious confidence.

Comparing the 2015 firm-oriented survey with the 2016 archives-oriented survey, the four predominant software packages identified were Adobe Suite, Autodesk–AutoCAD, Autodesk–Revit, and GIS Software (Figure 5).

The 2004 Art Institute of Chicago survey, which consisted largely of North American design firms, and the 2017 Norwegian firm survey revealed some similarities with two of the four predominant software packages aligning with the 2015 and 2016 surveys: Adobe Suite and Autodesk–AutoCAD. The 2004 survey (Figure 6) included the full suite of office software called the Microsoft Suite, which was an oversight in the other four surveys. Although Autodesk–Revit was not as highly ranked in the 2004 survey, the 2017 Norwegian survey's

---

[17] "Survey Results Digital Design Holdings," Society of American Archivists Design Records Section's Annual Meeting, 2016, https://www2.archivists.org/sites/all/files/20160508_SurveyResultsDigitalDesignHoldings.pdf, captured at https://perma.cc/95HS-S6YN.

[18] Birgitte Sauge, *Digital Design Media in Norwegian Architect's current Practice, Survey 2016–2017* (Oslo: National Museum of Art, Architecture and Design and Cultural Heritage Mediascapes–Architecture Museums and Digital Design Media, 2019).

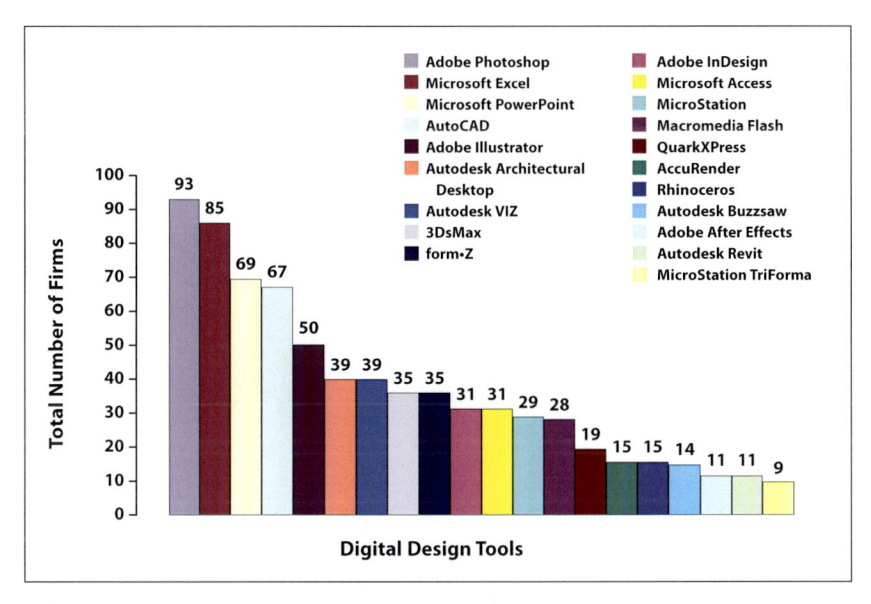

Navigating the Technical Landscape of Born-Digital Design Records   **47**

Figure 6: Most frequently used digital design tools from the 2004 survey by Kristine Fallon Associates for the Art Institute of Chicago's Department of Architecture. *Image courtesy of KFA, Inc.*

responses (Figure 7) confirmed that this BIM software has secured its place in the architect's toolkit.

Other notable differences between the 2015 and 2016 U.S.-based surveys and the 2017 Norway-based survey included GIS software and the variety of CAD and BIM software in the surveys. While GIS software had been in the top four in the previous North American surveys, it was listed seventh in the Norwegian survey and tied with Rhinoceros,

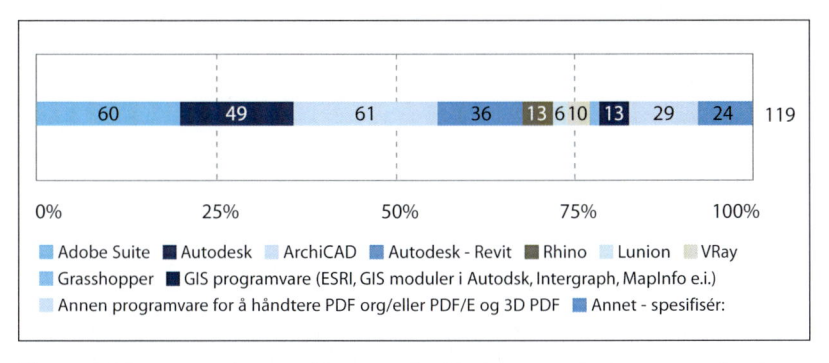

Figure 7: Responses from architects to the Birgitte Sauge's 2017 survey for the Norwegian National Museet. *Image courtesy of Birgitte Sauge.*

a 3D modeling software package. The fourth predominant software package from the Norwegian survey was ArchiCAD, a CAD/BIM software developed by the Hungarian company Graphisoft, now a Nemetschek company. Knowing a designer used Autodesk's AutoCAD vs. Graphisoft's ArchiCAD does offer insights and can influence the way an institution approaches the interpretation and access of those files; however, for the purposes of this module, the critical information gleaned from these surveys is the types of software and file types they utilize. Knowing the software used by a firm gives the accessioning or processing archivist valuable context as to the variety of file types to expect.

In 2019, this module's authors revisited the questions posed by these previous surveys to see whether there were any continuing trends or major changes in file type usage. The 2019 Survey of North American Archivists provided a more granular selection of software for respondents, exposing richer context in the use of the software making up the Adobe Suite. Our findings confirmed that the general software use patterns of 2016 have continued. The software packages most selected by respondents were Adobe Acrobat, Adobe Photoshop

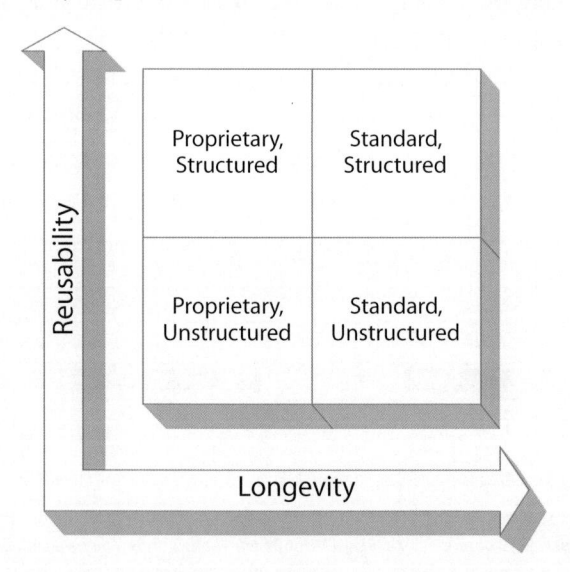

	Proprietary, Structured	Standard, Structured
	Proprietary, Unstructured	Standard, Unstructured

Reusability (vertical axis) / Longevity (horizontal axis)

Figure 8: Longevity and reusability of information forms and formats. From Kristine K. Fallon and Mark E. Palmer, *General Buildings Information Handover Guide: Principles, Methodology and Case Studies* (Gaithersburg, MD: U.S. Department of Commerce, National Institute of Standards and Technology, 2007), 57

and Autodesk-AutoCAD (tying for second), Microsoft Suite and Autodesk-DWG TrueView (tying for third). The most prevalent file types of JPG (image), TIF (image), DWG (model), and BMP (raster image) identified in the respondents' holdings shed additional light on the workflow of designers. These four file types vary slightly from the responses to the question of "the five most prevalent file types," which included DWG, JPG, TIF, and PDF tying with DXF (an exchange format for DWG and other related file types).

Information Forms and Formats

The number of design software titles and file extensions produced is daunting. However, it is helpful to categorize the data into a few big groups to permit quick assessment of suitability for archival purposes. See Figure 8.

The following discussion is condensed from the *General Buildings Information Handover Guide: Principles, Methodology and Case Studies*, published by the National Institute of Standards and Technology in conjunction with FIATECH (Fully Integrated and Automated Technologies for Construction) in 2007[19] and edited for relevance.

Unstructured Form

Although design information is now produced and managed electronically, much electronic information is still held in electronic documents that do not have a formal structure: the only way to interpret the contents is for someone to actually read them. Most CAD drawings fall into this category. Although the data might be compatible with multiple software products, some human effort is required to interpret the data for the receiving system. A good example is the work that firms do to reach agreement on layering for a particular project. This creates the appearance of structure in the CAD files. However, the structure is not intrinsic—there is nothing in the software that prevents a user from placing a floor drain on the wall layer.

---

19 Kristine K. Fallon and Mark E. Palmer, *General Buildings Information Handover Guide: Principles, Methodology and Case Studies* (Gaithersburg, MD: U.S. Department of Commerce, National Institute of Standards and Technology, 2007), 22–24.

Structured Form

Some types of software, including BIM applications, create information in a structured form that is immediately machine-interpretable. For example, the data structure indicates if a graphic element such as a circle is a manhole, a window, a water tank, a column bubble, and so on. This permits the use of computer tools to assist in managing, querying, and analyzing the data, which is useful for both archivists and researchers. Structured form reduces ambiguity about the designer's intent.

Proprietary Format

A proprietary format is any data format defined and owned by a specific software company. Most software outputs data in a proprietary format, sometimes referred to as the **native format**. *Proprietary* is the more significant term, however, because it means that the format is the property of a single software developer. At any time, the developer can modify the format. If this happens, archived data maintained in that format may no longer be usable in current versions of software. Also, a developer may cease doing business or discontinue the products that read and output the format. Either circumstance threatens to render the proprietary data unusable. From the perspective of long-term access and manipulation, proprietary formats are problematic.

Proprietary formats may have structured or unstructured form. For example, BIM authoring products create structured data in proprietary formats. Traditional CAD systems create unstructured data in proprietary formats.

Standard Format

Standard formats are preferred for any data that will be archived for an extended period. There are two types of standard formats:
- *De facto* standards refer to formats that may have originated with a single software developer but have been made publicly available and are supported by multiple companies and products. A good example of a *de facto* standard format is DXF. Since the format specification is published, anyone can write an application to access data stored in that format. The organization can be assured that its data will be retrievable. However, Autodesk, a major CAD software developer and originator of

the DXF format, decided not to extend the DXF format to include its complete product data structure, limiting the format's future utility in the design industry.
- *De jure* standards are those maintained by a standards development organization, such as the International Organization for Standardization (ISO), buildingSMART International (bSI), or the Open Geospatial Consortium (OGC). In addition to the advantage of data longevity, *de jure* standards are typically developed through a consensus process that considers the requirements of many organizations. Thus, *de jure* standard formats may be more flexible and useful. Also, the consensus process ensures that there are multiple organizations that have an interest in the standard. Thus, a unilateral decision by one developer will not halt support for or the extension of the standard. The downside to *de jure* standards is that the consensus process is slower than a single developer's development process.

Baseline Competencies for Archivists

The technical landscape of contemporary design work and the born-digital design records it produces is broad and complex. To some extent, archivists can navigate this complexity with the assistance of standards and other resources maintained by the design professions. Many of the challenges discussed in previous chapters can be approached with these resources, even if the challenge itself cannot be entirely overcome immediately.

Design Data Production Standards

In the design industry, practice standards have been developed primarily by professional organizations. The AIA is an example. With the advent of CAD and BIM, and the concomitant desire to share data easily, cross-organizational and professional efforts emerged. Early on, they proposed standardizing file naming and layering, as well as CAD drafting (line weights, line styles, symbology, etc.), to compensate for the unstructured nature of CAD data and to enable the multiple firms working on a project to overlay their CAD files and produce a coherent merged drawing.

Probably the most useful design data production standard for the archivist is the U.S. National CAD Standard (NCS), which was initially intended to bridge best practices from manual drafting to computer-aided drawing.[20] Parts of this standard began development in the 1990s under the auspices of the AIA, Construction Specifications Institute (CSI), and government agencies. By the late 1990s, these groups agreed to pool and harmonize the content they had developed. NCS version 1 was published in 1999. In version 6 as of this writing, NCS continues to be extended, updated, and distributed by the National CAD Standard Project Committee (NCSPC) of the National Institute of Building Sciences.[21] Membership is open.

NCS provides guidance on the layout and organization of drawing sheets. Most important, it defines standard naming—including of CAD files and layers. Although no firm follows the NCS to the letter, the standards have broadly influenced design practice, and knowing the NCS naming standards will help an archivist navigate both file and layer naming. An example is the standard discipline designator used in both file and layer names: A for Architecture, S for Structure, E for Electrical, I for Interiors, C for Civil, L for Landscape, and so on. These are the same discipline designators used for manual drawings.

Although originally focused on 2D CAD, NCS has always incorporated the concept of a model file—a file that is the source of multiple drawings, often at varying scales. This has provided the path for NCS to address BIM and to harmonize CAD and BIM practices, since many firms still use both technologies but need their output to be consistent. Recent NCS versions have explicitly addressed BIM.

The U.S. National BIM Standard (NBIMS-US) is a more technical standard, defining **model views** for typical design/construction processes—such as building electrical system design, energy analysis, and data turnover to facility management—and standardizing their representation in the Industry Foundation Classes (IFC) (ISO 16739). Like NCS, NBIMS-US is a product of the National Institute of Building Sciences (NIBS).

Although it is just coming into adoption by building projects, the BIMFORUM's Level of Development (LOD) Specification may

---

20 See the United National CAD Standard's website at www.nationalcadstandard.org.
21 The National Institute of Building Sciences' website is at www.nibs.org.

be a useful practice standard going forward. The LOD Specification uses the LOD definitions from the *AIA Document G202™-2013 Building Information Modeling Protocol Form*,[22] with some modifications, and is organized by the Construction Specifications Institute and Construction Specifications Canada's **UniFormat**. The LOD Specification defines and illustrates characteristics of model elements of different building systems at each Level of Development. The LOD Specification is intended to be used during design and construction to identify the following:

- The organization responsible for the design or construction of each building element at each project phase,
- The completeness of design or detailing of each building element in the BIM at each project milestone, and
- The extent to which other members of the team may rely on the digital information about each building element at each project milestone.

This specification is directed toward clarifying contractual and legal issues but could be of great utility in answering a researcher's questions, such as:

- Which design firm was responsible for the selection of the light fixtures?
- At what design phase was the specific exterior cladding selection made?
- Does the spiral staircase in the SD model represent a design idea that was abandoned, or was it only considered a placeholder for a vertical circulation element?

Although objects in a building model can look very detailed and even carry large amounts of information concerning manufacturer, performance capacity, price, and more, they may be objects borrowed from a library or previous project. The designer's intention in placing these objects in the building model may be simply to show that some type of heating unit, kitchen appliance, office configuration, etc., is required. Knowing the LOD of such objects in a BIM of interest will save the researcher from drawing the wrong conclusions.

---

22 American Institute of Architects, *AIA Document G202™-2013: Building Information Modeling Protocol Form* (Washington, DC: American Institute of Architects, 2013), Sections 2.2–2.6.

The reference document for the Levels of Development is the BIMFORUM *Level of Development Specification Guide*. It is updated on a regular basis. The current version as of this publication is December 2020:[23]

At this time, six Levels of Development have been defined:
- LOD 100 model elements are not intended to be true representations. They indicate the existence of certain building components, but not their precise type, size, shape, appearance, or location. Any information derived from LOD 100 elements is only approximate.
- LOD 200 model elements are generic. They indicate approximate size, shape, orientation, location, and quantities. They may be recognizable or may be shown as simple geometric volumes. Any information derived from LOD 200 elements is still approximate.
- LOD 300 model elements are specific building components. Their appearance, type, quantity, size, shape, location, and orientation, as designed, can be determined directly from the model. They may also contain nongraphic information (e.g., manufacturer).
- LOD 350 model elements contain additional information to allow them to be spatially coordinated with other building components and systems. In addition to their type, quantity, size, shape, location, and orientation, additional items necessary for coordination are modeled. These may include items such as operating or servicing clearances, supports, and connections. All items can be measured directly from the model without referring to non-modeled information such as notes or annotated dimensions.
- LOD 400 model elements are also specific building components. In addition to their appearance, type, size, shape, location, and orientation being precise, they contain additional information, graphic and nongraphic, to support their fabrication, assembly, and/or installation. In the twenty-first century,

---

23 BIMFORUM, "Level of Development (LOD) Specification, Part I and Commentary for Building Information Models and Data," December 2020, 15–16, https://bimforum.org/resources/Documents/LOD%20Spec%202020%20Part%20I%202020-12-31.pdf, captured at https://perma.cc/C5L3-3KMS.

the industry has seen an increase in the custom fabrication of building components from design data.
- LOD 500 is not used by the BIMForum but is included in the AIA LOD definitions. LOD 500 model elements are field-verified as to size, shape, quantity, location, and orientation. Nongraphic information may also be included (e.g., manufacturer, model).

As of 2020, it was still unclear whether the use of the LOD Specification would become a widespread industry practice. If an LOD Specification exists for a project, it will assist the archivist in distinguishing the work of the various project participants and also in determining how definitive various building elements are in the models saved at the project milestones. The unfortunate aspect from the archivist's perspective is that UniFormat is extremely detailed. A project LOD Specification will require careful examination and analysis to yield the basic information sought by the archivist.

Format Standards

Format standards emerged in the 1990s and early 2000s as the use of CAD became ubiquitous. The Initial Graphics Exchange Specification (IGES), is the exception. Nevertheless, some firms were drawing with computers in the 1970s, and universities were experimenting in the 1960s. Standards did not exist. There were two generations of CAD before the emergence of the PC–mainframe-based CAD, using specialized computer graphics terminals, and UNIX workstation-based CAD. Few software products from these generations made the transition to PC. Often, pre-PC CAD systems relied on specialized hardware: input via a 36" x 48" digitizer using a twelve-button puck, specialized computer circuits for graphic transformations, and so on. If design data from these generations is just being discovered now, an archivist will find dealing with it to be especially problematic.

There are multiple places to find information about the sustainability and preservation practices for digital files. The Library of Congress and the National Archives and Record Administration have each developed their own lists that provide detailed descriptions of file types, as well as each organization's collecting and preservation practices.[24] Several of the file types discussed here are included in the lists of both organizations.

As discussed above, to preserve data for the long term, a standard format is preferred. The following are key considerations in identifying and selecting a suitable standard format for computer graphic design data:

- Non-encrypted format or published format specification
- Free of patents and other legal restrictions on use
- Independent of specific underlying operating system or hardware functions
- Preserves the appearance and view characteristics of the original:
  ○ Layout
  ○ Fonts
  ○ Images
  ○ Line work
  ○ Resolution
  ○ Color
  ○ Scale
- Contains no externally referenced files
- Broadly used in the archival community
- Readily available viewers

Following are file formats suitable for long-term archiving of born-digital design data. If not international standards, they are industry standards or products of multi-organizational initiatives. For video data, the most commonly used standards do have patent restrictions, even though they are a product of multi-organizational industry initiatives. The patent restrictions are noted.

Data Type: Drawings, Documents, and Presentations (Without Audio or Video)

Standard: PDF/A (ISO 19005)

File extension: .pdf

---

24 Library of Congress, "Sustainability of Digital Formats: Planning for Library of Congress Collections," 2021, https://www.loc.gov/preservation/digital/formats/fdd/descriptions.shtml; National Archives and Records Administration, "Preservation Action Plan for Digital Design and Vector Graphics Records," January 12, 2022, https://github.com/usnationalarchives/digital-preservation/blob/master/Digital_Design_Formats/NARA_PreservationActionPlan_DigitalDesignVectorGraphics_20210525.pdf.

Description: PDF/A is an ISO standard version of Adobe's PDF, now in the public domain, targeted to archiving and long-term preservation of electronic documents by prohibiting reliance on information external to the file, such as external text fonts. It handles text, raster and vector graphics, embedded fonts, and color management. It explicitly prohibits audio and video content. As such, it is an excellent choice for technical drawings, renderings, and presentations that do not include audio and video. Its great advantage is that it is familiar and accessible to any computer user.

There are a number of confusing sub-standards—PDF/A-1, PDF/A-2, PDF/A-3, and PDF/A-4. PDF/A-1 (ISO 19005.1-2005) is based on PDF version 1.4. PDF/A-2 (ISO 19005.2-2011) is based on PDF version 1.7 (ISO 32000-1). PDF/A-2 allows the embedding of PDF/A-compliant attachments. PDF/A-3 added embedding of a file or files in any format. This seems to some to contradict the core goal of PDF/A—to eliminate external dependencies.

A related standard, PDF/E, is targeted specifically to documents used in geospatial, construction, and manufacturing contexts. It is intended to handle 3D, dynamic content, including video and embedded data such as attributes. The current ISO standard, ISO 24517-1:2008, does not yet address these content types. However, PDF/E is a standard to watch.

Data Type: Raster Graphics

Standard: TIFF (ISO 12639) – uncompressed

File extension: .tif, .tiff

Description: The Tagged Image File Format (TIFF) describes and stores raster image data that comes from scanners. It also describes and stores image data from CAD and BIM renderers, digital photography, and programs that allow the compositing and editing of image data, such as Photoshop. TIFF is able to describe bi-level (two-color only), grayscale, and full-color image data in several color spaces and embed a color profile.

Standard: PNG (ISO/IEC 15948)

File extension: .png

Description: Portable Network Graphics (PNG) is a bitmapped graphics format that employs a **lossless data compression** method. It was developed for the purpose of transferring images on the internet in a patent-free format. PNG supports palette-based (24-bit) color, grayscale, or RGB (red, green, blue) color modes. It does not support other color spaces, such as CMYK (cyan, magenta, yellow, and black), but does support embedding International Color Consortium (ICC) color profiles. Although uncompressed TIFF is the preferred archival format for still images, PNG is an acceptable format because its compression is lossless and it is open, documented, and patent-free. Its advantage is that it is supported in many popular graphics applications on multiple operating systems.

Standard: JPEG (ISO/IEC 10918, ISO/IEC 14495 and ISO/IEC 18477)

File extension: .jpg, .jpeg

Description: The Joint Photographic Experts Group (JPEG) has defined multiple standards related to the JPEG format—ISO/IEC 10918, ISO/IEC 14495, and ISO/IEC 18477. JPEG is a ubiquitous format for continuous color images, such as digital photographs. According to the 2019 survey cited above, it was also the most common format in digital design archives. This format comes with a few problems, the first being that it is a **lossy compression** standard. Although lossless and near-lossless options are included in the standards, it is difficult to know, either when creating or when receiving a JPEG image, whether the lossless option was used. The second problem with JPEG as an archival format is that there are patents on some of the compression algorithms. Although it is an excellent format for dissemination, particularly for web publication, JPEG is *not recommended* as a long-term archival format.

Data Type: *Vector Graphics*

Standard: IGES (NBSIR 80-1978, ASME Y14.26M)

File extension: .igs

Description: The IGES is a vendor-neutral file format developed in the early years of computer-aided design to support the transfer of very precise geometric information between unlike CAD systems. Its development was driven by the aerospace and manufacturing industry and conducted under the auspices of the U.S. National Bureau of Standards, now the National Institute of Standards and Technology (NIST). Because it was a very early data exchange standard, it is broadly supported in commercial CAD software. If there is a need to preserve very complex 3D CAD geometry, such as NURBS surfaces, IGES is a good option.

Data Type: Born-Digital Video

Video poses some unique archival problems. Early digital video was hardware-dependent. This stemmed from the need to rapidly compress video data for storage and decompress it for viewing. The term for this is **codec**, short for "compress/decompress." With earlier computational speed limitations, this could only be handled by special-purpose hardware. Such hardware dependence made digital video data very difficult to preserve for long periods of time. More recently, software codec, which provides a better preservation path, has become available. In addition to the codec, digital video requires what is called a "container"—a file format for storing the content. Thus, the archivist must pay attention to the suitability of both the codec and the container (file format).

Uncompressed Audio Video Interleave (AVI) is a video export option that bypasses the use of codec entirely. It creates a huge file but is lossless. Unfortunately, support for this option has been dropped by many digital design software products.

Codec standard: FFV1 (Internet Engineering Task Force [IETF] Internet-Draft)

File extension: Multiple containers, including .mkv, .avi, and .mov

Description: Fast Forward Video codec 1 (FFV1) is a lossless software codec. It has been part of the free, open-source library—libavcodec—of the FFmpeg project (ffmpeg.org) since 2003. In 2015, the IETF began working on making FFV1 an internet standard. As of 2019, its IETF status was Internet-Draft.[25] The IETF Codec Encoding for LossLess Archiving and Realtime

---

25 "FFV1 Video Coding Format Version 4," November 27, 2021, https://datatracker.ietf.org/doc/html/draft-ietf-cellar-ffv1-v4., accessed January 24, 2022

transmission (CELLAR) project, of which FFV1 is a part, was prompted by the European PREFORMA project, which focuses on long-term preservation of data.

Container standard: Matroska-03 (IETF Internet-Draft)
File extension: .mkv, .mk3d, .mka, .mks
Description: Like FFV1, the Matroska Multimedia Container is part of the IETF CELLAR project. It is a free, open standard container (file) format for storing common multimedia content, including movies and born-digital video. It is based on EBML (Extensible Binary Meta Language), a binary derivative of XML.[26]

Codec standard: H.264 (MPEG-4 AVC)
File extension: Multiple containers, including .mp4, .flv, .mov, and .qt
Description: H.264 is MPEG-4 Part 10, Advanced Video Coding, a lossy video compression standard. It is possibly the most commonly used codec on the web. MPEG-4 (ISO/IEC 14496—Coding of audio-visual objects) was introduced in late 1998 as a standard for a group of audio and video coding formats and related technology by the ISO/IEC Moving Picture Experts Group (MPEG). Despite its extensive use, H.264 is both lossy and encumbered by patents from multiple companies, making it a questionable choice for long-term archiving. However, it may be the only codec available in the authoring software for exporting a video.

Container standard: MPEG-4 Part 14
File extension: .mp4
Description: MPEG-4 Part 14 (MP4) is a container format developed by the Motion Pictures Expert Group. Videos inside MP4 files are encoded with H.264. Audio is usually encoded with Advanced Audio Coding (AAC), but other audio standards can also be used.

---

26 Steve Lhomme, Moritz Bunkus, and Dave Rice, Matroska Specifications, IETF Trust, 2019, accessed July 22, 2019, tools.ietf.org/html/draft-ietf-cellar-matroska-03.

Data Type: Geospatial

Standard: Georeferenced Tagged Image File Format (GeoTIFF)
File extension: .tif
Description: GeoTIFF is an open file format and *de facto* standard based on the TIFF format used as an interchange format for georeferenced raster imagery. NASA uses GeoTIFF in its earth science data systems.[27]

The GeoTIFF Standards Working Group of the OGC is working to update the specification, bring it into conformance with current OGC practices, and provide a forum for evolving the standard in the future, as necessary.[28]

Standard: GeoJSON (IETF RFC 7946, Standards Track)
File extension: .json, .geojson
Description: GeoJSON is a geospatial data interchange format based on JavaScript Object Notation (JSON). It represents data about geographic features, their attributes, and their spatial extents. GeoJSON uses a geographic coordinate reference system—the World Geodetic System 1984—and units of decimal degrees.[29]

Data Type: Building Information Modeling (BIM)

Standard: IFC (ISO 16739)
File extension: .ifc, .ifcXML, .ifcZIP
Description: Since the mid-1990s, buildingSMART[30] and its predecessor organizations (Industry Alliance for Interoperability, International Alliance for Interoperability) have been developing an international standard for information sharing and interoperability of structured digital building models. The Industry Foundation Classes define an object-based **information model**, or **schema**, for the architecture, engineering, and construction industry. They constitute a set of definitions of

---

27 NASA Earth Science Data and Information System Project, GeoTIFF, last updated March 1, 2021, earthdata.nasa.gov/esdis/eso/standards-and-references/geotiff.
28 Open Geospatial Consortium, GeoTIFF SWG, 2021, www.opengeospatial.org/projects/groups/geotiffswg.
29 Howard Butler, Martin Daly, Allan Doyle, Sean Gillies, Stefan Hagen, and Tim Schaub, The GeoJSON Format, IETF Trust, 2016, tools.ietf.org/html/rfc7946.
30 The buildingSMART website is at www.buildingsmart.org.

all the objects encountered in the building industry. The IFC core concepts became an ISO standard in 2013. As of 2019, the current version is ISO 16739-2018. The exchange file formats for exchanging and sharing data according to the conceptual schema are: clear text encoding defined in ISO 10303-21 and Extensible Markup Language (XML), defined in the XML W3C Recommendation.[31] Alternative exchange file formats may be used if they conform to the data schemas.[32]

The IFC coverage includes many types of information, such as the following:
- geometry (volume, areas)
- building elements (walls, openings, stairs, doors)
- spaces and spatial structure (space, building story, building site)
- equipment (ducting, piping, fans)
- furniture (furniture items, furniture systems)
- costing (cost planning, estimates, budget)
- asset identification (maintenance history, inventories)
- associated documents
- work plans (schedules, resource allocation)

The IFC specifications also include support for visualization, such as surface style rendering, materials, and lighting specifications.

Because IFC coverage is so broad, none of the commonly used BIM software products supports the full schema. This can lead to incomplete export of BIM data into IFC format, unless the information content desired and the capabilities and limitations of the software are well understood. A subset of the schema and attribute data is referred to as a "model view definition." A particular model view definition is defined to support one or many recognized workflows in the building construction and facility management industry sector. Each workflow identifies data exchange requirements for software applications. Conforming software applications need to identify the model view definition(s) they support.

---

31 W3C, "XML Essentials," 2015, www.w3.org/standards/xml/core.
32 International Organization for Standardization, ISO 16739-1:2018: Industry Foundation Classes (IFC) for data sharing in the construction and facility management industries—Part 1: Data schema, 2018, www.iso.org/standard/70303.html.

Basic Considerations for Archivists

Once grounded in an understanding of the practices, technologies, and standards employed by the design disciplines, archivists can turn to challenges and considerations that they will likely encounter when working with the born-digital records produced by the design disciplines.

Common Challenges in Establishing File Integrity

Moving born-digital design records through the archival processes of appraisal, acquisition, arrangement, description, reference and access, and preservation (to name the most central processes) can be less than straightforward. The challenges outlined below can be further exacerbated if the archivist does not conduct a thorough interview with the donor, and ideally with additional members of their firm, to understand how they organized their design data.

File integrity is a well-known topic for those who currently practice digital preservation.[33] Digital objects (usually represented as files in a computer interface) are more susceptible to change than analog information resources, and digital archivists have developed a suite of workflows and tools to respond to this situation.[34] More often than not, these tools and workflows establish, record, or verify that a file has not changed since it was acquired by the archive and that the file is what it claims to be (integrity as reliability and authenticity, respectively).[35]

With born-digital design records, however, archivists cannot rely only on **checksum** tools to ensure that the content will display properly. It is true that if an archivist can document a designer's technological ecosystem (ideally through interviews) and any software dependencies, most immediate pitfalls can be avoided. But as more work is done with the records, and especially the CAD and BIM data, more integrity issues will likely arise, as discussed in Modules 25 and 26.

---

33 Diane Dietrich and Frank Adelstein, "Archival Science, Digital Forensics, and New Media Art," *Digital Investigation* 14, no. 1 (August 2015): S138–S141.

34 COPTR, "Community Owned digital Preservation Tool Registry (COPTR)," last modified April 26, 2019, https://coptr.digipres.org/Main_Page, captured at https://perma.cc/LN3J-85EA.

35 Luciana Duranti, "The Reliability and Authenticity of Electronic Records," in *Preservation of the Integrity of Electronic Records*, ed. Terry Eastwood (Dordrecht, Germany: Springer Science+Business Media, 2002), 23–30.

For instance, born-digital design records can rarely, if ever, be considered at the individual file level. Adopting a group-level perspective of records is not new to archivists, but such a perspective often operates at a conceptual or semantic level. That is, users and archivists can often derive a richer sense or meaning from records when they are considered as part of a group. With born-digital design records, a group-level perspective is essential at the technological level. Design files will often not *work* (or, perhaps worse, they may display but be missing information, unbeknownst to the archivist or eventual user) if their integrity as a group of files is not established and verified.

The component files that play the most prevalent role in this sort of integrity is reference drawings. Essentially consisting of a file path to another drawing (and also known as an X-Ref/ in AutoCAD and other Autodesk products), reference drawings allow design practitioners to collaborate more easily and more effectively but have the effect of creating external dependencies on one or more individual design drawing files. Elements of a design—say, a roof or a mechanical system—can be stored in a different file but, for all intents and purposes, exist in the file where it is referenced. When the references are broken, the referenced elements are no longer available to the reference drawing—and this is where the integrity can be affected. Sometimes error messages in the authoring software can indicate whether the apparently missing content is intentional or a problem. It is worth noting that reference drawings can be merged with the drawings that reference them; ideally, the designer or design firm can be persuaded to do this before acquisition.

References can be broken in several ways. Not surprisingly, if a reference drawing is somehow separated from a file that references it (for example, by storing the two drawings on separate hard drives or servers), the connection between the two will likely be broken. Similarly, if a reference drawing's file path is an absolute file path (as opposed to a relative file path; see Figure 9), the connection will almost certainly be broken when the design files are transferred to the archive, which will have its own root directory structure and naming conventions.[36]

In both of these examples, the archivist should maintain file groups together and be aware of the references that files are assuming. But

---

36 Alex Ball, *Preserving Computer-Aided Design (CAD)*, Digital Preservation Coalition Technology Watch Report (Great Britain: Digital Preservation Coalition, 2013), 11, http://dx.doi.org/10.7207/twr13-02.

Navigating the Technical Landscape of Born-Digital Design Records   65

Mac Example

Absolute:

/Macintosh HD/Users/user/Projects/180/180_2012_WJB Naming Renderings/WJBCFS.ai

Relative:

180/180_2012_WJB Naming Renderings/WJBCFS.ai

Windows Example

Absolute:

C:\Users\user\Documents\Projects\180\180_2012_WJB Naming Renderings/WJBCFS.ai

Relative:

180\180_2012_WJB Naming Renderings/WJBCFS.ai

Figure 9: Examples of absolute and relative directory paths in Mac and Windows environments

what constitutes a file group? Appraisal and preliminary descriptive analysis should help the archivist make decisions on what drawings are related to each other. However, it is possible for reference drawings to be referenced by many different projects, some of which may not be immediately related to one another. For instance, a firm designing for a multi-branch client may share a core set of files for color palettes, furniture, and font types. In such cases, file groups that encompass every external reference may be too large in terms of file size to be accommodated in a typical server share or archival processing storage directory.

Archivists can check for the presence of reference drawings in a design file, or they can discover how many design files are using a particular reference drawing. For instance, for AutoCAD files (.dwg), archivists can make use of the DOSLib library and its dos_xreflist function to generate a list of reference drawings for a given .dwg file.[37] This particular library requires knowledge of the Microsoft Visual Studio

---

37   Dale Fugier, dos_xreflist, GitHub, last modified November 30, 2018, accessed July 12, 2019, https://github.com/dalefugier/DOSLib/wiki/dos_xreflist.

2017 programming interface, but such automated tools may be preferable to more manual methods that may also rely on access to and knowledge of the file's native software environment.

Reference drawings are not the only possible threat to born-digital design file integrity. Other references, such as to external databases, documents, or websites, may be embedded in a design file. Spreadsheets and GIS databases, in particular, can be essential to a design, whether the spreadsheet is providing information that determines the parameters of a model or the database is used to modify the design's display.[38]

A design file can contain all the information it was meant to contain but *appear* to be incomplete. Such a case would be an example of a designer intentionally leaving areas of a design unfinished or filling in design areas with stock imagery and product information. The appearance of incompleteness may lead an archivist to question the file's integrity—and with good reason. However, a more comprehensive analysis of the project data in which the design file is found, as well as input and guidance from the record creators, should provide confirmation on whether the file is displaying all of the design that it was meant to display. Indeed, an archivist should exercise caution before making a final assessment of integrity based exclusively on a visual inspection of a design file in native format. This is an example of how validating the native format file against related outputs can be particularly helpful.

Color management is a fast-moving area of technology that is of interest to both filmmakers and archivists. However, it presents another potential threat to file integrity, and with color often playing a significant role in design, any changes to a design's color may result in the loss of the object's significant properties.[39] A number of variables can alter the color that a designer perceived on their workstation display, after it has been transferred to a collecting organization and viewed on one of the organization's many workstations or public displays. Those variables include the color profiles used by the designer and those used by the collecting organization; whether or not the profiles have been embedded in the design files; whether or not the display hard-

---

38 Ball, *Preserving Computer-Aided Design*, 12.
39 Geoffrey Yeo, "'Nothing Is the Same as Something Else': Significant Properties and Notions of Identity and Originality," *Archival Science* 10, no. 2 (June 2010): 86–90, https://doi.org /10.1007/s10502-010-9119-9. As Yeo notes, the idea of significance is subjective.

ware (monitors) is calibrated; whether or not there is a profile connection space (PCS) that can translate the designer's profile (especially if it is non-standard or specialized) to the organization's profile; and the capability of the organization's software and operating systems' color management systems to convert color spaces appropriately.[40]

Taken as a whole, the tools to maintain color integrity from the initial computer monitor where the design was developed to the final output, printed or digital, is referred to as a Color Matching Module (CMM). The International Color Consortium (color.org) has developed an open standard CMM at the operating system level, and both Macs and PCs now incorporate a CMM at the operating system level. Adobe offers their own CMM, which can be downloaded from their website. Color management is likely to be more problematic with born-digital design data created before the mid-1990s.

Archivists familiar with digitization best practices will likely also be familiar with one other design file integrity issue: image resolution. Specifically, raster images (TIFF, JPEG, PNG, GIF, etc.) are at issue here, because the concept of resolution does not apply to vector images (as they are not composed of pixels). Raster images, however, are made of pixels. And raster images are not confined to photographic images—they can be design drawings exported from CAD software. In fact, any rendering created by digital design software is a raster image. Raster images can also be maps and embedded in a variety of formats like PDF and Microsoft PowerPoint. Often, the embedding process will apply lossy compression to an image, which will literally obscure details in the image and thereby affect the integrity of the image file. In such cases, the archivist should document where the highest-resolution files reside in the collection.

One must also bear in mind image resolution when migrating image files to an archival format. Almost by definition, archival image formats will not apply lossy compression (rather, they use lossless compression). But again, consider the situation in which an image is embedded in a Microsoft Word document: care must be taken when converting the file to PDF, making sure that the Adobe Acrobat settings will not apply lossy compression.

---

40 Kristine Fallon Associates, Inc., *Collecting, Archiving and Exhibiting Digital Design Data*, 2, 5–7. This passage provides a thorough discussion of color management.

Navigating Software Dependencies

Much like the preservation challenges related to file integrity, software dependency is not a challenge unique to born-digital design records; however, design records are unique in their degree and scale of software dependence. Although the intent of the architect or designer can be well understood through schematic and other project-as-designed drawings found in ubiquitous file formats like PDF and Microsoft PowerPoint, and many organizations and researchers will be satisfied consulting presentation deliverables, the desire for deeper analysis calls for consulting the original design data. There is no substitute for extensive knowledge of the intended information content and the computer application that created the data. If a researcher wanted to understand the designer's interaction with the software, the availability of that software is indispensable, as is the original environment in which that software existed. A detailed discussion of emulation and virtualization of software is discussed in Module 25.

At the individual file level, archivists should be aware that the native software title will provide the closest rendering of the design; knowing the last used version of the software title can be just as important. As Alex Ball notes in *Preserving Computer-Aided Design*, different versions of the same software title may contain different modeling and feature logic (buried in the software's internal architecture and not apparent to the end user), which can produce different displays of the same design file.[41]

Taking a project-level view, archivists will discover that many groups of design files are created by many different types of software (as described by the surveys discussed earlier). Besides CAD and BIM file formats, image files, document files, database files, and others are typically found in a project. Furthermore, a single design file may be created with several different software titles. This does not necessarily mean that an archivist will need more than one title to access the file, but it does mean that the archivist will need to make a choice when documenting dependencies or engage in time-consuming trial-by-error activities to confirm.

Many design software titles also allow designers to extend the software's features through the development of custom software code

---

41 Ball, *Preserving Computer-Aided Design*, 10.

(usually written in a scripting language and known as a **script**). This practice has matured to the point that **visual scripting** programs now exist to facilitate the development of this type of code. For instance, Grasshopper produces scripts for Rhino, while Dynamo is made to work with Revit. However the scripts are developed, the resulting source code may be as essential to a design file's generation as the native software title itself. A good working relationship with the designer or design firm donating the records can be the most efficient way to find out about the use of such custom scripts. If the scripts are included, though, archivists may ask: How are they used in the software? Is it as simple as opening a design file to ensure that the custom script is deployed? Or are other settings or configurations necessary? What intrinsic value is there in a .gh file created with Grasshopper?

Archivists should be aware that some firms may consider the scripts proprietary to their practice and may balk at including them in a donation. Custom parametric objects, sometimes used in object-oriented design software, are another type of content that firms may not want included in an archive. (However, this objection should not extend to the outputs—the drawings, renderings, videos, etc.—because these show the results but do not reveal the underlying proprietary logic.)

With all of these perspectives in mind, any processing plan for an accession of born-digital design records should include a thorough review of, at minimum, file extensions and last-modified dates found in the accession. Such information will give archivists enough context to begin attempting educated guesses of the software that was used to create the design records. Understanding of file extensions and headers of certain scripting languages will assist archivists in identifying the presence of scripts. File characterization tools will strengthen the accuracy of the review, as file extensions can sometimes be misleading or arbitrary. Work on automating the recognition of software title, version, and operating system is in progress,[42] but in the meantime archivists can ease many aspects of their workflow by compiling a list of software programs used in each project or group of design records.

---

42   Euan Cochrane, "Designing a Universal Virtual Interactor (UVI) for digital objects," *Digital Preservation Coalition* (blog), November 23, 2018, https://www.dpconline.org/blog/idpd/designing-a-uvi-for-digital-objects, captured at https://perma.cc/HN28-V4NL.

It is worth noting that some software titles in the CAD/BIM market are so complex that they contain more than one software license. A partner company, for instance, may have contributed a function or feature that the partner company licenses to the main software title's publisher. At the time of the main software title's publication and distribution, these licenses-in-licenses are not an issue, because end-user licenses will likely include the subsidiary licenses. As time passes, intellectual property changes hands from one rights holder to another, and licenses lapse and renew, a license acquired by the archive may not be as comprehensive as the original license.

Cloud-Based Applications

The design workflow for the built environment is a heavily collaborative work process that requires software that can support both in-office and across-office collaboration. Reflecting the connectivity capable by technology today, designers are rapidly adopting software that facilitates multiple offices of the same firm, as well as offices of multiple firms, to contribute to the same model or documents.

Platforms such as Office 365, Box, DropBox, SharePoint, and GoogleDrive are all examples of this type of collaborative working space, posing levels of complication that are further heightened when the files become more complex, such as building models. These platforms support hierarchical file organization that is comparable to that of project folders on a network drive. Note that syncing these platforms to the network drive's folders can potentially cause additional records management challenges with duplicative storage or misalignment, depending on a project team's file backup practices. It is imperative that design firms and project teams document, establish, and implement policies and workflows for how they are using cloud-based storage platforms independently or in tandem with more traditional network drives.

Over the past decade, industry-leading Autodesk has developed cloud-based services that include modeling software, BIM360, which enables consultants and sub-contractors to contribute directly to the lead design firm's model, as well as supporting remote collaboration in a firm. This practice keeps all of the design players abreast of changing information and design parameters, and, while authorship is fairly trackable, there are longer-term concerns around the records management of these shared files stored (at least one copy) on Autodesk's servers. This multiple-location storage, while often lauded as the appropriate way to ensure the security of the files (**Lots of Copies Keeps Stuff Safe, or LOCKSS**), the reality for collecting institutions will be murky waters to confirm rights restrictions and ownership. The same issues of connecting reference files and keeping linked files in alignment persist in this new platform but are further strained by the variability of storage and workflow practices with this new platform. The design and output workflows are just as important to understand as what the software is used to produce, and the former is often much more challenging to document or understand without being embedded in the project work or office environment.

Adobe Creative Cloud is another major piece of cloud-based software used by designers. Similar to concerns about BIM360, there are concerns about linking files and establishing workflows to ensure that the entirety of the file's content are captured. Consistently listed as one of the most-used software programs in surveys conducted since 2015, the shift of the Adobe Suite to the cloud will have significant ramifications for collecting institutions, depending on their collection policies and the anticipated uses of collections by their designated communities. An additional consideration is the subscription model, or Software-as-a-Service (SaaS), that these cloud-based platforms require, presenting a precarious model for ensuring that files are not lost because of an unpaid bill. When a project closes out, the designer of record should move the project archive to internal servers from the cloud. This requires the archivist to be more proactive and have earlier conversations with potential donors, as well as to potentially provide recommendations for records management and file capture to ensure that these files are included in any donation.

Free Readers

The cost of acquiring and maintaining all of the software used to render or experience the information contained in born-digital design files has already proven untenable for even the most financially stable and supported institutions. Luckily, free readers, which are software programs available through web browsers or for free download, are available for many of the mainstream and prevalent software and file types. These have existed for much of the past decade and, in some cases, even longer. Many of these free readers are provided by the software companies themselves—not with archives and archival research in mind but to provide reading capabilities to former and current customers who are unable to access older files in current versions of software.

Many of these free readers offer high-quality rendering capabilities and fulfill many of the basic requirements for providing access that concern archival institutions. Autodesk,[43] SketchUp,[44] Rhinoceros 3D,[45] and form•Z[46] are four software companies who provide high fidelity and functionality in their free readers for users to experience a wide swath of the files produced by their proprietary software. This is of utmost importance, as Matthew Allen explained during the 2017 "Designing the Future Landscape" summit at the Library of Congress: "software is sometimes visible in the architecture," meaning that a viewer who is proficient with the tools can glean additional information based on the functionality visible in the digital object.[47]

Similar to how quickly the design software experiences patches/updates and new version releases, the available free readers continue to evolve, and offerings change. Archivists should look for free reader lists that are often published in 3D printing publications or design software forums.[48] Free reader resource pages often provide directions or links to tutorials to introduce functionality to the user.

Recommendations

Archival Approaches

The most important factor in the successful ingest of born-digital design data is the interest and support of the donor. As demonstrated in the case studies included in this module, each firm maintains its

---

[43] Autodesk, Inc., Autodesk Viewer, https://viewer.autodesk.com; Autodesk, Inc., Navisworks 3D Viewer, https://www.autodesk.com/products/navisworks/3d-viewers.
[44] Trimble, SketchUp, https://www.sketchup.com/plans-and-pricing/sketchup-free.
[45] Robert McNeel & Associates, "Downloads," Rhinoceros, https://www.rhino3d.com/download.
[46] AutoDesSys, "form•Z free," www.formz.com/products/formzfree.html.
[47] Matthew Allen, "Expanded Archives of Digital Culture" (paper presented at "Designing the Future Landscape: Digital Architecture, Design and Engineering Assets," Washington, DC, November 16, 2017).
[48] "Best Free DWG Viewers of 2021 (Online and Offline)," All3DP, January 12, 2022, https://all3dp.com/2/best-free-dwg-viewers-autocad, captured at https://perma.cc/DG7B-ZKUA.

data in an organized fashion but not in exactly the same way. The archivist needs to understand that firm-specific organization. It is also in a designer's business interest to ensure that the firm can retrieve data from previous projects. A design firm ensuring its own access to design data from past projects goes a long way toward ensuring access for the archivist as well.

Even granting full cooperation and interest from the record donors, it may be useful for archivists to conceive the options for archiving and providing long-term access to born-digital design records as beginning with a basic approach and building from there to more complex and resource-intense approaches. The following are three options, which are by no means the only three options, but may serve as templates from which a more organization-specific approach (guided by the organization's collection development policy) can be developed.

At the most basic level, archivists may consider collecting only what the designer would consider their "outputs"—that is, documents, 2D drawings, presentations, photographs, and videos that the designer has delivered to the client or other constituent. Every design phase produces such outputs, so this approach will not necessarily include less coverage of the design process. Indeed, examples of such outputs can be found in each phase: high-resolution images, videos, or static renderings from the Pre-Contract phase or presentation slides that bring together different design options in the Schematic Design phase; the outline specification during the Design Development phase; 2D exports from a BIM software program during the Construction Documents phase; addenda from designers or proposed changes from successful bidder during the Procurement phase; or scanned copies of redlined drawings during the Construction phase.

With this basic approach, one can follow general digital preservation practices without much deviation. Collecting or migrating to archival formats can be more or less straightforward, with file formats such as PDF, TIFF, JPEG, Microsoft Word, and Microsoft PowerPoint being predominant. To maintain file integrity, archivists would assess a design firm's color management practice and make certain that resolution is not lost during any conversion to archival formats. A collection curated by such an approach will likely result in design files that are not problematic for online viewers and discovery systems and, if necessary or appropriate, print out in paper form with no loss of information. In addition, migration from these archival formats over time will be less problematic.

Building on this basic approach, archivists and their organizations can adopt what the 2004 Art Institute of Chicago study labeled as a "two-tier" approach.[49] On one hand (or tier), archivists will follow the basic approach as though that were the only approach they were following (the outputs would look the same). On the other hand, archivists would also accession original design data. Ideally, the designer will provide the design data in a standard format, as well as native format, and it is worth noting that an archivist sufficiently trained in design practices and software can migrate design data in proprietary formats to standard formats. However, there may be cases in which archivists find that the design data remains stored in its native (proprietary) format.

In this scenario, not only would it suffice for archivists to collect and ensure the bit-level preservation of the digital design data (such as 3D CAD drawings and BIM models), but, in anticipation of requests for such data in its native environment, archivists would need to document as thoroughly as possible (1) the practices and workflows of the designer or design firm and (2) the hardware and software used to create the design data.[50]

This sort of upfront documentation can mitigate (though not eliminate) the challenges associated with emulating obsolete software environments and improve response times to research requests. For instance, if the designer can only document linked or referenced files before accessioning, archivists will still need to resolve the links and references before providing access. Given these challenges, proactive promotion and advertisement of born-digital design data in collections may not be advisable. Rather, it is possible to quietly offer access services (which could include access to data migrated to standard formats) when a researcher requests it. Finally, the end goal of this second tier of the "two-tiered" approach is not to resolve all questions surrounding authenticity, screen fidelity, and information loss when

---

[49] Kristine Fallon Associates, Inc., *Collecting, Archiving and Exhibiting Digital Design Data*.
[50] Some hardware, such as Wacom and other electronic drawing surfaces, or virtual reality headsets and handsets, may be helpful for viewing or experiencing the design files as intended.

researchers request access to born-digital design data. Rather, the goal would be to provide direct access to the data in its native format, in whatever ways that current technology allows and aided by the mitigation measures described above.

Many organizations will find the two-tiered approach suitable for their mission.

A third "full-service" approach lies at the far end of the spectrum. With this approach, an organization would collect in a similar manner as described above, acquiring both the archival outputs and the native born-digital design data. However, instead of adopting an access-on-demand service for the native data, organizations following this full-service approach would allocate more resources toward proactive and preemptive rendering of the native data. The reasons for such proactive work on the native born-digital design data are typically curatorial—that is, an organization collects the design records to display, interpret, and interrogate the design process and its artifacts. But there is no doubt that substantial resources are required to pursue this approach.

Not only that, but the approach will inevitably lead the organization directly into the middle of the technical and legal challenges associated with software preservation and emulation. A more focused software collecting initiative would need to be pursued alongside this "full-service" approach. Whether the organization collects on its own or joins a consortia initiative such as the SPN, the organization will need to allocate more resources to pursuing legal and technical solutions to broadening access to obsolete, legacy software. Ideally, multiple coordinated efforts from a variety of organizations (such as those that collect born-digital design records) should be involved in developing the infrastructure necessary for legacy software access. That said, infrastructure building is a slow, long-term process, and the patience required for gradual progress may be at odds with the pace an organization requires in the short-term.

Recommendations for the Design Office

The Art Institute of Chicago's 2004 *Collecting, Archiving, and Exhibiting Digital Design Data* study formulated comprehensive recommendations for both design firms and archivists to support successful ingest of born-digital design data by archival institutions.[51] Following is a list of recommendations from the study, with some additions and updates that address the changing technology landscape.

- Maintain checkpoint data that corresponds to each major project milestone, documenting the relationship between output and native data at that point.
- Follow standard or well-documented digital data organization and naming conventions.
- Provide output images, such as renderings and Photoshop montages at print-quality resolution in uncompressed TIFF format.
- Export animations and videos in uncompressed AVI format. If the software does not support uncompressed AVI, the preferred codec is FFV1 and file format is .mkv. FFV1 can also be used in conjunction with the .avi and .mov formats.
- Provide CAD drawings, PowerPoint presentations, and hybrid outputs in PDF/A format.
- For most current information on recommended formats for 3D and design files, consult the Library of Congress Recommended Format Statement website at https://www.loc.gov/preservation/resources/rfs/design3D.html and the National Archives and Records Administration website at https://www.archives.gov/recordsmgmt/policy/transfer-guidance-tables.html.
- Embed source color profiles in all files.
- Embed all components of compound files—particularly externally referenced files in CAD and BIM—in a single file when possible.
- Document all linked or referenced files, if embedding of components is impossible.
- Provide native data in original format.
- If the receiving organization has a requirement for updating the information over the long term, that data should also be delivered in a standard format (such as IFC).

Recommendations for archival practices related to born-digital design records, including use of Archival Information Packages (AIP),

---

51   Kristine Fallon Associates, Inc., *Collecting, Archiving and Exhibiting Digital Design Data.*

delivery requirements and procedures, and actions that archivists should take after accessioning and ingest of records, are addressed in Modules 25 and 26.

Conclusion

There are many factors, ranging from technological expertise to access to the donor to budgetary capacities, that need to be taken into account before collections of born-digital design records are accessioned. There are different intentions and levels of investment an organization must consider when establishing its collection, preservation, and access policies. Each organization's mission varies to support its designated community, and incorporating born-digital design records into its collection should not fundamentally alter this scope and mission. This may result in a feeling that more could be done to support born-digital records included in a collection, but as an organization conducts cost-benefit analyses to determine acceptable storage and service spaces for analog/paper-based collections, its archival staff members must also decide what is a reasonable expectation for stewardship of born-digital design records they can provide, given limitations.

Whatever decision-making processes need to take place, it is critical to not delay engaging with these records. Engaging with donors early and often through initial donor interviews, establishing the Deed of Gift, and facilitating the accession raises donors' awareness of the preservation and access challenges their records will present in the future. Such actions would provide archival professionals opportunities to document and assess the practices and critical information and files in the collection. Organizations that include design records in their collecting scope should not shy away from collecting born-digital design records, or a gap in the collective archival holdings of design processes and projects may develop. Concerns about the known costly complications, as well as the fear of the unknown complexities of born-digital design records, are valid; however, these issues should not result in total inaction, but rather inspire testing and outreach to explore and better understand the dual visual-technological literacy required to appreciate and place born-digital design records in the context of an organization's larger design records holdings.

Appendix: Glossary of Terminology

addendum. An additional document that modifies a contract; the change can be administrative (e.g., deadline) or technical (e.g., a change of material or product)

algorithmic generation of form. An algorithm is a procedure for solving a mathematical problem in a finite number of steps that frequently involves repetition of an operation.[52] Algorithmic generation of form, sometimes referred to as generative design, leverages algorithmic procedures to create complex geometries from small amounts of input data.

Architect's Sketch (ASK). Issued to clarify design intent, typically in response to a contractor question

attribute. Non-geometric information associated with a specific element of the design; an example is descriptive information (e.g., manufacturer, model, cost) of building products and equipment

behavior. In object technology, the way an object reacts to other objects in a file—for example, the bottom of a door is always at floor level; if the floor level is changed, the door will move with it

born-digital design records. Design data that was originally created using software, which contrasts to digital design data that was created on paper or as a physical model and then scanned or digitized

Building Information Model (BIM). Building representation created by BIM software

Building Information Modeling (BIM). Software that uses structured data, wherein the software objects correspond to real-world building elements. There is an underlying schema that describes the objects included in a building as well as their relationships. BIM software is also capable of managing many

---

[52] Merriam-Webster, "algorithm," in *Merriam-Webster Dictionary*, 2021, https://www.merriam-webster.com/dictionary/algorithm, captured at https://perma.cc/KK5T-XB8P.

attributes (also known as "properties") in the model. The vision is that a BIM could be a complete electronic description of an intended building, used for design, construction, and facility management. As of 2019, this vision had not been realized. BIM may also refer to the process of creating a Building Information Model.

change directive. Document that directs the contractor to perform additional work when the time and/or cost of the work has not been agreed on by the owner and the contractor performing the work

change order. A contractual document that makes changes to the work as agreed to by the owner, contractor and designer.

checksum. A unique alphanumeric value generated by an algorithm interacting with a digital file. If the same algorithm is used more than once on the same digital file, the same checksum value will be generated.

codec. Short for "compress/decompress," referring to the need to compress video frames for storage and decompress them for display. A codec is the mechanism by which this compress/decompress activity takes place. A codec can be implemented in hardware or software.

computer-aided design (CAD). Also referred to "computer-aided drafting" in the 1970s and 80s. CAD software provides on-screen tools for design activities, with a focus on the production of 2D technical drawings. CAD software can also incorporate 3D capabilities, attributes, and linkages to design analyses such as structural and energy analyses.

deliverable. Something that is required by contract to be provided

electronic flythrough. Computer animation for visualizing a building, site, city, and so on, that involves movement through the computer model of the environment, typically from a helicopter's perspective

Geographic Information System (GIS). Software that provides a visual representation of geospatial data. GIS handles storing those data in a database, querying them and visualizing them in a mapped format.

information model. A representation of concepts and the relationships, constraints, rules, and operations to specify data semantics for a chosen domain of discourse. "Data semantics" means that the model describes the meaning of its data objects by relating them to the real world.

lossless data compression. One type of algorithm that reduces the size of a file. Lossless data compression achieves size reduction while maintaining the same amount of information. In the case of an image file, this means that the original resolution of the image is maintained.

lossy data compression. One type of algorithm that reduces the size of a file. Lossy compression reduces file size at the expense of some amount of information in the file. In the case of an image file, this means that it will be impossible to restore the image to its original resolution.

Lots of Copies Keep Stuff Safe (LOCKSS). Widely accepted best practices in the digital preservation field and beyond for ensuring the persistence of digital information. Familiar risks such as media failure and format obsolescence are accounted for, as well as important but less considered factors, such as human error, malicious attack, and organizational failure.

model view. A subset of the data schema and object data defined to support one or many recognized workflows, such as structural analysis or cost estimating

native format. The data format of the software application that originally produced the data. For example, a BIM produced in Revit would have a native format of .rvt, even though it may have been exported to .ifc and its drawings may have been saved as .dwg.

object class. In object technology, the class packages all the attributes and methods of an object, including its geometry if it has a graphic representation. Methods are the functions and code that operate on the data and express the behavior of the object.

object instance. While the object class provides the "template" for an object, the object instance is the concrete occurrence of the object within the file and provides values for its attributes.

object-based. The elements manipulated by the software are objects. See "object class" and "object instance" above.

outputs. Images or other digital artifacts that designers choose to communicate to their team or client

parametric modeling/parametric design. The creation of a digital design model based on a series of pre-programmed rules or algorithms known as "parameters." Parametric rules create relationships between different elements of the design so that a change in one element can automatically update elements such as size and configuration of other elements.

program. In the architectural or interior design sense, the documentation of the functional requirements of the project, primarily the number and types of spaces needed

properties. Descriptions of the characteristics of an object; used synonymously with *attributes*

punchlist. A document prepared by the designer near the end of construction listing outstanding work that the contractor must complete before final payment

record drawings. Drawings that reflect the as-constructed building's changes from the Construction Drawings; typically prepared by the architect based on the contractor's field mark-ups

Request for Information (RFI). A formal process used during construction whereby the contractor asks the designer to clarify or to fill any information gaps in the drawings, specifications, contract, or other documents

schedule. Tabular listing of all products of the same type (e.g., doors, windows, light fixtures) required for a project, along with their relevant attributes

schema. In this text, used synonymously with *information model*

script. In this context, a computer program that executes in another program

submittals. Information, such as shop drawings, material data, samples, and product data that the contractor is required to supply to the designer for approval before procurement or installation. At the end of construction, there are additional submittals of documents such as warranties and maintenance manuals that are submitted "For Record."

systems. Refers to building systems—structural, mechanical, electrical, and so on

UniFormat. A classification system published by the Construction Specifications Institute (CSI) and Construction Specifications Canada (CSC) that arranges construction information based on functional elements, without regard to the materials and methods used to accomplish them

visual scripting. Technique that allows users to create computer programs by sequencing and connecting program elements graphically, rather than by specifying them textually

Bibliography

"Best Free DWG Viewers of 2021 (Online and Offline)." All3DP, January 12, 2022. https://all3dp.com/2/best-free-dwg-viewers-autocad, captured at https://perma.cc/DG7B-ZKUA.

Allen, Matthew. "Expanded Archives of Digital Culture." Paper presented at "Designing the Future Landscape: Digital Architecture, Design & Engineering Assets," Library of Congress, Washington, DC, November 16, 2017.

American Institute of Architects. *AIA Document B101™-2017: Standard Agreement Between Owner and Architect.* Washington, DC: American Institute of Architects, 2017.

—————. *AIA Document G202™-2013 Building Information Modeling Protocol Form.* Washington, DC: American Institute of Architects, 2013.

Art Institute of Chicago. "Project Update, October 2007." Digital Design Data. October 2007. https://web.archive.org/web/20071228102829/http://www.artic.edu/aic/collections/dept_architecture/ddd.html

"Autodesk Viewer: Free Online File Viewer." Autodesk Viewer | Free Online File Viewer. Accessed August 27, 2019. https://viewer.autodesk.com.

Ball, Alex. *Preserving Computer-Aided Design (CAD).* Digital Preservation Coalition Technology Watch Report. Great Britain: Digital Preservation Coalition, April 2013. http://dx.doi.org/10.7207/twr13-02.

BIMFORUM. "Level of Development (LOD) Specification Part I & Commentary for Building Information Models and Data." December 2020. https://bimforum.org/resources/Documents/LOD%20Spec%202020%20Part%20I%202020-12-31.pdf, captured at https://perma.cc/C5L3-3KMS.

Cochrane, Euan. "Designing a Universal Virtual Interactor (UVI) for digital objects." *Digital Preservation Coalition* (blog), November 23, 2018, https://www.dpconline.org/blog/idpd/designing-a-uvi-for-digital-objects, captured at https://perma.cc/HN28-V4NL.

Construction Specifications Institute and Construction Specifications Canada. *UniFormat: A Uniform Classification of Construction Systems and Assemblies.* https://www.csiresources.org/standards/uniformat.

COPTR. "Community Owned digital Preservation Tool Registry (COPTR)." Last modified April 26, 2019, https://coptr.digipres.org/Main_Page, captured at https://perma.cc/LN3J-85EA.

Construction Specifications Institute and Construction Specifications Canada, *CSI Uniformat 2010.* https://www.csiresources.org/standards/uniformat.

Designing the Future Landscape: Digital Architecture, Design & Engineering Assets Morning Session." Library of Congress, November 16, 2017. Video. 3 hours 2 minutes. https://www.loc.gov/item/webcast-8280.

Designing the Future Landscape: Digital Architecture, Design & Engineering Assets (Morning Session). Library of Congress, n.d., https://www.youtube.com/watch?v=8XMko7E49E4.

Dietrich, Diane, and Frank Adelstein. "Archival Science, Digital Forensics, and New Media Art." *Digital Investigation* 14, no. 1 (August 2015): S138–S141.

"Downloads." Rhino. Accessed August 27, 2019. https://www.rhino3d.com/download.

Duranti, Luciana. "The Reliability and Authenticity of Electronic Records." In *Preservation of the Integrity of Electronic Records.* Edited by Terry Eastwood. Dordrecht, Germany: Springer Science+Business Media, 2002.

Eastman, Chuck, Paul Teicholz, Rafael Sacks, and Kathleen Liston. *BIM Handbook (A Guide to Building Information Modeling for Owners, Managers, Designers, Engineers and Contractors).* 2nd ed. Hoboken, NJ: John Wiley & Sons, Inc., 2011.

Fallon, Kristine K., and Mark E. Palmer. *Capital Facilities Information Handover Guide, Part 1.* Gaithersburg, MD: U.S. Department of Commerce, National Institute of Standards and Technology, 2006)

———. *General Buildings Information Handover Guide: Principles, Methodology and Case Studies.* Gaithersburg, MD: U.S. Department of Commerce, National Institute of Standards and Technology, 2007.

"*File Information Tool Set (FITS): Introduction,*" Projects at Harvard, accessed August 27, 2019, https://projects.iq.harvard.edu/fits/home.

"form•Z free." form•Z free. AutoDesSys, n.d. http://www.formz.com/products/formzfree.html.

"Free 3D Modeling Software: 3D Design Online: SketchUp Free Subscription." SketchUp. Accessed August 27, 2019. https://www.sketchup.com/plans-and-pricing/sketchup-free.

"Introduction." *File Information Tool Set (FITS).* Harvard University. https://projects.iq.harvard.edu/fits/home.

Itami, Robert M., and Robert J. Raulings. *SAGE Introductory Guidebook.* Melbourne, Australia: Digital Land Systems Research, 1993. Excerpt at www.cs.upc.edu/~lpv/general.dir/whatgis.html, captured at https://perma.cc/U54B-26B2.

Kristine Fallon Associates, Inc. *Collecting, Archiving and Exhibiting Digital Design Data* (Chicago: Art Institute of Chicago, 2004).

Lehane, Richard. "Siegfried." *IT for Archivists*, accessed August 27, 2019, https://www.itforarchivists.com/siegfried.

Leventhal, Aliza. *Designing the Future Landscape: Digital Architecture, Design & Engineering Assets.* Washington, DC: Library of Congress, March 12, 2018.

National Archives (UK), *DROID: User Guide* (July 2017), accessed July 25, 2019, captured at https://perma.cc/9W5L-5R7D.

National Institute of Building Sciences, "National BIM Standard-United States V3." Accessed August 30, 2019. https://www.nationalbimstandard.org.

———. "U.S. National CAD Standard (NCS) - V6." Accessed August 30, 2019. https://www.nationalcadstandard.org/ncs6.

Sauge, Birgitte. *Digital Design Media in Norwegian Architect's Current Practice, Survey 2016–2017.* Oslo: National Museum of Art, Architecture and Design and Cultural Heritage Mediascapes–Architecture Museums and Digital Design Media, 2019.

"Welcome to PRONOM," The National Archives (UK), accessed August 27, 2019.

Yeo, Geoffrey. "'Nothing Is the Same as Something Else': Significant Properties and Notions of Identity and Originality." *Archival Science* 10, no. 2 (June 2010): 86–116, https://doi.org/10.1007/s10502-010-9119-9.

MODULE 25
EMERGING BEST PRACTICES IN THE ACCESSION, PRESERVATION, AND EMULATION OF BORN-DIGITAL DESIGN MATERIALS

Jody Thompson, Euan Cochrane, Aliza Leventhal, Laura Schroffel, and Emily Vigor

Module 25 Contents

Introduction • 91

Ingest • 93
    Assessing Organization Capacity • 93
    Discussion with Donors • 99
    Deed of Gift • 103
    Dependencies • 106
        Software and Hardware Obsolescence • 106
        Software Licenses • 107
        Versioning/Patches • 107
        Understanding the Technological Ecosystem • 108
        Cloud-Based Platforms • 109

Preservation Fundamentals • 109
    Digital Preservation Frameworks • 109
    Content Preservation Approaches • 117
        Migration • 117
        Migration via Emulation Environments • 118
        Recompiling • 119
        Maintaining a Hardware Museum • 120

Emulation and Virtualization • 121
    Emulation • 121
    Virtualization • 124
        Traditional Use Cases for Virtualization • 124
        Virtualization with VirtualBox, VMWare, or KVM • 125

Digital Forensics Processing • 126

Emulation for Access • 128
    Applications of Emulation and Virtualization for the Preservation of
        and Access to Born-Digital Design Records • 128
    Local Emulation • 130
    Emulation-as-a-Service • 131
    Acquiring Legacy Software • 133
    Complex Records and Dependencies • 133

Potential for Emulation and Virtualization • 135
    Pausing and Citing Views on Designs/Models • 137
    Emulating Networked Environments • 138
    Migration by Emulation • 138

Conclusion • 139

Appendix A: Digital Material Donor Survey • 141

Appendix B: Sample Deed of Gift • 145
    Exhibit A: Description of Collection Materials • 153
    Exhibit B: Transfer of Collection Method • 154
    Exhibit C: Donor Permission • 156
    Exhibit D: Collection Materials That May Contain Sensitive Information and Require Access Restriction • 157
    Exhibit E: Credentials and Permissions • 158

Bibliography • 159

ABOUT THE AUTHORS

Jody Thompson is head of the Archives, Special Collections, and Digital Curation department at Georgia Institute of Technology's Library. She co-authored the Digital Preservation Coalition's Tech Watch Report, *Preserving Born-Digital Design and Construction Records,* in 2021. She is co-chair of the Digital Design Records Task Force, which is part of the Society of American Archivists' Design Records Section. She holds a masters' degree in history from Georgia Southern University.

Euan Cochrane is an information management and long-term digital preservation practitioner with experience in the public, private, and nonprofit sectors. Cochrane leads Yale University Library's digital preservation team, which provides digital preservation infrastructure and services across Yale University's libraries, archives, and museums. Cochrane also has a long history with, and passion for, emulation and software preservation and is leading a number of projects that ensure historic software is preserved and made accessible for future generations.

Aliza Leventhal contributed to this module in her previous role as the corporate archivist and librarian for Sasaki, a Boston-based interdisciplinary design firm (2014–2019). She currently is the head of the Prints and Photographs Division's Technical Services Section at the Library of Congress. Leventhal is the co-founder and co-chair of the Society of American Archivists' (SAA) Design Records Section's Digital Design Records Task Force, and has written and presented extensively in a variety of forums including SAA, the Visual Resources Association, International Confederation of Architectural Museums, and the Library of Congress. She is the co-author of the Digital Preservation Coalition *Preserving Born-Digital Design and Construction Records* Technology Watch Report. She holds an MLIS and an MA in history from Simmons University's Archives Management Program.

Laura Schroffel is the digital archivist in the Getty Research Institute's Special Collections, Collections Management department, where she has worked since 2016. Active in both the Digital Library Federation (DLF) and the Society of American Archivists (SAA), Schroffel is a member of the DLF Born-Digital Access working group as well as SAA's Design Records Section's Digital Design Records subgroup.

Emily Vigor is the archives manager at the Eames Institute. She previously worked as the digital and collections archivist at the Environmental Design Archives at the University of California at Berkeley. She holds an MLIS from San José State University and an MA in art history from Richmond University in London. She has served as a consultant for managing and preserving design records in California and the United Kingdom.

Introduction

Over the past twenty years, archival institutions in North America have slowly developed the practice of collecting and preserving born-digital design records. Members of the archival community have not collectively addressed these files, despite born-digital records occasionally sneaking into collections as ancillary materials of larger design collections or as tests/experiments by the institutions to understand their capacity to collect such materials in the future. This is partially due to the inherent latency of when these materials are collected to when their creators are prepared to donate them to an institution. It is also the result of the gradual and hesitant marriage of subject expertise and digital archives skills in the archival profession.

In the first two decades of the 2000s, the archival profession began to explore the challenges of developing these joint skills and attempting to ask and answer questions about the significant attributes of digital design files and how best to provide long-term access to these files. Each research effort or exhibition has further opened up the conversation, removed some mystery, and clarified the nuance around the creation and use of born-digital design files.

As the landscape has become better understood by archivists, cross-disciplinary conversations have begun among the design record creators, archivists, digital preservationists, academics, and technologists. The year 2017 was significant for such conversations: the Library of Congress, the Architect of the Capitol, and the National Gallery of Art hosted "Designing the Future Landscape: Digital Architecture, Design & Engineering Assets," and Harvard University's Graduate School of Design (GSD) hosted the IMLS-funded "Building for Tomorrow" project.[1] Both brought together stakeholders from the entire lifecycle of born-digital design files to identify opportunities for symbiotic collaboration across industries.

With this corpus of research as an ever-growing and solidifying foundation, institutions have increasingly begun to intentionally collect born-digital design records and are sharing their experiences and

---

[1] Aliza Leventhal, *Designing the Future Landscape: Digital Architecture, Design & Engineering Assets* (Washington, DC: Library of Congress, March 12, 2018); Ann Whiteside, et al., "Building for Tomorrow," Institute of Museum and Library Services, June 16, 2021, https://projects.iq.harvard.edu/files/buildingtomorrow/files/building_for_tomorrow_whitepaper_version_1.0-final2.pdf, captured at https://perma.cc/G4DH-S3CJ.

lessons learned through myriad outlets, including Society of American Archivists (SAA) sessions.[2] Each of these presentations or educational offerings have combined the expertise of digital preservationists/archivists with architecture, design, and engineering subject-expert archivists establishing a shared vocabulary and blended perspective.

This melded perspective is presented throughout this cluster of modules, and especially in this second installment. Through the viewpoint of archivists from public and private academic institutions, as well as private research organizations and corporate archives, this module discusses the challenges and opportunities that collecting born-digital design files present. The following pages walk through the issues and practices to consider for ingest and accessioning, preservation and providing access, from the various institutions collecting born-digital design files. The structure of this module is aligned with the lifecycle of archival collections. However, for born-digital records, this is rarely a purely linear experience; therefore, the discussion will weave elements of preservation and access throughout the module to reflect the reality of the contributing authors. Archivists will gain a better understanding of elements to take into consideration when developing a collection plan and working with a donor.

The information provided in this module reflects a specific moment in time from the experience of only a few archival practitioners. The rapid rate of development and growth in the field of digital preservation means that standards and tools are regularly evolving and being expanded by an active and interested community of diverse practitioners. Archivists must recognize that there are limitations and challenges to what archival organizations are capable of when it comes to the preservation of born-digital design files. However, being prepared with clear missions, collection policies, and expectations for providing

---

2   Examples include a session at the 2016 SAA Annual Meeting, "DWG, RVT, BIM: A New Kind of Alphabet Soup, with a Lot More Heartburn," https://archives2016.sched.com/event/6mYV/309-dwg-rvt-bim-a-new-kind-of-alphabet-soup-with-a-lot-more-heartburn; the Pecha Kucha session at 2018 International Committee of Architecture Museums "Designing and Preserving Digital Architecture – Correlations between Architecture Firms and Collecting Repositories," https://dac.dk/wp-content/uploads/2018/04/ICAM19_official-program.pdf?_ga=2.85152666.2095085305.1522923843-1210852451.1522923843; the 2018 SAA Education course, "Managing Physical & Digital Architecture, Design, and Construction Records," www2.archivists.org/prof-education/course-catalog/managing-physical-digital-architecture-design-and-construction-records, captured at https://perma.cc/A2NK-5QFM; and the 2018 LYRASIS webinar "Introduction to Computer Aided Design (CAD) for Archivists" by Tessa Walsh.

access to born-digital design files, as well as being proactively engaged with donors and design record creators, will help to ensure the long-term access of these files. A 1997 quote by American business consultant icon Peter Drucker states the overall theme of this module:

> In human affairs ... it is pointless to try to predict the future, let alone attempt to look ahead 75 years. But it is possible—and fruitful—to identify major events that have already happened, irrevocably, and that will have predictable effects in the next decade or two. It is possible, in other words, to identify and prepare for the future that *has already happened* [emphasis is the author's].[3]

Ingest

Assessing Organizational Capacity

The capacity of an organization to ingest born-digital design files is reliant on a variety of factors that are essential for the preservation of these records, including technological and financial barriers, and the ability to move files from their original storage media. The preservation of digital content requires the creation of preservation packages to inform archival description, processing, and research. To meet these demands, archival organizations need to ensure that they are prepared to support a variety of means to ingest records.

Firms and individual designers have stored their work in a variety of ways throughout the late twentieth and early twenty-first centuries. They have used physical external media such as floppy discs, compact discs, or Zip™ cartridges, magnetic hard drives, cloud storage services, and myriad other technologies. When it comes time to transfer records to an archival organization, firms' personnel may be amenable to transferring physical media for imaging, they may want an archivist to capture certain files in-house, or they may want to handle the migration of data themselves via a transfer over the internet using a method such as File Transfer Protocol (FTP). Organizations will need to ensure that they are capable of supporting the preferred transfer methodology and assess what equipment they may need to capture this data, or they will need a strong preservation policy in place clearly indicating the breadth of their capacity to transfer or receive files. Records housed on

---

3   Peter F. Drucker, "The Future That Has Already Happened," *Harvard Business Review* (September–October 1997): 2000.

physical digital storage media include inherent risks, such as chemical, mechanical, and magnetic failures that over time renders media unreadable. This means that data on external media should be copied to a robust storage solution as soon as possible. Technological obsolescence may also require the use of legacy equipment to be deployed to retrieve content, re-creating the intended experience of using legacy software, as well as many types of legacy media, from which the data will need to be migrated. Applying prescribed frameworks and approaches to the preservation of born-digital design records requires carrying out a set of integral tasks. These tasks can be carried out as a whole, at one time, or iteratively.

Appraisal and the establishment of physical control should be carried out shortly after an organization acquires content. These efforts include the tasks of surveying the materials, identifying physical media, and/or assigning unique identifiers.[4] After appraisal, ingest activities can be facilitated by enterprise software environments, such as the open-source toolkit BitCurator or the commercial software AccessData Forensic Toolkit. It is also possible for an organization to compile its own software in an à la carte manner to fit its needs.

Capturing digital content off of storage media and transferring it to a "workbench" storage space is a fundamental step in the digital preservation framework. There are several means of capturing digital content. For bit-level preservation, the media can be connected to a processing computer using a hardware write blocker, and the data can be moved from one location to another. To ensure robust verifiable transfer, it may be worthwhile to work with the donor to package the content to be transferred into packages that include data-verifiability and documentation features. This can be achieved by referring to the BagIt specification and assisted further by the Bagger graphic user interface, as well as bagit-python and bagit-ruby, which are scripts that execute BagIt packaging and validation. The BagIt specification is derived from work by the Library of Congress and the California Digital Library. It is a hierarchical file packaging format used for storing and transferring digital content for the creation of standardized digital containers, called "bags." The bag consists of a "payload" of digital content made of arbitrary groups of files and "tags" comprising

---

4   Surveying could include looking for physical signs of deterioration and/or photographing labels.

metadata that describe the files.[5] Bags are packaged in a folder structure along with description of the file groups and checksums for the files. A checksum is then made for the package of files as well. A checksum or hash is a fixity tool. Checksums are typically expressed as a text string or hash value output that is generated by a mathematical algorithm. For example, the MD5 checksum is thirty-two characters long and the SHA256 is sixty-four characters long. Generating a checksum for files establishes a fixity baseline against which any changes can be measured. The BagIt folder structure then allows for the files to be validated against the checksums with a simple command or click.

Transferring files using operating system tools or the BagIt specification does not by default account for deleted files and unpartitioned slack space, which are not represented in a directory. Disk imaging can capture hidden content, while BagIt and general moving/copying normally does not. A disk image is a copy of a storage disk that perfectly replicates the content and structure of the storage medium and retains all the bits included on the original medium. Disk imaging is also known as *bitstream imaging*, because it is a bit-for-bit copy of the original medium.[6] There are several disk image formats, all with their own advantages and disadvantages: Raw (dd), Advanced Forensics Format (AFF), Expert Witness Format/EnCase (E01), and the International Organization for Standardization (ISO) image are some examples. Selecting the right disk image format depends on the type of software being used, the file system of the medium, or even the time and storage space available to a practitioner. Thankfully, there are many reliable open-source software applications that facilitate disk imaging.

An additional way to capture digital content off of legacy magnetic media is to extract raw stream files from the media object. One tool for achieving this is a KryoFlux device, which can read 8", 3.5", and 5.25" floppy disks, media types that are not readily accessed with contemporary computers. The KryoFlux is a Universal Serial Bus (USB)-compatible floppy disk controller developed by the Software Preservation Society (SPS) that was designed specifically to read the

---

5 "The BagIt Library," Digital Curation Centre, last modified November 24, 2014, https://web.archive.org/web/20190405141208/https://www.dcc.ac.uk/resources/external/bagit-library.
6 National Institute for Standards and Technology, "Bit Stream Imaging," in Computer Security Resource Center Glossary, https://csrc.nist.gov/glossary/term/bit_stream_imaging, captured at https://perma.cc/KF3Q-EF6L.

magnetic flux that represents the data stored on floppy disks and store it as raw stream files.[7] However, some concerns have been raised about the licensing associated with the KryoFlux, and users may want to consider alternatives, such as the SuperCard Pro.[8] Like other tools, a KryoFlux device can create disk images, but its advantage over other hardware is that it allows the practitioner to capture a copy of the raw magnetic flux on the disk and then process that flux at a later point in time to make an image of the disk from the stream file. This is beneficial as it enables the practitioner to try creating many different image formats from the flux capture without having to physically image a disk multiple times (which is often the case for 8" and 5.25" disks when the file system and encoding are often unknown). Furthermore, if no method yet exists to convert the flux to an image file, which is unfortunately the case for some rare older disk types, the practitioner can still save the raw flux and work to create a converter, safe in the knowledge that any data that was on the disk is now captured and not susceptible to the decay of the disk itself. Disk imaging is particularly useful for acquiring content stored on legacy media that modern operating systems cannot access directly but should not be seen as necessary for all transfers. Imaging external hard drives can create large image files that contain a lot of empty space or may contain deleted files that inadvertently introduce intellectual property and privacy issues. There are many tools available for transferring data from external hard drives and optical media that ensure no changes to the files transferred, and use of these tools may be a better option for any newer media that can be read directly by modern operating systems.

A succeeding ingest activity after disk imaging or file transfer is to assess the transferred files or disk image(s). If a disk image was made, the individual files should be extracted to the organization's temporary storage space and analyzed. All extracted/transferred files should have associated checksums generated at this point, and, if possible, those checksums should be validated against what was on the original storage media. There are several open-source programs that can validate or compare checksums, and all modern operating systems include

---

[7] Jennifer Allen, et al., "The Archivist's Guide to KryoFlux," GitHub, accessed October 1, 2019, https://github.com/archivistsguidetokryoflux/archivists-guide-to-kryoflux.

[8] Archive Team, "Rescuing Floppy Disks," https://www.archiveteam.org/index.php?title=Rescuing_Floppy_Disks.

checksum creation/comparison tools built into their terminal/command-line interfaces. Collecting policies can be impacted by checksum generation, which will indicate when there are duplicate files and trigger an organization to make decisions about weeding. An open-source program might even facilitate the identification and deletion of duplicate files.[9] Alternatively, if there is a checksum mismatch, an organization must confront how it addresses corrupt content. The mismatched checksum can trigger organization policy not to acquire the invalid file. It might also force the organization to go back to the donor to get another verified copy, or it can instigate an investigation into the file that could reveal a negligible change to the content, making no action necessary.

Identifying formats also impacts an organization's collecting policies and how files are retained based on scope or format type. File format identification has the largest impact on an organization's content preservation approach and how the organization's personnel intend to preserve and support digital content in the long term. As discussed in Module 24: Navigating the Technical Landscape of Born-Digital Design Records, there are several ways to determine format types. Hexadecimal code is a compact and humanly readable translation of the bits that constitute a file. A hexadecimal editor typically displays the hex code of a file along with a separate view to the right that presents the American Standard Code for Information Interchange (ASCII), the equivalent of all bytes, legible to the human eye. Often a string of bytes of a file, usually found in the header, indicates its format. This particular string of bytes is referred to as a *file signature*. File signatures are used in format identification tools that scan sets of digital files and look for the signatures to match the files to file format identifiers. These tools provide a more streamlined and scalable approach than reading the hex of each file.

Several robust open-source file format identification tools utilize or rely on the PRONOM Technical Registry.[10] PRONOM (Public Record Office and Nôm) was developed by the National Archives of the United Kingdom and is an extensive and dynamic database of technical information that is regularly growing from contributions of new

---

9   One example is FSlint in the BitCurator environment.
10 DROID, FITS, and Siegfried use the PRONOM technical registry.

file signatures from preservation practitioners.[11] Some preservation management systems rely on the PRONOM registry for their technical metadata extraction tasks.

Assessing the files should also include the activity of scanning digital content for Personal Identifiable Information (PII) and other sensitive materials. Due to the standardized formatting of PII data (e.g., social security numbers, passwords, credit card numbers, financial records, or medical records), searching across digital content is relatively easy using regular expressions (a sequence of characters that define a search pattern) and can be accomplished with several open-source software tools. If these tools identify PII or other restricted content that needs to be removed, redacted, or restricted, there are preservation framework implications to be aware of. If the disk image is retained as part of the preservation package, the simple act of deleting content will not delete it from the disk image file. However, the BitCurator Access Redaction Tool, which was developed recently, can redact portions of a disk image. Plans for governing term restrictions should be addressed, at least in documentation. Some preservation management systems have automated retention policies, but if restriction terms are only noted in descriptive documentation, a long-term plan on how to technically make the previously restricted digital content newly accessible should also be documented and retained.

Before completing the ingest process, files need to be checked for viruses. To prevent accidentally infecting an organizational network with a computer virus when transferring files, transfer of data from the original storage media to a temporary storage space should be carried out on a non-networked computer with Wi-Fi capabilities disabled. After file extraction, a practitioner should run a virus scan on the content. An organization can consider repairing or deleting infected files, but as with PII and sensitive materials, deleting an extracted file does not account for that content in a disk image if it is not being addressed by a disk redaction tool. Documentation is key to ensuring the successful quarantine of infected files on disk images and to properly convey the provenance of that digital content for access. Creating a prioritization workflow and understanding the preservation risks for each format expedites the fulfillment of an organization's preservation

---

11 "The Technical Registry PRONOM," The National Archives (UK), accessed July 12, 2019, https://www.nationalarchives.gov.uk/PRONOM/Default.aspx.

policy that assists in the future acquisition of additional obsolete formats. Capturing data off media creates many unique challenges, and archivists must consider their organization's ability to recover the data, either by purchasing the necessary equipment or considering the possibility of imaging through a third-party company. Although there are excellent proprietary resources, they are not essential for successfully capturing data.

The unique challenges of setting up a born-digital workstation with hardware and software often require additional support outside an archivist's skill set. While digital archivists have more resources available to them to support the new technological demands of their work, organizations often require additional assistance from information technology (IT) professionals. In academic and museum settings, IT is often an internal department, but in smaller independent organizations, this type of support may be outsourced, and all organizations should consider the financial cost of this work.[12]

Discussion with Donors

Design records are often donated at the end of a career or when a firm closes, making this information potentially difficult to receive. As mentioned by archivist Aliza Leventhal, the tradition of waiting to accept records can often be detrimental when it comes to born-digital design content, in part because of the obsolescence or new editions of design software. Archivists should consider taking a more proactive approach to acquiring the accessioning materials and work with donors to establish a donation schedule closer to the creation date of these files.[13] This will allow for a better understanding of all aspects of the technology used to create the records. To manage the early stages of the acquisition process, open and extensive conversations with the donor or creator is key when considering the transfer of new materials.[14] These conversations can impact the collection of files and formats that the collecting organization may want or are able to support

---

12 Recommendations for hardware and software can be found at the POWRR Tool Grid page, https://digitalpowrr.niu.edu/digital-preservation-101/tool-grid/; the DigiPres Commons Resources page, www.digipres.org/; and on the page for the Digital Preservation Coalition's Handbook, https://dpconline.org/handbook.
13 Aliza Leventhal, "Architectural and Design Collections," in *The Digital Archives Handbook*, ed. Aaron Purcell (Lanham, MD: Rowman and Littlefield, 2019), 169.
14 In some situations, the donor and creator may be one person; however, there are times when the donor could be a family member or partner of the creator.

and offer a level of information needed during the arrangement and description process.

The creator often has critical information about the creation of born-digital design records, which can be captured in information sessions and donor surveys (see Appendix A for a sample donor survey). They can be conducted in person, over the phone, or via email; however, it is recommended that the interview be conducted in person, as the interviewee can demonstrate the use of their files and software. The archivists conducting interviews and surveys can aid in the acquisition process and ultimately add to the research experience. When creating the interview or survey, some of the areas to consider include context; content; organization; technical information; storage, transfer, and backup; deleted information; and preservation intent.

With context, it is important to think of the who, how, when, and why these records were created. Born-digital design files are created at multiple stages of a project, including during the Design Development phase, for presentation to clients, and as construction documents. Understanding who and why may help describe the donor or creator's intent, techniques, and workflows, which may assist the archivists during description, access, and management of the collection. This knowledge will be useful in preparing repositories to better understand their internal needs to process, preserve, and provide access to these records.[15] The years the records were created are also important, as they may give insight to any closeout files or retention schedules that may have been applied. Last, the interconnected network of the technological ecosystem needs to be addressed to support the storage areas and software tools in which they were created and used by the donor.

As important as understanding the hardware and software used to create born-digital design files is an understanding of how content has been migrated between files of different formats in the past, how content is currently stored by the creator, and how content should be transferred to an organization. Design record creators store content on hard drives and other removable media, networked servers, and in cloud-based storage. That content may have potentially undergone scheduled format migration, especially at firms that have been active

---

15 Archivist Aliza Leventhal suggests that "a new collection of design files may result in an organizations investing in hardware, software, storage, or preservation services." Leventhal, "Architectural and Design Collections," 186.

for longer periods of time. Understanding how and where files are stored is essential to retrieval, especially as there may be multiple storage options in use for a single project.

"Content" covers what the records contain and why they are valuable. It is important to have a discussion with the creator about the collection scope of the organization to ensure that the transfer of files includes relevant content. The project list of files, if available, can be beneficial. If starting from the beginning, the donor may find the appraisal grid in Waverly Lowell and Tawny Ryan Nelb's *Architectural Records: Managing Design and Construction Records* helpful for determining the records an organization may be interested in and the potential research value. Building on Lowell and Nelb's work, "Design Records and Appraisal Tools" by Aliza Leventhal, Jody Thompson, Alison Anderson, Sarah Schubert, and Andi Altenbach is another useful resource.[16] When interviewing the donor, it is extremely important that the archivist inquire about any potentially sensitive information (personal and private) that may be transferred to the collecting organization.[17] Imaging media can recover deleted information, potentially sensitive content, or files that are outside the organization's collecting scope. Donors should be notified that the potential for recovering these types of files exists, and they should be asked how this material should be treated, whether deleted, suppressed, or returned. This conversation should be clearly outlined, and a summary of the decisions made should be covered in the donor agreement, including the possibility that files with sensitive information may be found even after the archivist's screening. This should also be clearly outlined in the Deed of Gift or Donor Agreement. For born-digital design records, PII may also include what the content of files describes physically, such as in the case for projects including banks, prisons, transportation, and urban planning situations in which plans may need to be restricted.[18]

It is also important that the organization is aware of the file formats, software, and hardware used in the donor's collection. Depending on

---

16 Aliza Leventhal, Jody Thompson, Alison Anderson, Sarah Schubert, and Andi Altenbach, "Design Records and Appraisal Tools," *American Archivist* 84, no. 2 (2021): 320–354, https://doi.org/10.17723/0360-9081-84.2.320.
17 Waverly Lowell and Tawny Ryan Nelb, *Architectural Records: Managing Design and Construction Records* (Chicago: Society of American Archivists, 2006), 84–85.
18 "PII Considerations in Screening Archival Records," National Archives and Records Administration, https://www.archives.gov/files/Before-Screening-Records.pdf, captured at https://perma.cc/S25S-LFPC.

the age of the firm, numerous file formats could be deposited that might depend on many different software applications, fonts, software add-ons, and other technical dependencies. In addition, software rights management must be addressed with the donor. As Menzi Behrnd-Klodt notes in "Balancing Access and Privacy in Manuscript Collections," "Rights management issues also should be addressed and negotiated with donors and IT staff at the time of acquisition, as archivists need to understand the limits imposed by digital rights management, subscriptions, or other external technological access controls."[19] Another critical topic to address is the total file size. If the firm has an IT department, a conversation with the staff about typical file sizes and the total volume to be transferred can make for a smooth transfer and assist in determining any storage needs and preparations for the archives.

Assessing the organization of a creator's born-digital files is incredibly useful. Similar to physical materials, the structure of born-digital content is often unique to a specific collection. This is especially the case when it comes to the file structures used by design firms. Talking with the donor to better understand the hardware, file naming conventions, file structures, and hierarchies is essential to helping the archivist better understand the files' creation. It also sets the stage for increased accessibility for the researcher once the collection is made available. When preserving born-digital content, preservation practitioners often have to make changes to both the files in which the content is stored and the software and hardware used in creating the final experience of the content for the end user. These decisions can be significantly hampered if the archivist is not informed as to what the creators of the content intended to have preserved. A discussion of preservation intent should form part of the donor interview process. This discussion should include documenting the creators' intentions related to what content must be preserved and what can be lost through changes made over time.

---

19 Menzi L. Behrnd-Klodt, "Balancing Access and Privacy in Manuscript Collections," in *Rights in the Digital Era*, ed. Menzi Behrnd and Christopher Prom (Chicago: Society of American Archivists, 2015), 94.

Deed of Gift

Due to the complex nature of born-digital design records, it is important to capture all necessary info about the born-digital design files in the form of a Deed of Gift (see Appendix B for an example of a detailed Deed of Gift). SAA defines the deed as a "formal and legal agreement between the donor and the representative that transfers ownership and legal rights to the donated materials."[20] Some archivists view this document as "the first opportunity for archivists to establish an understanding and set expectations with the donor."[21]

The Deed of Gift confirms expectations and context about how the records were created and how to best reflect the creator's specific practices and interests. Without a relationship between the creator and archives, the archivist may be unable to access or preserve the born-digital files as they were intended to be experienced. Archivists need to understand the type and size of files created and their technical dependencies to ensure all project files are preserved.

When crafting a Deed of Gift for born-digital materials, archivists should consider several descriptive and logistical components. In the past, recommendations for general Deeds of Gift include title and description of materials donated and transfer of ownership.[22] However, there are no set standards or guidelines for what a Deed of Gift must cover in the acquisition of born-digital design materials. It is really up to each organization and its policies. In 2018, Aliza Leventhal, Laura Schroffel, and Jody Thompson presented research on this topic during SAA's Research Forum. They recommended that the Deed of Gift include standard sections on the description of digital files, transfer of ownership, intellectual property (IP), preservation, and access but also include disk imaging, methods of transfer, and copyright.[23]

The document's section on description should categorize the born-digital design files at a high level, such as office records, project

---

20 Society of American Archivists, "A Guide to Deeds of Gift," 2021, www2.archivists.org /publications/brochures/deeds-of-gift, captured at https://perma.cc/C75G-WVDV.
21 Aliza Leventhal, Laura Schroffel, and Jody Thompson, "Deeds of Gift as a Tool to Facilitate Born Digital Design File Processing and Preservation" (Chicago: Society of American Archivists, 2019), 1, www2.archivists.org/sites/all/files/Leventhal_Schroffel_Thompson _Deeds%20FINAL.pdf, captured at https://perma.cc/B6Z2-U3ZY.
22 Society of American Archivists, "A Guide to Deeds of Gift."
23 Leventhal, Schroffel, and Thompson, "Deeds of Gift as a Tool." The subjects are not listed in any particular order of importance. For all formal and legal contracts, it would be best to research other archives' Deeds of Gifts and seek legal assistance.

files, and construction drawings. It is not necessary to describe at the item level on ingest, as this will be addressed during the other stages in the lifecycle of the collection. It is also important to note whether the materials were created or acquired by the donor or creator. The Deed of Gift should also include a section on the transfer of ownership. This is what Aprille McKay has defined as the "passing of title and possession of materials in the collection."[24] The transfer needs to describe, in detail, the sole lawful owner of the digital files, acknowledge the transfer of rights to the organization, and state that deposited files will become the property of that organization.

IP rights should be given a good deal of attention in the document, as they will describe the many possible issues around born-digital design records. The document should ask the donor whether they own or control all or some of the IP of the digital files. If the rights will be transferred to the organization, the creator must be made aware that reproducing, licensing, publishing, altering, or displaying the files could take place. Any necessary limitations should also be addressed in this section. This could include not transferring IP and contact information that would be required for access or licensing purposes. Where and when possible, licenses for software that is being transferred with the donation should also be included in the transfer.

The document's preservation section should state that the receiving organization will be responsible for all aspects of preservation. Although the archivist will most likely discuss the organization's preservation activities with the donor during the interview process, the organization will have discretion on such stages as stabilization, storage, retention, emulation, migration, and transfer. A statement about contracting with a third-party vendor for storage and management would also be useful.

The issues of copyright can be confusing for all parties involved, so questions and concerns about who can access the born-digital records should be addressed in the Deed of Gift. There are numerous copyright resources available online, as well as organizational legal counsel. Since many of the born-digital design files will be accessed by researchers in the organization, it is critical to cover all possible aspects, such as reproduction rights, the creation of adaptations or derivative works,

---

24 Aprille McKay, "Managing Rights and Permission," in *Rights in the Digital Era*, ed. Menzi Behrnd and Christopher Prom (Chicago: Society of American Archivists, 2015), 180.

distribution of copies of the work to the public, and display to the public. However, there are copyright exceptions with fair use of which the creator should be made aware. SAA's *Dictionary of Archives Terminology* states that fair use is "a provision in copyright law that allows the limited use of copyrighted materials without permission of the rights holder for noncommercial teaching, research, scholarship, or news reporting purposes."[25] The organization's Deed of Gift should cover copyright as it applies to the specific donation, so key research by the archivist must be applied with the best practices and possible discussion with legal experts in the field.[26]

The document should also address sensitive and privacy issues with a statement about how PII—including social security numbers, passwords, and financial records, such as bank statements—will be dealt with. The Deed of Gift can indicate the organization's preservation policy and whether staff members will weed, redact, or restrict the content. In addition to U.S. laws governing privacy that will apply to the donated materials, the Deed of Gift might lay out specific restriction requests from a creator.[27] The organization's staff members need to ensure that the Deed of Gift covers how to access any files when encountering login information, encryption, and access keys. Last, the document should address how files in publicly available collections will be made available, either on a local network or for institutional use only.

The Deed of Gift should also cover disk imaging, as most creators are not aware of this practice. As mentioned earlier, if disk imaging recovers deleted or log files, the creator should be contacted and determine the outcome of the files—namely, giving or declining access. To get to the disk imaging phase, the archivist can give the creator several options for transferring digital files. The donor may prefer to transmit the files via an external storage medium, such as a flash drive or an external hard drive, or may choose to donate the storage medium

---

25 Society of American Archivists, "Fair Use," in *Dictionary of Archives Terminology* (Chicago: Society of American Archivists, 2021), https://dictionary.archivists.org/entry/fair-use.html.
26 Heather Briston, "Understanding Copyright Law," in *Rights in the Digital Era*, ed. Menzi Behrnd and Christopher Prom (Chicago: Society of American Archivists, 2015), 45.
27 U.S. laws governing privacy include the Family Educational Rights and Privacy Act (FERPA), Health Insurance Portability and Accountability Act (HIPPA), Privacy Act of 1974, Video Privacy Protection Act (VCPA), Electronic Communications Privacy Act, Telephone Consumer Protection Act (TCPA), Driver's Privacy Protection Act (DPPA), Children's Online Privacy Protection Act (COPPA), and Gramm-Leach-Bliley Act (GLB).

or place it on temporary loan with the archives until data has been captured. Transmitting an entire computer for donation or capture may also be an option. As Aaron D. Purcell states, "The relationship between the donors and archives is complex and does not end when the donor delivers his or her materials to the archives. The use of digital forensic tools and processes in acquiring digital content compounds this complexity."[28]

Dependencies

The technological dependencies and their associated challenges presented by born-digital design records are not so different from the standard concerns of digital preservation. Issues around hardware and software obsolescence, licenses, and versioning concerns are present in any born-digital collection created by proprietary software that has continuously evolved over decades. The delayed point of entry of born-digital design software has hindered the archival community's timely ability to acquire and understand preceding versions of software that made up the early universe of design software, which subsequently influenced the development of later versions of software. The standard range of dependency concerns are exacerbated by the inconsistent use of the broad range of design-specific and related/adopted software by design record creators as a profession, as well as in an individual's own practice or a single project.

Software and Hardware Obsolescence. Also known as technological obsolescence, software and hardware obsolescence occurs when a technical product or service is no longer needed or wanted, generally the result of a new product being created to replace an older version. In the digital preservation sense, this also applies to hardware accessories required for accessing a particular software, such as authentication dongles.[29] The learning curve can be steep for anyone attempting to reverse engineer or create a surrogate dongle to access older programs and systems.

In addition to sometimes holding the literal key to accessing the data, the original hardware also supports the practitioners' experience

---

28 Aaron D. Purcell, *Donors and Archives: A Guidebook for Successful Program* (Lanham, MD: Rowman and Littlefield, 2015), 9.
29 A dongle is a small device that can be connected to and used with a computer, especially to allow access to wireless broadband or use of protected software.

in engaging with computers to create designs. The evolution of the interface between the designer and the software—including light pens, computer mice, keyed commands, and, more recently, designing in a virtual reality environment—can be an important factor in understanding the limitations and valuable qualities of design software.[30] Due to the rapidly evolving nature of computer hardware, it is challenging and often expensive to acquire the original interfaces of early software. If this aspect of design history is part of an organization's mission and scope, its archivists should attempt to document the intended original interface experience and explore modern equivalents or emulated controls.

Software Licenses. In the past, software used by designers has not always included documents with legally binding guidelines on its use and distribution. Several early technologically inclined designers were known for co-opting the purpose of a software (e.g., in the 1990s, Maya, a movie animation software, was used to create simulations of built environments) or actual "breaking" of software to use an unlicensed copy or add functionality to existing software. There is also the very real scenario of not being able to find older, less mainstream, and even custom-made software used by designers—especially as many of the original companies no longer exist because the field of design software has oscillated between a rich field of startups and a series of mergers or buyouts. When the software is still available, collecting organizations should acquire a copy and use it according to the Code of Best Practices in Fair Use for Software Preservation.[31] This Code offers guidance from legal and technical experts for preserving software within the parameters defined as fair use by the Copyright Law of the United States.

Versioning/Patches. All software, especially proprietary software, undergoes updates, patches, and, eventually, entirely new version releases. The continuous improvements, edits, and additions to a program over time can create a different experience of the interface and

---

30 A light pen is a computer input device in the form of a light-sensitive wand used in conjunction with a computer's cathode-ray tube display, used in Ivan Sutherland's PhD thesis project, and 1960s computer-aided design software "Sketchpad."
31 Center for Media & Social Impact, American University, and Association of Research Libraries, Code of Best Practices in Fair Use for Software Preservation, September 2018, revised February 2019, https://www.arl.org/wp-content/uploads/2018/09/2019.2.28-software-preservation-code-revised.pdf, captured at https://perma.cc/V56N-GRZD.

new functionality; these changes can also cause backward compatibility issues that require specific versions of software to be maintained to accurately view all the attributes of a born-digital design file. As demonstrated by Matthew Allen's research-cum-exhibit at Harvard University's GSD, the impact of every feature update and code patch is felt and noticed by the users.[32] This has immediate ramifications for any institution accessioning a collection of born-digital design files and the necessary software to support access.

Understanding the Technological Ecosystem. A designer or firm's technological ecosystem includes platform preferences (Mac vs. PC) and hardware preferences (desktop vs. laptop vs. tablet), as well as each designer's software suite and combination preferences. A designer's decision of which tools to use, alone and in combination, as well as for which parts of a project, can shed insight on how that designer approaches a project and develops their practice. While many designers will acknowledge that all the software programs at their disposal are just tools for doing the same work of envisioning and designing physical spaces that might eventually be built and experienced, the robust functionality of design software that has developed over the past forty-some years cannot be minimized as a secondary attribute to the buildings constructed.

There are some practical aspects of these decisions as well, including cost, scalability, and collaborative practices. The AIA's surveys of technology in practice through the 1990s and 2000s depicted adoption practices for firm sizes that ranged from large (500+ employees) to sole practitioners. Designers from firms of various sizes pointedly discussed the topic at the 2017 "Designing the Future Landscape: Digital Architecture, Design & Engineering Assets" symposium, reaffirming the understanding that experimentation with hardware and software is part of all practices.[33] The panel exposed that both smaller and larger firms have the capacity to adopt new technology despite overhead investments. In his 2012 book *Co-designers: Cultures of Computer*

---

32 Matthew Allen, "Tell Me About a Rhino Command. Software and Architectural History" (exhibition at Harvard GSD, April 2016), https://www.academia.edu/24720335/Exhibition_Tell_me_about_a_Rhino_command._Software_and_Architectural_History_Harvard_GSD_April_2016.

33 "Designing the Future Landscape: Digital Architecture, Design and Engineering Assets," Washington, DC, November 16, 2017, https://www.loc.gov/preservation/digital/meetings/ade/ade2017.html.

Simulation in Architecture, Yanni Loukissas sheds additional light on the significance of the relationship between a designer and their technological tools, affirming that the choices of what technology to use and the level of engagement a designer experiences with technology have a profound effect on their relationship to the design process and final outcome as well.[34]

Cloud-based Platforms. Collaboration has become a more desirable and necessary function of design software. To accommodate this, like many mainstream collaborative web-based software services such as Office 365 or Google Docs, design software companies have created cloud-based platforms, such as Autodesk BIM 360 and Adobe's Creative Cloud. Regardless of whether these software programs have desktop applications, it is clear that significant amounts of information are being saved to the servers of the cloud-based software company. This multi-location storage situation could present copyright and ownership issues for organizations that accept collections. In addition, because the software allows more collaboration, the issues of provenance and contributions to the files have become more complex. These issues will be universal of all cloud-based-software, rather than a unique issue for design software. Therefore, resources and workflows to address such technical and logistical features will be developed by the larger archival and digital preservationist community.

In addressing the ecosystem-level issues that born-digital design files present to collecting institutions, design records archivists need to leverage the collective wisdom and research developed by the broader digital preservation community. By building on the strong foundation for managing born-digital collections, design records archivists can focus their energy on the gaps between the norm and their niche records rather than independently establishing an existing standard.

Preservation Fundamentals

Digital Preservation Frameworks

Preservation is the set of activities, processes, and policies that safeguard materials and facilitate ongoing access to information, artifacts,

---
34 Yanni Alexander Loukissas, *Co-designers: Cultures of Computer Simulation in Architecture* (London: Routledge, 2012).

and evidence that constitute archival collections.[35] The most fundamental action that can be carried out on a digital object is bit-level preservation. This is the most basic form of preservation, because it essentially consists of caring for the needs of digital objects at the level of the bits that constitute them. Bit-level preservation allows for potential changes to a file to be monitored over time, but it does not ensure access and it does not capture context, meaning the ability to understand digital content in the long term. To determine whether a file is stable over time and has maintained all of its original bits, organizations rely on fixity checks. The most accessible tools for creating fixity information are cryptographic hash functions that generate checksums and hashes (like MD5 [message-digest algorithm] and SHA [Secure Hash Algorithm]), but there are other methods, such as recording expected file size and file count, that provide basic fixity information.[36] Organizations are encouraged to verify checksums whenever receiving digital content.[37] It is critical to be confident that the fixity baseline established when receiving digital content is reliable so that the files can be properly stewarded over time, assuring their provenance. If the fixity of an object has changed, then one or more of the characters in the checksum will be different when compared to the checksum of the original file. Changes to the bits of a file may not be apparent to the human eye in an image file or word-processing document, but if a checksum does not verify, then the integrity of the file has been compromised. Files are the most vulnerable to changes in their integrity during moves when data is transferred between storage systems. While most modern operating systems perform a reasonable level of integrity validation when copying and moving files, it is worthwhile for an archivist to check the integrity of content whenever moving it and to mitigate the potential for storing data in a place where moving it might be a common occurrence.

Digital preservation storage management is best understood as a risk management activity. When planning long-term digital preservation storage, an organization's staff members should evaluate the risks

---

35 Erin O'Meara and Kate Stratton, *Digital Preservation Essentials*, ed. Christopher J. Prom (Chicago: Society of American Archivists, 2016), 8.
36 Paula De Stefano, et al., "What Is Fixity, and When Should I Be Checking It?," in *Checking Your Digital Content* (National Digital Stewardship Alliance, 2014), http://hdl.loc.gov/loc.gdc/lcpub.2013655117.1.
37 De Stefano, et al., "What Is Fixity?"

they are trying to address and the methods they can use to mitigate those risks. For example, staff members may want to mitigate the risk of a storage administrator accidentally or deliberately destroying the copy(ies) of data stored in a system they have access to by making a copy in a separate system that is managed by different staff members. An organization may also want to mitigate the risk of a natural disaster by storing an additional copy of data in a location that has a different level of risk for natural disasters. There are many other risks an organization will likely want to mitigate, and these risks form a risk profile for each copy of data. An organization should be aiming to minimize the risk that any copy will be lost at any point in time. That way, if any copy is lost, it can be recovered from the additional copies.

A "good enough" best practice is to follow the 3-2-1 model.[38] This involves storing at least three separate copies of data on three different forms of media, using at least two different storage technologies (e.g., tape, disk, optical), and storing at least one copy in a location with a completely different risk profile.

Storage structure is of critical importance to preservation, and there are multiple frameworks available that can be used to plan for preservation and storage of digital files. The reference model framework process begins with the ingest of data and moves to data management and archival storage through access. Frameworks include the Open Archival Information System (OAIS) reference model, the National Digital Stewardship Alliance (NDSA) Levels, and Trustworthy Repositories Audit and Certification (TRAC). These three frameworks have emerged as the most prevalent in the field and can be implemented independently or in concert with one another; however, many other frameworks have also been developed.

The OAIS is considered the most comprehensive framework and explains digital preservation as a set of concepts, relationships, and processes. The model was first developed in 1995 as a joint project of The Consultative Committee for Space Data Systems (CCSDS) and the ISO to develop formal standards for the long-term storage of digital data generated from space missions.[39] It was later released in open public

---

38 Backblaze, "3-2-1 Backup Strategy," 2022, https://www.backblaze.com/blog/the-3-2-1-backup-strategy, captured at https://perma.cc/E8C2-5XKK; Princeton University Library, "Research Data Management at Princeton," 2021, https://libguides.princeton.edu/c.php?g=102546&p=665865, captured at https://perma.cc/6EXT-UDUN.
39 Brian Lavoie, *The Open Archival Information System (OAIS) Reference Model: Introductory Guide*, 2nd ed. (Digital Preservation Coalition, 2014).

forums and was officially published as ISO International Standard 14721 in 2003. The OAIS provides a conceptual framework and also defines the language used to describe digital preservation work, which facilitates unity and consistency among diverse practitioners and/or stakeholders in the field.

Before information is ingested into a framework, however, an organization may have to intervene with the donor to ensure the stability of the files and that the content can be appropriately ingested into a preservation management system following the organization's collecting policies. Through tools like Deeds of Gift, organizations can shape how files are received, allowing themselves to have a clear understanding of intent, rights, and dependencies, along with establishing requirements about how the files are received. The first stage of the OAIS, the SIP (Submission Information Package), is an information package that is transferred from the information producer to the preservation organization. The SIP represents the state of materials as they were received following all of the collecting organization's criteria. The acquisition of the SIP should not be a passive process. SIPs are processed using ingest tools that extract and record additional preservation metadata about the content and do not alter the integrity of the files.

The product of these ingest tools makes up the Access Information Package, or AIP, which the SAA describes as "the set of content and metadata managed by a preservation organization, and organized in a way that allows the organization to perform preservation services."[40] The AIP should be flexible enough that it allows for the digital objects to be accessible in the long term.

Finally, the last stage of the OAIS is the DIP, or Dissemination Information Package. The DIP is the package of digital objects that are available for access, the content that is delivered to patrons/users. This often includes some kind of descriptive metadata, and it can refer to content spanning one or multiple AIPs.

The National Digital Stewardship Alliance, or NDSA, developed a system called the Levels of Digital Preservation (LoP), which can be used as a self-assessment tool or as a basic framework for the development of a digital preservation system. The NDSA Levels are a tiered set

---

40 Society of American Archivists, "Open Archival Information System," 2021, www2.archivists.org/groups/standards-committee/open-archival-information-system-oais, captured at https://perma.cc/8W7W-E9V2.

of recommendations that allow organizations to create baseline workflows, measure how well they are currently meeting goals in an established system, or provide recommendations as to how to improve their preservation practices. The Levels are organized into five functional areas that are essential to preservation systems: storage, integrity, control, metadata, and content. Those five areas are then broken down laterally into four levels of compliance, with Level 4 considered the most stable. Like the OAIS, the LoP matrix is format- and systems-agnostic, allowing any type of digital preservation workflow to be evaluated.[41]

The LoP originated in 2012 when a group from NDSA thought that there was not sufficient practical technical guidance available for beginning preservationists.[42] The Levels were developed in a collaborative environment, and comments were accepted until 2013, when version 1 was published as part of the "Archiving (IS&T) Conference" held in Washington, DC, in April 2013 (Figure 1). The Levels of Digital Preservation project is ongoing, and, according to the group, revisions will be accepted until "the levels stabilize at a broad consensus view of the progression of technical steps recommended for decreasing the risk to digital materials."[43] Because organizations have been actively using the Levels and currently expanding them as necessary, the NDSA Levels of Digital Preservation Working Group published version 2 in 2019 (Figure 2). The categories were updated to describe actions that are independent of specific formats, content types, and storage systems, thus enhancing the Levels' usability across domains.[44]

The Trustworthy Repositories Audit and Certification (TRAC) is an additional preservation framework that uses a set of metrics that are based on the OAIS reference model and split into three subject groups: Organizational Infrastructure; Digital Object Management; and Technology, Technical Infrastructure, and Security. A TRAC audit consists of an organization's staff members completing the TRAC checklist by citing how they fulfill each metric. The checklist was developed by the Center for Research Libraries in 2007 and was revised and

---

41 National Digital Stewardship Alliance, "Levels of Digital Preservation," https://ndsa.org/activities/levels-of-digital-preservation, captured at https://perma.cc/RB2F-J5VH.
42 Megan Phillips, "The NDSA Levels of Digital Preservation: An Explanation and Uses," National Digital Stewardship Alliance, *Proceedings of the Archiving (IS&T) Conference*, Washington, DC, April 2013, 2.
43 Phillips, "NDSA Levels of Digital Preservation," 6.
44 National Digital Stewardship Alliance, "Levels."

	Level 1 (Protect your data)	Level 2 (Know your data)	Level 3 (Monitor your data)	Level 4 (Repair your data)
Storage and Geographic Location	- Two complete copies that are not collocated - For data on heterogeneous media (optical discs, hard drives, etc.) get the content off the medium and into your storage system	- At least three complete copies - At least one copy in a different geographic location - Document your storage system(s) and storage media and what you need to use them	- At least one copy in a geographic location with a different disaster threat - Obsolescence monitoring process for your storage system(s) and media	- At least three copies in geographic locations with different disaster threats - Have a comprehensive plan in place that will keep files and metadata on currently accessible media or systems
File Fixity and Data Integrity	- Check file fixity on ingest if it has been provided with the content - Create fixity info if it wasn't provided with the content	- Check fixity on all ingests - Use write-blockers when working with original media - Virus-check high risk content	- Check fixity of content at fixed intervals - Maintain logs of fixity info; supply audit on demand - Ability to detect corrupt data - Virus-check all content	- Check fixity of all content in response to specific events or activities - Ability to replace/repair corrupted data - Ensure no one person has write access to all copies
Information Security	- Identify who has read, write, move and delete authorization to individual files - Restrict who has those authorizations to individual files	- Document access restrictions for content	- Maintain logs of who performed what actions on files, including deletions and preservation actions	- Perform audit of logs
Metadata	- Inventory of content and its storage location - Ensure backup and non-collocation of inventory	- Store administrative metadata - Store transformative metadata and log events	- Store standard technical and descriptive metadata	- Store standard preservation metadata
File Formats	- When you can give input into the creation of digital files encourage use of a limited set of known open formats and codecs	- Inventory of file formats in use	- Monitor file format obsolescence issues	- Perform format migrations, emulation and similar activities as needed

Figure 1: Matrix for version 1 of the NDSA's Levels of Digital Preservation. From Megan Phillips, "The NDSA Levels of Digital Preservation: An Explanation and Uses," National Digital Stewardship Alliance, Proceedings of the Archiving (IS&T) Conference, Washington, DC, April 2013, https://mfr.osf.io/render?url=https://osf.io/dpnqs/?direct%26mode=render%26action=download%26mode=render, captured at https://perma.cc/CDX6-GW5P. Image used with Creative Commons Attribution 4.0 International License.

Emerging Best Practices in the Accession, Preservation, and Emulation of Born-Digital Design Materials

Functional Area	Level 1 (Know Your Content)	Level 2 (Protect Your Content)	Level 3 (Monitor Your Content)	Level 4 (Sustain Your Content)
Storage	Put content into stable storage Document all storage media where content is stored Have two complete copies in separate locations	Have three complete copies with at least one copy in a separate geographic location Document storage and storage media indicating the resources and dependencies they require to function	Have at least one copy in a geographic location with a different disaster threat than the other copies Have at least one copy on a different storage media type Track the obsolescence of storage and media	Have at least three copies in separate geographic locations, each with a different disaster threat Maximize storage diversification to avoid single points of failure Have a plan and execute actions to address obsolescence of storage hardware, software, and media
Integrity	Verify integrity information if it has been provided with the content Generate integrity information if not provided with the content Virus check all content; isolate content for quarantine as needed	Verify integrity information when moving or copying content Use write-blockers when working with original media Back up integrity information and store copy in a separate location from the content	Verify integrity information of content at fixed intervals Document integrity information verification processes and outcomes Perform audit of integrity information on demand	Verify integrity information in response to specific events or activities Replace or repair corrupted content as necessary
Control	Determine the human and software agents that should be authorized to read, write, move, and delete content	Document the human and software agents authorized to read, write, move, and delete content and apply these	Maintain logs and identify the human and software agents that performed actions on content	Perform periodic review of actions/access logs
Metadata	Create inventory of content, also documenting current storage locations Back up inventory and store at least one copy separately from content	Store enough metadata to know what the content is (this might include some combination of administrative, technical, descriptive, preservation, and structural)	Determine what metadata standards to apply Find and fill gaps in your metadata to meet those standards	Record preservation actions associated with content and when those actions occur Implement metadata standards chosen
Content	Document file formats and other essential content characteristics including how and when these were identified	Verify file formats and other essential content characteristics Build relationships with content creators to encourage sustainable file choices	Monitor for obsolescence, and changes in technologies on which content is dependent	Perform migrations, normalizations, emulation, and similar activities that ensure content can be accessed

Figure 2: Matrix for version 2 of the NDSA's Levels of Digital Preservation. From National Digital Stewardship Alliance, "Levels of Digital Preservation," https://ndsa.org/activities/levels-of-digital-preservation, captured at https://perma.cc/RB2F-J5VH. Image used with Creative Commons Attribution 4.0 International License.

updated as an ISO standard in 2012, now referred to as a TDR, or Trusted Digital Repositories, audit.[45] The checklist can be completed as a self-audit, or a private group called the Primary Trustworthy Digital Repository Authorization Body Ltd. (PTAB) can evaluate organizations for hire. The certification by an outside body can provide an organization with a degree of credibility, but it is an expensive and complex undertaking.

The three frameworks provide options for building and enhancing preservation management systems, but all of those systems require standardization for the documentation of digital objects. A data dictionary called Preservation Metadata: Implementation Strategies (PREMIS) is a metadata standard for digital content that builds on the OAIS reference model. PREMIS takes its name from an international working group sponsored by the Online Computer Library Center and Research Libraries Group from 2003 to 2005. That working group produced a report called *PREMIS Data Dictionary for Preservation Metadata*. The Library of Congress then published a set of PREMIS schemas for representing metadata elements in the *Data Dictionary* in XML. The Library of Congress schemas were updated from 2008 through 2015.[46] The *PREMIS Data Dictionary* defines a core set of metadata elements used to perform preservation functions to ensure that digital objects remain viable, renderable, and not inadvertently altered, as well as to document any changes to those objects. The semantic units from PREMIS version 3.0 are Object Entity (file object, bitstream objects, representation objects, intellectual entity objects), Events, Agents, and Rights. By documenting digital preservation metadata, an organization conveys full transparency about the content of the files and any processing or changes carried out on them. All trustworthy digital preservation systems automate the generation and capture of PREMIS compliant metadata.

The option to serialize PREMIS-compliant metadata into an XML file compliant with the available PREMIS schema allows the metadata to be transferable between systems. PREMIS XML is flexible and can be incorporated into other types of common XML records, such as

---

45 Center for Research Libraries, "Digital Preservation Metrics," accessed July 12, 2019, www.crl.edu/archiving-preservation/digital-archives/metrics.
46 Priscilla Caplan, *Understanding PREMIS*, rev. ed. (Washington, DC: Library of Congress Network Development and MARC Standards Office, 2017), 1–2.

Metadata Encoding and Transmission Standard (METS), which is often used to process the ingest of SIPs.

Content Preservation Approaches

Because born-digital design records are intrinsically complex and tend to be reliant on proprietary software, organizations should consider a strategic plan for specific preservation needs. There are several content preservation approaches available, and each one offers its own set of benefits and drawbacks. A preservation approach is one of the concepts that bit-level preservation alone does not consider. Some digital content, and especially content of born-digital design files, can only be viewed in its original structure with all intended components connected by means of software applications. However, software quickly obsolesces, breaks, or "versions out" without backward compatibility, so digital objects are no longer immediately accessible. To ensure long-term access to digital objects, it is necessary for them to exist independently of storage and delivery systems, and a content preservation approach frames how that long-term access is implemented.

Migration. One prominent preservation approach is migration. A migration plan accounts for how an organization might move digital objects out of one system or file type and into another by transferring the digital content from one hardware/software configuration to another. Some digital preservation system software can facilitate automated migration by performing regular transfer of content from files that have an older format to files that have a newer format. However it is carried out, a migration plan relies heavily on documentation that accurately and consistently describes digital objects in an organization. An organization's staff members must understand what content they have and whether it includes behavior or functions, as well as its dependencies, to reformat it. Once a new stable format—preferably an open-source format—has been determined, documentation must account for the fact that new files with different formats have been created to replace the original ones. This is typically captured in PREMIS documentation. Migration should be thoroughly tested before new format types are identified to ensure that migrated objects behave in the way they are intended in their newly reformatted state. In addition, migration must be a continuous process as renderable formats and

Figure 3: Full record set for the renovation of the Irving S. Gilmore Music Library between 1992–1998, shown attached in a CD-ROM in an emulated Microsoft® Windows 98 computer. *Example courtesy of the Irving S. Gilmore Music Library at Yale University.*

compatibility change over time. The investment in maintaining the continuous migration of content between files over time is immense, and, as the technology stack used to present the content to users over time moves farther away from its original state, the integrity of the content will ultimately decline.

Migration via Emulation Environments. It is possible that migration can never properly reflect the context of a digital object's origination. A migrated object might lack the ability to convey the look and feel that it had on its original platform, or the software required to present the new digital object may alter, remove, or add content compared to the original. The risk of data loss is also quite high for migration approaches. An option for maintaining the long-term integrity of digital content is to do so via emulation environments. An emulator is a software application that can simulate the hardware of one or more computers. For example, when Yale University renovated the Irving S. Gilmore Music Library, many digital records were created, including both CAD files and supporting documentation in various other office file formats (Figure 3). By providing all of the files in a single emulated computer containing all the necessary software, archivists can simplify provision of access to legacy design projects like this one.

In addition to re-enabling authentic access to legacy born-digital design records, emulation and a related process, virtualization, can give users a single consolidated mechanism for accessing a full set of legacy records associated with a design project, with all the software dependencies included in it. Both processes are discussed in detail later in this module.

Recompiling. A third preservation approach is recompiling. This is a kind of migration process in which the software source code is recompiled or rebuilt directly from the original source. The code typically requires updating to configuration scripts to accommodate contemporary differences in build systems, system libraries, or programming languages and versions.[47] To ethically execute the recompiling method, any changes to the source code should be documented in a transparent manner, such as in PREMIS documentation. Considering the breadth of changes to a complex digital object, such as born-digital design files, that might be required, organizations such as the Guggenheim have commented out the original source code of a recompiled project so that it remains legible and embedded in the code of the new version.[48] Obviously, recompiling depends on access to the original source code, which is sometimes not transferred to the collecting organizations. Open lines of communication with living digital content producers or access to organizations that archive source code are essential to this approach. Recompiling also requires that staff members have the technical expertise to carry out this type of migration. When recompiling is insufficient, there is also the option of creating a new software from scratch. Developing a fresh interaction software means compiling new code to make it properly function in a current computing environment. Reprogramming might be considered a form of migration as well, and, like general format migration, it requires a detailed understanding of intended behaviors of digital content. This

---

47 Esther Conway, et al., "Towards a Methodology for Software Preservation" (paper presented at the 6th International Conference on the Preservation of Digital Objects, iPRES, San Francisco, California, 2009).
48 Joanna Phillips, Deena Engel, Emma Dickson, and Jonathan Farbowitz, "Restoring Brandon, Shu Lea Cheang's Early Web Artwork," *Checklist* (blog), The Guggenheim Museums and Foundation, https://www.guggenheim.org/blogs/checklist/restoring-brandon-shu-lea-cheangs-early-web-artwork, captured at https://perma.cc/DS4B-YB48.

methodology requires substantial technical expertise to re-create the exact behavior of a complex digital object in new systems, entailing a great effort that might never truly express all the idiosyncrasies of the original language. Recompiling and reprogramming would most typically be applied in cases where the design software was custom built or did not achieve long-term commercial success in the marketplace so that options like free readers or migration do not exist for it. Typically, the best-fitting approach is a combination of multiple options. For example, an approach may be to migrate content into files with newer formats to ensure that the content can be readily reused in modern tools and, simultaneously, provide access to the original objects using emulation to ensure that the full integrity of the content can always be experienced and verified. An organization's staff members should consider a good balance for themselves, one that considers the research value of the digital content in relation to the effort that the chosen approach(es) require(s).

Maintaining a Hardware Museum. Another preservation approach is to practice technology preservation and maintain what some refer to as a "hardware museum."[49] Technology preservation requires the active maintenance of outdated equipment. With this approach, data that is saved in its native format can be accessible in its original operating environment creating the least amount of intervention and deviation for the original data. But collecting hardware requires a great deal of physical space, not only are originals needed but backups are needed in case they fail, and, considering the age of some currently obsolescent technology, failure can be commonplace. Hardware museums also require a financial investment of time and patience to find all the right products because, as time passes, computing hardware becomes more and more scarce and often more expensive as a result. Yet, some organizations base their preservation strategy on this methodology, retaining multiple reserve computers and hardware/peripherals, such as a mouse, camera, and screen. The Zentrum für Kunst und Medien (the ZKM, or Center for Art and Media) even goes so far as to maintain backups of digital artworks on spare computers,

---

[49] Patrick Ngulube, *Handbook of Research on Heritage Management and Preservation* (Hershey, PA: IGI Global 2018), 153.

rather than on servers or tape.[50] It should be kept in mind that there are also organizations whose sole mandate is to preserve technology. The Computer History Museum (Mountain View, California), the Centre for Computing History (Cambridge, England), and the Living Computer Museum (Seattle, Washington), all have large collections of computing artifacts and offer additional collection materials supporting those artifacts, such as guides, software, and in some cases original source code. Before an organization's staff members commit to technology preservation, they should evaluate how their collection needs might be supported by the work already being done in emulation or in other technology preservation organizations.

Emulation and Virtualization

Emulation

As discussed earlier, an emulator is a software application that can simulate the hardware of one or more computers. For example, the UAE (Unusable Amiga Emulator) simulates, or "emulates," the hardware of various Amiga computers from the 1980s and 1990s.[51] An emulated computer is a computer that is simulated or "emulated" using an emulator software application. Emulators are most often used to simulate computers that have a "hardware architecture" that is different from the computers that the emulators are being run on. This allows the user of the emulator to run software that is compatible with the emulated hardware *but not compatible with* the hardware that the emulator is running on (see Figure 4 for an example).

When a user installs and runs software on an emulated computer, the software sends commands to the emulated hardware. These commands are accepted by the emulator software that is simulating the emulated hardware and translated into commands that the system running the emulator can interpret and respond to. This translation process can be relatively slow and uses extra CPU cycles (processing

---

50 Daniel Heiss, Morgane Stricot, and Matthieu Vlaminck, "Open the Museum's Gates to Pirates: Hacking for the Sake of Digital Art Preservation" (paper presented at the 15th International Conference on Digital Preservation, iPRES, Boston, Massachusetts, 2018).
51 UAE is a computer emulator that emulates the hardware of Commodore International's Amiga range of computers. At various times, the U has stood for Unusable, Unix, Universal, Ultimate, and Ubiquitous. https://en.wikipedia.org/w/index.php?title=UAE _(emulator)&oldid=886217765, captured at https://perma.cc/ZQ2N-KPK3.

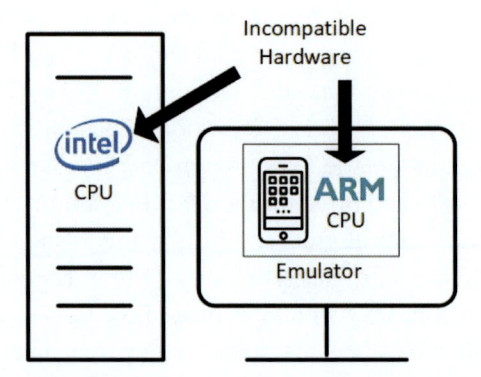

Figure 4: A host computer with an Intel central processing unit (CPU) is able to use an emulator to run software made for a mobile device with an ARM CPU that would not run directly on the host computer's Intel CPU

capacity) that wouldn't be necessary if the commands were running directly on the physical hardware. Therefore, for an emulator to be most useful, the hardware they are being run on should be at least a generation newer and faster than the hardware being emulated. Without the extra processing capacity of the newer hardware, the emulators often run so slowly that they are not practical for everyday usage.

There are some use cases in which the hardware to be emulated is modern but is normally somewhat slower than the hardware that the emulator is being run on, so the slow-down "tax" of emulating the hardware is less of a problem. In particular, mobile phone hardware is often slower or more limited in capacity than the hardware of desktop PCs and workstations, so the slow-down "tax" of emulating mobile hardware on desktop computers is not as large a problem as it might be otherwise.

Emulators are often used by developers of mobile phone applications. For example, the software development kit for the Android operating system comes with the Quick EMUlator (QEMU) bundled in it. The reason the mobile-software developers need emulators is because mobile phones generally have architecture that is different from most laptops and desktop PCs, but developers use PCs to create mobile applications. So, during the development process, to test mobile applications on their PCs, developers emulate the phone hardware using an emulator and run the mobile application on the emulated hardware.

Another important use case for emulators is to access legacy video games. Video games often have large and/or dedicated user communities and fan groups, which are often highly motivated to keep their games playable over time. Unfortunately, old games often don't run on newer hardware as changes in the hardware mean the old games are no longer compatible. This has led to dedicated enthusiasts developing their own emulators to emulate the hardware of legacy gaming systems on modern PCs and other devices. Fortunately, these emulators have often been released with open and/or free license terms that enable reuse of the emulators for other purposes. The existence of openly licensed emulators allows the archival community to freely make use of the emulators to, for example, ensure long-term access to archived born-digital design records using their original software environments. For example, the Internet Archive has an online "Internet Arcade," where users can play legacy video games by seamlessly downloading them and running them in a web browser.[52]

Emulation may be particularly useful for born-digital design records in situations in which there is no non-destructive migration path. While many born-digital design record file formats have options available for migrating content to newer formats to maintain access, the content can be altered or parts of it lost during this process. In other cases, born-digital design record file formats have no migration pathway—meaning that emulation is the only currently viable option for ensuring long-term access to them. Where multiple systems need to come together to provide meaningful access to born-digital design records (such as client software, server-based applications, and server-based databases), a new approach is fortunately becoming available.[53] With emulated network technology being added to the open-source Emulation-as-a-Service Infrastructure (EaaSI) platform, archivists will soon have an option for preserving access to entire networks of machines on which born-digital design records are dependent.

---

52 "Internet Arcade," Internet Archive, accessed July 22, 2019, https://archive.org/details/internetarcade.
53 Klaus Rechert, "Emulating Networks – Preserving Access to Webservers," *Open Preservation Foundation* (blog), November 5, 2020, https://openpreservation.org/blogs/emulating-networks-preserving-access-to-webservers/?order=date%3ADESC&page=1, captured at https://perma.cc/S46L-Q56K.

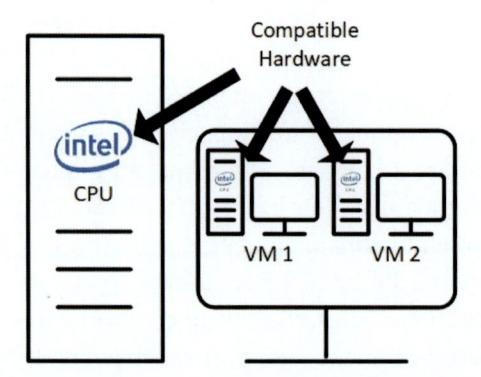

Figure 5: Virtualization allows users to run multiple alternative operating systems on the same host computer at the same time, provided those operating systems are compatible with the hardware on the host computer

Virtualization

Like emulation, *virtualization* describes a situation in which a computer is simulated or "virtualized" on another computer. Unlike emulators and emulation, when software is installed on a virtualized computer, it sends commands to the virtualization software that are predominantly passed to the underlying hardware and run on it directly (Figure 5).[54] This has two significant impacts:

1. It means the software runs with minimal slow-down tax, meaning that the software runs at roughly the same speed as it runs when installed directly on the physical hardware.
2. It means that the software run on a virtualized computer has to be compatible with the hardware that the virtualization software is running on. That means that the archivist cannot run a mobile application made for ARM hardware in virtualization on a PC running on x86_64-based hardware. In that scenario, the archivist would have to use an emulator.

Traditional Use Cases for Virtualization. Virtualization is most often used to enable the hardware of server-computers (servers) to be used

---

54 Some components in virtualized hardware, such as network components, are fully emulated. In the case of emulated network hardware, this is necessary as the virtual computers each need their own network card, and the host computers usually can't provide enough dedicated network cards to support the multiple virtual computers that they may host. To resolve this issue, the virtualization software created fully emulated network cards in software and an emulated network "switch" in the software to connect them to the network connection of the host computer.

more efficiently. Multiple virtualized computers, or Virtual Machines (VMs), can be created and run on the same physical server, and they can share the underlying hardware. The hardware can also be "over-provisioned," which means that the VMs running on the hardware can be assigned more resources (e.g., memory/RAM) than the server actually has. This is possible because the administrators of these systems assume that most of the time the VMs do not fully utilize their assigned resources, and, at any point in time, not all the VMs will need all their assigned resources. Overprovisioning the physical hardware enables administrators to ensure that they get the most value from the physical hardware, as a greater proportion of the underlying hardware is used at any point in time than would be used if each of the VMs instead ran on its own dedicated machine. For example, an administrator might provision VMs with 164GB of total memory shared between them on a physical server that has only 128GB of memory. This is possible, as most of the time most VMs don't use all the memory they are provisioned.

Another common case for virtualization is to be able to test or actively use software applications that are not compatible with a computer's operating system. For example, web developers will often use computers that run a Mac operating system or Linux to develop their websites but also have a need to test the sites in versions of the Internet Explorer or Edge web browsers that only run on a Microsoft Windows operating system. By creating a VM that runs Microsoft Windows, the developers can then install or run Internet Explorer in the VM running on their MacOS or Linux-based computer and use it to test how the website functions in Internet Explorer.

Virtualization with VirtualBox, VMWare, or KVM (Kernel-based Virtual Machine). One approachable method to getting experience with running legacy software is to use one of the free virtualization tools that are available from VMWare and Oracle/Virtualbox (cross-platform tools) or through KVM in Linux. These tools enable users to install older operating systems and software and import files into them to be opened and interacted with using that legacy software. Some of these tools also allow for pausing running VMs and saving the state so users can return directly to that machine with the software already opened and an object accessible in it.

Approaching and implementing emulation or virtualization-based preservation and access strategies can be daunting. Fortunately, practitioners who do not have extensive training or background knowledge can get experience with these tools. In addition, emerging services further facilitate access to emulation and legacy software.

Digital Forensics Processing

Once a preservation approach has been determined and the SIP has been appraised and ingested, the digital content, and all associated descriptive documents, is ready to become an AIP and be deposited into a preservation management system or other appropriate long-term storage option. At this point, the management of the digital data requires alignment to other facets of preservation planning, including providing access to content and description so that users understand what the digital organization has, what is available to them, and how they might access it. For born-digital design records in particular, this is one of the most challenging phases of digital preservation. The content preservation approach that organizations' staff members choose to apply to their digital collections has a profound impact on how the files are served to researchers.

The complex digital objects that tend to make up design records are increasingly platform/software dependent. When they are normalized for viewing, they are stripped of their digital integrity. An example of this might be normalizing content in a drawing (DWG) file, a proprietary, but open, file type native to AutoCAD, by transforming it to a PDF. Unfortunately, the PDF capabilities are much more limited than viewing the file in its native AutoCAD software, and a single PDF will not accurately represent a multitude of external reference (xref) files to which a single DWG file might refer. For some organizations, this type of normalization is the only option available, and if it fits the research needs of the individuals using those records, then it should sufficiently comply with fulfilling the dissemination requirements of a digital preservation framework at the organization. This type of simple-format migration is also very automatable, and it can be carried out at the batch level using open-source software.

Similarly, content can be migrated to files with more contemporary formats. Some design software companies have learned over time the value of offering backward compatibility and migration options for file types that they generate in the form of free readers. With proper licensure in place, archival formats can be converted or versioned up so that they can be opened in the current version of the software that will be provided for access. As that file type has been updated over time, the commercial entity that supports the format revisions has not necessarily been keeping preservation goals in mind, and a freshly migrated file will not be an authentic representation of an older format. Yet, providing access in a comparable platform offers users a nearly authentic experience, which can have value for some users.

Another approach to digital access is to allow individuals to view digital content in original native software supported by an emulation platform. This would be ideal for born-digital design files. Users can see and perhaps even engage with files as they were intended at the point of creation. The scalability of providing myriad operating systems and software versions to serve a suite of born-digital design files makes emulation a more challenging approach.[55]

Whatever access approach is applied, digital content requires transparent description so researchers can locate the digital content they require and understand how the context for access being provided to them at the organization might differ from how the organization originally received that digital content. Local guidelines for digital description are being developed by organizations at a rapid pace, but a national standard for archival digital description has not yet emerged. The best set of guidelines in circulation right now are the University of California Libraries' "UC Guidelines for Born-Digital Archival Description," developed by the UC Born-Digital Content Common Knowledge Group (CKG) in 2017.[56] The guidelines give instruction and make recommendations based on the structured fields of Encoded Archival Description (EAD), the descriptive standards of *Describing Archives: A Content Standard* (DACS), and the General International Standard Archival Description (ISAD[G]). A finding aid is typically the system of record of all processing carried out on an archive. However,

---

55 The following section, "Emulation for Access," explains how EaaSI is able to deploy an emulation environment that supports varying operating systems and software environments available on a network to offer access to many types of obsolete design file formats.
56 University of California Systemwide Libraries, "The UC Guidelines for Born-Digital Archival Description," GitHub, accessed October 1, 2019, https://github.com/uc-borndigital-ckg/uc-guidelines.

for digital content, a surfeit of descriptive and technical metadata is generated during processing, even if the collection of digital materials is quite small. The UC guidelines offer recommendations for how to write a technical description that doesn't overwhelm a finding aid and how to provide an essential amount of transparency so that content can be accessed. The guidelines suggest that often description can be reconciled by attaching a container list to the finding aid. Accurate archival description depends on the level and intensity of processing carried out on the digital content. Files can be described and arranged in aggregate (for example, by attaching a container list), at the storage object level, or, in very rare cases, at the file level. Describing digital content at the file level is an incredibly labor-intensive undertaking for an organization and most likely an unsustainable practice.

To measure the sustainability of an organization's access plans another framework has been developed, the Digital Library Federation's (DLF) Levels of Born-Digital Access. DLF's Born Digital Access Working Group created a framework covering six categories of access across three levels of intensity.[57] The categories are Description, Tools, Research Support & Discovery, Security, and Accessibility. While the Levels of Access prompt an organization to consider text description in a finding aid and the infrastructure of digital content viewers, it also motivates organizations to confront some of the physical conditions and interpersonal dependencies that serving digital content also relies on. Due to their intrinsic complexities, born-digital design records might require more intensive access considerations across the spectrum of needs that the Levels of Access address.

Emulation for Access

Applications of Emulation and Virtualization for the Preservation of and Access to Born-Digital Design Records

Born-digital design records include everything from CAD files; to software add-on configuration files; to GIS data; to spreadsheets, emails, and documents supporting the development and implementation of design projects. These files are often tied to the software they

---

57 Digital Library Federation, "Born-Digital Access Working Group," accessed December 19, 2019, https://www.diglib.org/groups/born-digital-access-group. [The linked page https://osf.io/r5f78/ seems to be more germane?]

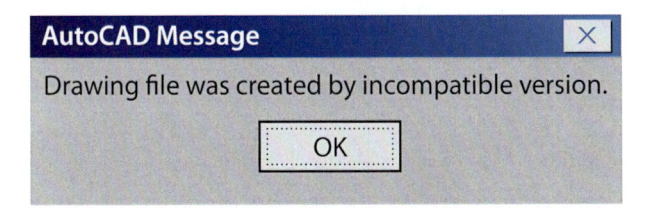

Emerging Best Practices in the Accession, Preservation, and Emulation of Born-Digital Design Materials **129**

Figure 6: AutoCAD 2002 error message produced when an older AutoCAD file was opened in a newer version of AutoCAD. *Used according to fair-use terms of the Copyright Act.*

were originally used in significant and often unexpected ways. In some cases, the original software is the only software that can open the files involved (Figure 6). In other cases, opening a file in a newer application may either change the content presented or uncover previously hidden content (Figures 7 and 8). In both scenarios, it can be essential to be able to run the original software so as to preserve access to the legacy born-digital design records. Emulation and virtualization offer

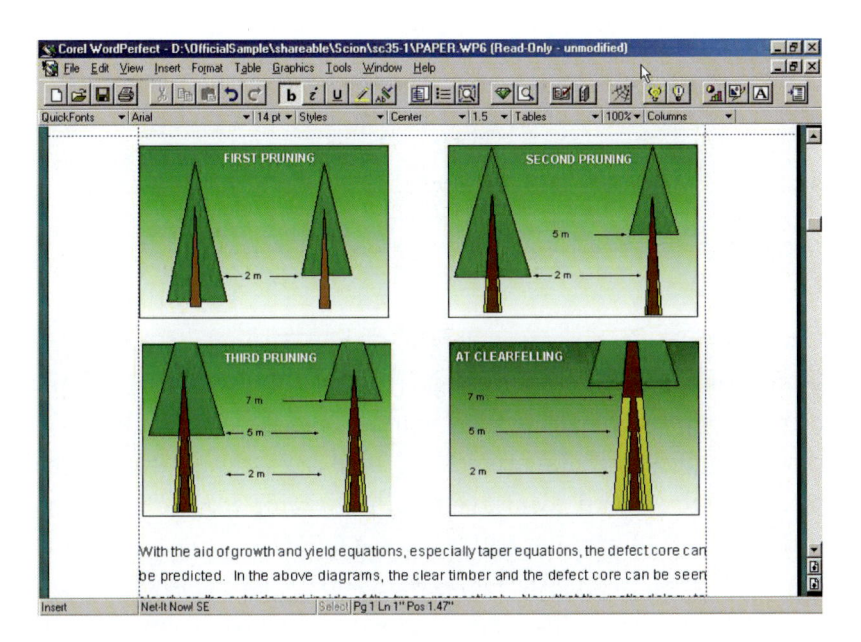

Figure 7: A research report written in Corel WordPerfect 7 in Windows 98. *Image courtesy of Archives New Zealand, https://web.archive.org/web /20150128104350/http://archives.govt.nz/rendering-matters-report-results -research-digital-object-rendering. Creative Commons Attribution 3.0 New Zealand License.*

130   BORN-DIGITAL DESIGN RECORDS

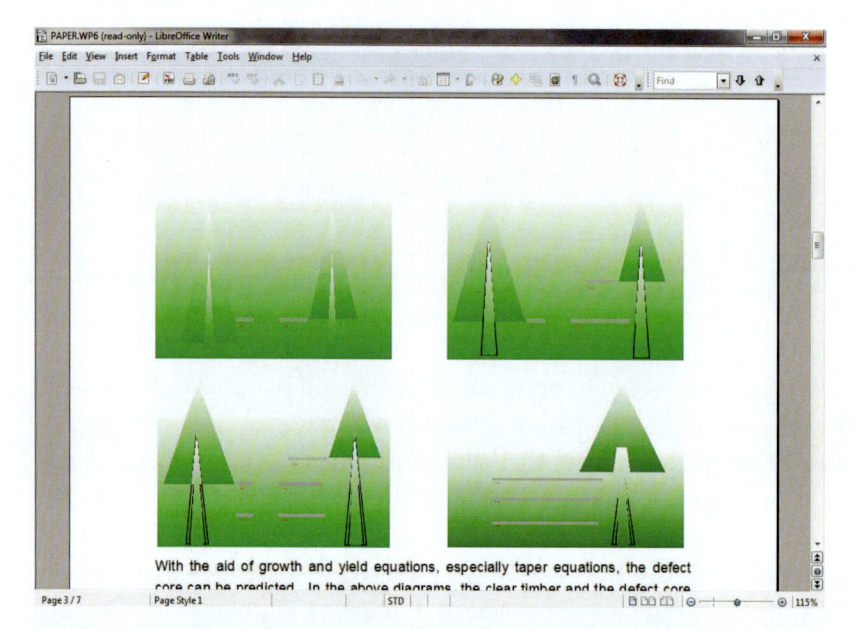

Figure 8: The same WordPerfect report opened in LibreOffice Writer 3.3.0 in Windows Vista. *Image courtesy of Archives New Zealand, https://web.archive.org/web/20150128104350/http://archives.govt.nz/rendering-matters-report-results-research-digital-object-rendering. Creative Commons Attribution 3.0 New Zealand License.*

options for ensuring that born-digital design records can be accessed using the original software.

Local Emulation

Until recently, most archives, libraries, and museums that have been using emulation had been configuring and running emulators on-demand or pre-configuring them and then providing access on dedicated machines in reading rooms. In some cases, this process can be more straightforward than in others. For example, Figure 9 shows some of the configuration options in the QEMU manager Graphical User Interface (GUI) for the QEMU emulator. This can be quite intimidating for anyone who has never worked with emulation or virtualization before. Weighing the costs of resources, including developing staff technical and content expertise, must be considered when determining what level of access an organization intends to provide in the near and long term.

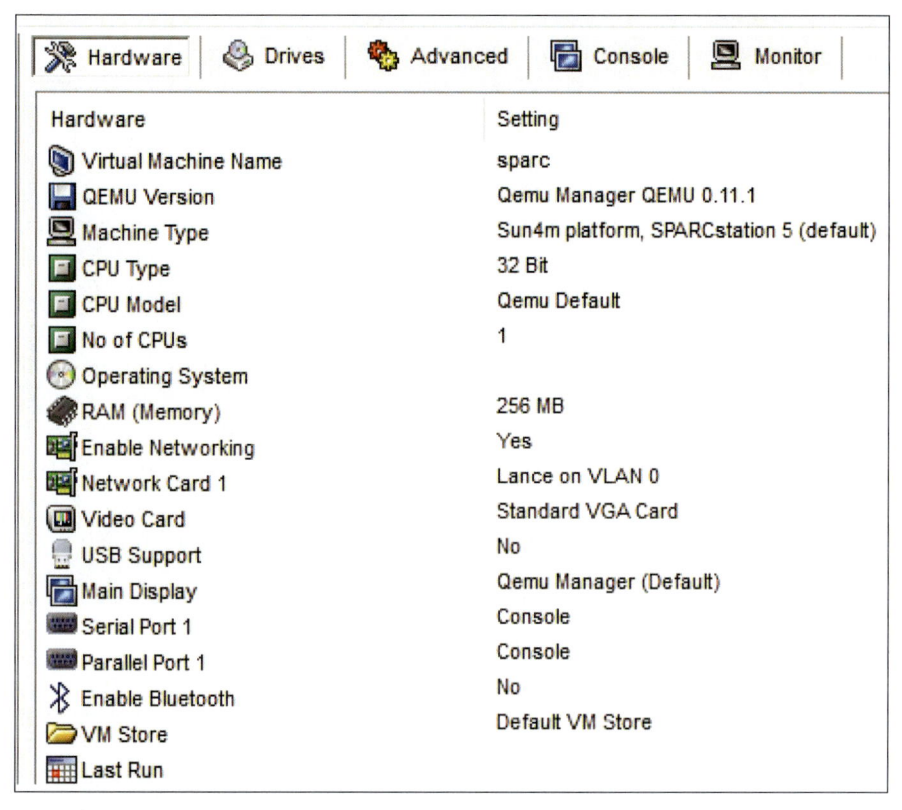

Hardware	Setting
Virtual Machine Name	sparc
QEMU Version	Qemu Manager QEMU 0.11.1
Machine Type	Sun4m platform, SPARCstation 5 (default)
CPU Type	32 Bit
CPU Model	Qemu Default
No of CPUs	1
Operating System	
RAM (Memory)	256 MB
Enable Networking	Yes
Network Card 1	Lance on VLAN 0
Video Card	Standard VGA Card
USB Support	No
Main Display	Qemu Manager (Default)
Serial Port 1	Console
Parallel Port 1	Console
Enable Bluetooth	No
VM Store	Default VM Store
Last Run	

Figure 9: Configuration options in the QEMU manager GUI for the QEMU emulator show how complicated configuring emulators can be for novice users. *Screenshot captured and used according to fair-use terms of the Copyright Act.*

Emulation-as-a-Service

Emulation-as-a-Service (EaaS), a web-based interface that requires no custom software to be installed on users' computers, was developed to make emulators and emulation easier to access. EaaS pre-configures emulators for a variety of use cases while also providing customizability, if needed, making them simpler for novice users, who only need to choose from a list of pre-configured options based on the operating systems they are going to be using in the emulator. EaaS provides access to configure and use the emulated environments via a web

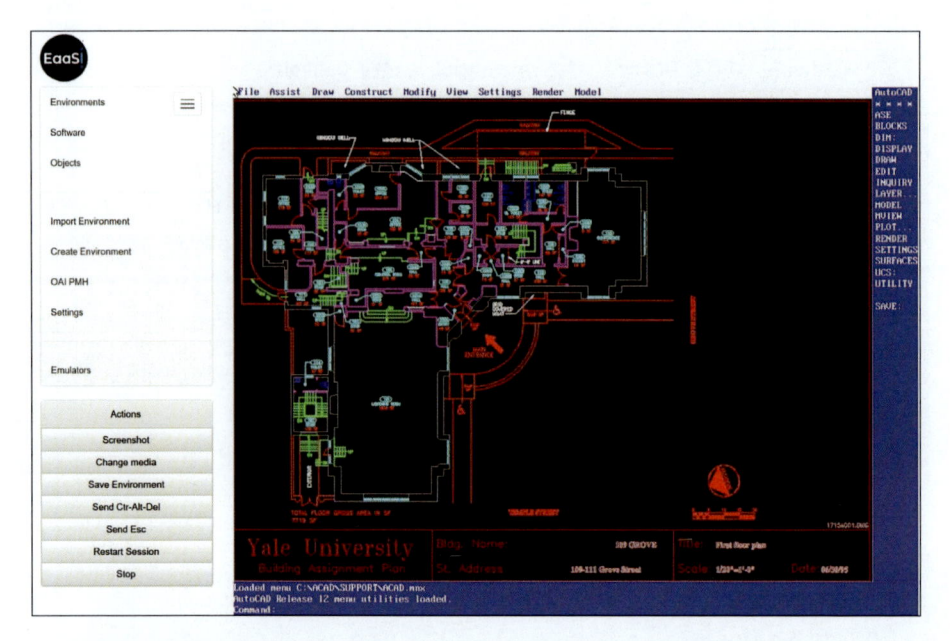

Figure 10: An AutoCAD R12 file opened in AutoCAD R12 in MS-DOS 6.22 in the EaaS/EaaSI interface. *Image provided courtesy of Manuscripts and Archives, Yale University Library.*

browser and enables users to share pre-configured environments via static URLs/web links. (See the example in Figure 10.)[58]

EaaS also enables users to create "derivative" emulated computers that are derived from an existing emulated computer ("environment") but only contains changes a user may have made to it when configuring it for another use. For example, a user may take an existing computer running Windows 98, install AutoCAD Release 14 on it, and save a new "derivative" environment. The files that are saved for that derivative will contain only the new content added by installing AutoCAD R14. When the user wants to re-run that environment, EaaS brings together the original environment and the derivative and seamlessly joins them at run-time. This saves a great deal of space, as all the data from the Windows 98 installation does not need to be replicated in the files that make up the second derivative environment.

---

58 Emulation-as-a-Service (EaaS) was originally developed at the University of Freiburg.

EaaS also contains a variety of powerful and valuable ancillary features, such as the ability to print a PDF from any environment and the ability to import and export data from environments. These additional features present a more comprehensive access strategy for even the most complex digital files, including born-digital design records.

Acquiring Legacy Software

A challenge for anyone working with emulation is to acquire the software needed to make use of emulators and to open and interact with archived digital objects. Archivists should work with donors to ensure that they capture original software whenever possible or at least work with the creators (where/when possible) to develop an inventory of software that was originally used to create and interact with the objects being deposited.

It is sometimes possible to acquire legacy software from online auction sites or other online vendors. However, these can be unreliable and may have unacceptable problematic Digital Rights Management (DRM) features associated with them. The EaaSI program (Scaling Emulation and Software Preservation Infrastructure) is aiming to reduce the effort required to find and use legacy software by enabling easy sharing of software between participating organizations and by pre-populating the EaaSI software catalog with many legacy software applications.[59] To support this kind of work, the SPN worked with the Association of Research Libraries (ARL) to develop a "Code of Best Practices in Fair Use for Software Preservation." The code outlines various affordances that the copyright law allows for preserving and using legacy software to ensure access to digital archives.[60]

Complex Records and Dependencies

The complexity and interdependent bricolage of files depicting a design project's born-digital records can cause problems when one tries to

---

59 The EaaSI program began in 2018 with $2,000,000 of funding from the Alfred P. Sloan Foundation and the Andrew W. Mellon Foundation. It builds on EaaS and adds functionality.
60 "Code of Best Practices for Fair Use in Software Preservation," Software Preservation Network, revised 2019, https://www.softwarepreservationnetwork.org/wp-content/uploads/2020/02/2019.2.28-software-preservation-code-revised.pdf, captured at https://perma.cc/FK5K-MWJR.

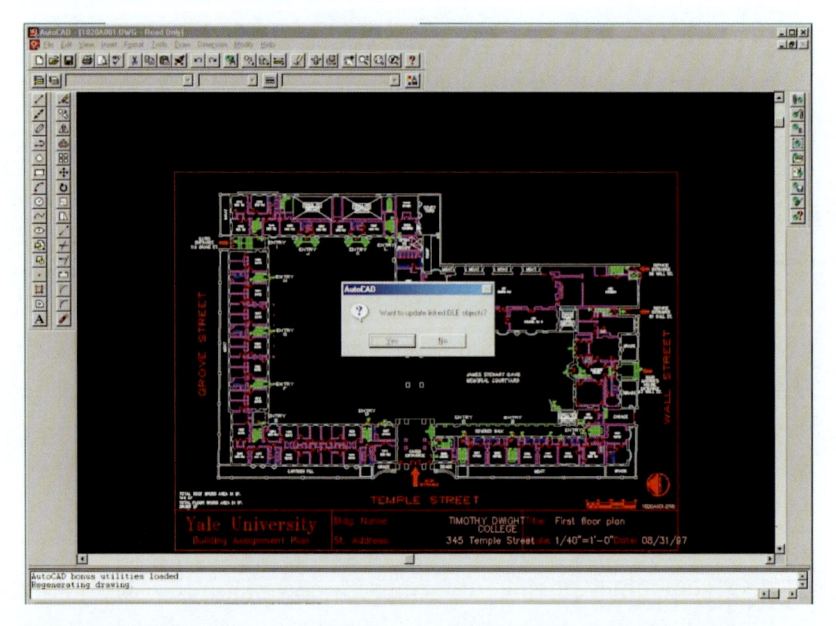

Figure 11: AutoCAD R14 requesting access to objects linked via the Object Linking and Embedding (OLE) protocol. *Image provided courtesy of Manuscripts and Archives, Yale University Library.*

open a file in the original software but the contextualizing files are not present, as shown in Figure 11.

In addition, the software applications used to create the files may have had various add-ons or features installed or there may be multiple applications that work in concert when creating born-digital design records that have to be present when users interact with those records in the future. Without those external expansions, the software may present error messages and use proxies to present a version of the object that may differ from what the original looked and/or behaved like (Figure 12).

Archivists should work with donors to ensure that dependencies of their born-digital design records are included in the materials being acquired. Once again, this issue reinforces the value of donor discussions and the binding legal agreement that the Deed of Gift provides.

Potential for Emulation and Virtualization

The goal of the EaaSI program is to increase access to emulation and software preservation infrastructure. To that end, the EaaSI team is building off EaaS to develop a number of services, including (though not limited to) the following:

- *Easier access to legacy software:* An open (but membership-based) network of nonprofit organizations sharing pre-configured virtual computers with thousands of pre-installed

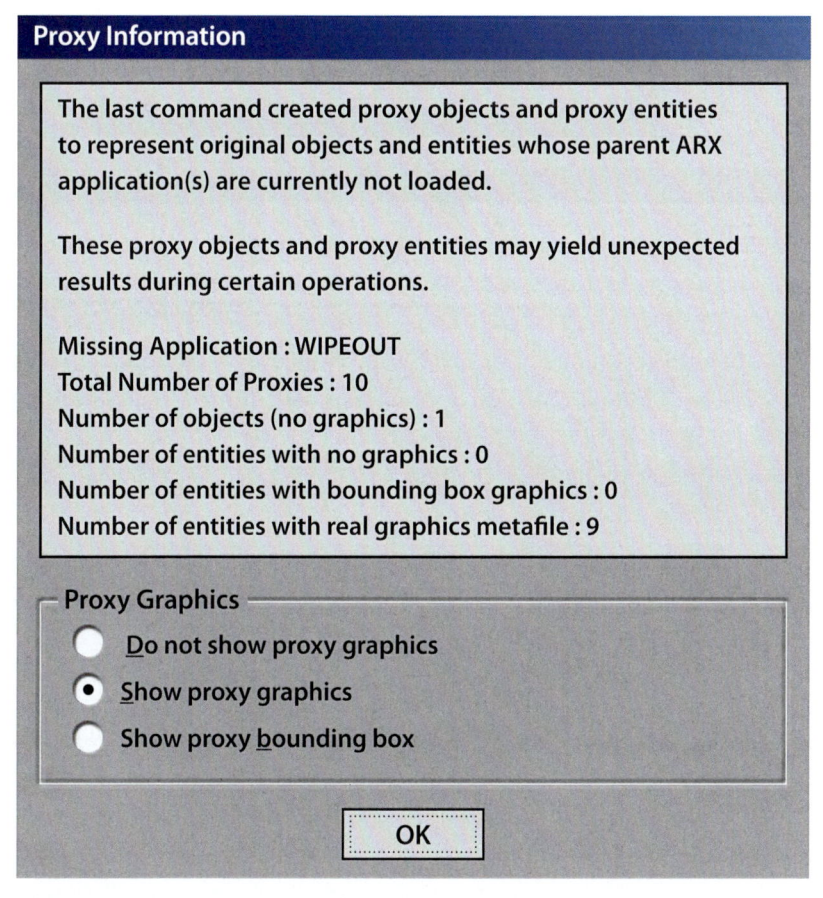

Figure 12: Error resolution message presented by AutoCAD R14 when a dependent application, WIPEOUT, is missing from the environment used to open a CAD file. *Screenshot captured and used according to fair-use terms of the Copyright Act.*

136 BORN-DIGITAL DESIGN RECORDS

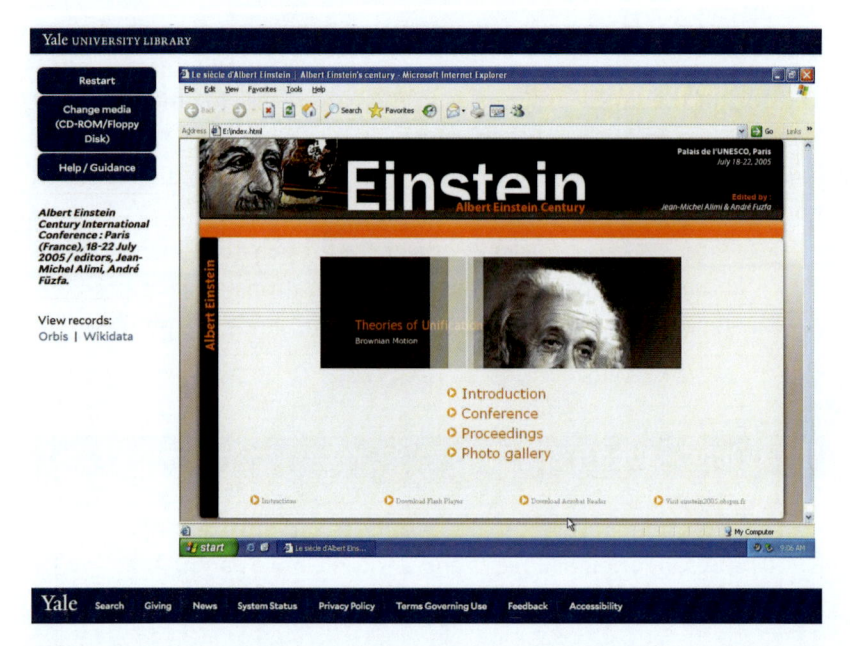

Figure 13: An emulated environment embedded via the EaaSI API in a library access interface. *Image provided courtesy of Yale University Library.*

software applications that can be run in EaaS instances at each organization or via an optional remotely hosted EaaS instance
- *Automatic identification of software dependencies:* A service to scan digital files or their metadata and identify what pre-configured virtual computers in the EaaSI network have the software installed on them that is most appropriate for interacting with them in an "original" presentation
- *Automatic opening and interaction with objects in "original" software:* A Universal Virtual Interactor (UVI) service that can be integrated with discovery and access systems that enable "one-click" opening of a digital object in an original software context in a user's web browser via Emulation-as-a-Service (Figure 13 shows an example environment accessed via a web browser)
- *Easier provisioning of controlled access to legacy digital records via virtual reading rooms:* A virtual reading room service to enable dedicated emulated environments to be assigned to users for periods of time, with requested digital archives

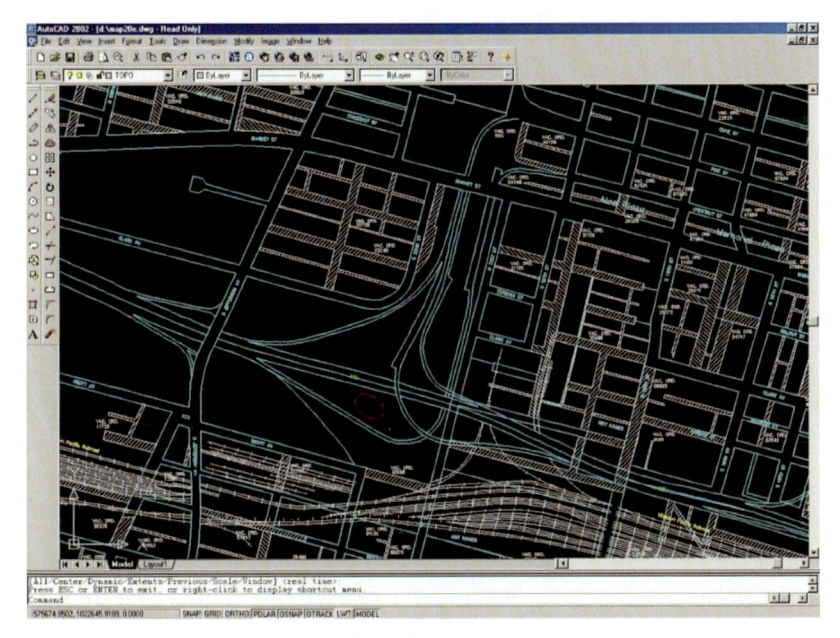

Emerging Best Practices in the Accession, Preservation, and Emulation of Born-Digital Design Materials **137**

Figure 14: 2D CAD file zoomed and navigated to display a particular section of the design. *Image provided courtesy of Manuscripts and Archives, Yale University Library, and Balmori Architects.*

attached to them so they can be accessed and used for the users' research in a controlled and contained manner. Any printouts or changed files a user wishes to take away can be automatically intercepted and vetted before being passed on to the user, and access can be restricted to particular contexts (e.g., particular machines in a physical reading room, an organizational network, etc.). Users can make changes to the environment and save and come back to it over time, and the changes can be discarded or kept by administrators, who can also refresh the environment back to the original state. All of this can be accomplished with a web browser.

Pausing and Citing Views on Designs/Models

The developers of EaaSI are working to enable environments running in EaaS to be paused, cited, and returned to at any point in time using a single URL. This will enable both two-dimensional born-digital design records and three-dimensional models to be rotated, zoomed, or navigated to display a particular view on the object that a user wishes to link to and cite. This opens new options for citation and referencing of born-digital design records. Figure 14 shows an example of a CAD file zoomed in on by a user to a particular view. This view can be saved, cited, and shared using this new approach, something that previously was not easily done.

Emulating Networked Environments

Modern design software tools can often use resources that come from multiple computers or servers in real time, such as at the point at which the file is being interacted with. Reproducing these configurations for future researchers in an archival setting can be challenging, as it can require combining multiple emulated computers or servers and networking them with each other.[61] Fortunately the team at the University of Freiburg are working to add features to EaaS to make this much less complicated. Future practitioners will be able to easily configure networks of computers and servers and have them share data in a way that can be isolated from external networks but still made easily accessible via a web browser or a secure local connection application. This should make archiving and preserving access to the complex digital records from modern design agencies and architecture firms much more feasible.

Migration by Emulation

Digital preservation content is often migrated from a file in one format (e.g., Wordstar or .wsd) and put into a file with another format (e.g., Open Document Text or .odt) so that it can be reused and opened in modern software. This is sometimes impossible if there is no modern software that will open the old format. However, legacy software can often open older formats and can save the content in a file type that is either openable by modern software, or slightly newer software that can open and then move to a newer format. This can be a challenging, if not impossible, undertaking when working with large quantities of files created with obsolete software. Due to the variability of content of the files and the robust commands required by the software, it

---

61 Claudia Roeck, et. al, "Preservation Strategies for an Internet-based Artwork Yesterday, Today and Tomorrow" (paper presented at the 16th International Conference on Digital Preservation, iPRES, Amsterdam, the Netherlands, 2019, https://ipres2019.org/static/pdf/iPres2019_paper_125.pdf, captured at https://perma.cc/6XTS-B59H.

becomes a significant and time-consuming undertaking to open each file individually and save some of the contents into a file with a newer or more open format.

The Planets (Preservation and Long-term Access through Networked Services) project, a four-year project co-funded by the European Union under the Sixth Framework Program to address core digital preservation challenges starting in 2006, demonstrated an implementation of automated migration via emulation in EaaS in 2011.[62] Using this feature allows users to open a file in an emulated environment with legacy software, save the contents into a newer format, and shut down the computer. The EaaS software records those interactions and is able to replay them automatically over an unlimited number of similar files without requiring user-input. This approach is possible because software applications often will open a few, but not all, legacy formats, so they can be used to migrate the previous one to three generations of file formats.

This feature will be added back to EaaS in a future release and will enable two important workflows:

1. As practitioners will likely keep the legacy software available for authenticating and accessing legacy records, they will also be able to use it to migrate content to more modern formats for reuse-purposes (despite the likelihood of losing some content it may be useful for future users to be able to reuse-what can be migrated in modern applications). By doing this on demand rather than at point of acquisition, the archive will not have to preserve multiple copies of a similar object, thus saving storage space.
2. These workflows could also be chained together to enable migrating content consecutively from one format to another in bulk to arrive at a modern file format.

Conclusion

When presented with born-digital design files, an organization must strive to consider the fundamental implications of the context; content;

---

62 Klaus Rechert, Dirk von Suchodoletz, and Isgandar Valizada, "Migration-by-Emulation Planets Web-Service" (poster presented at the 8th International Conference on Preservation of Digital Objects, iPRES, Singapore, 2011), http://eprints.rclis.org/16263.

organization; technical information; storage, transfer, and backup; deleted information; and preservation of that material. These areas of consideration inform outcomes for all aspects of the acquisition, preservation, and access processes. While there are fundamental models to follow, it is in the best interest of organizations to choose sustainable practices to steward any digital objects, but especially for the scale and complexity of born-digital design files.

This sustainability extends beyond the collections on an organization's immediate horizon and should include a degree of flexibility that is critical to account for future accessions that will most definitely include new software and file types and uses of both. Proactively planning outreach to potential donors should include both expressing interest in the collection and raising awareness of the collecting repository's concerns, both technical and cultural. Having the potential donor answer questions about their past and current practices, as well as explaining how those files will be preserved and accessed in the repository's setting, will enrich both parties' experience, and hopefully enhance the repository's ability to receive and support current and future collections of born-digital design records. As the design world continues to evolve, it behooves archivists and collecting repositories to act on their curiosity and establish long-term dialogues with their donor community and to recognize that the preservation and access of these collections are more intimately connected than are analog or paper-based records.

Appendix A: Digital Material Donor Survey

Digital Material Creation and Function
1. What functions and activities led to the creation of your digital materials?
2. What kinds of records were created? (Microsoft Word documents, spreadsheets, databases, email, images, video, web materials, etc.)
3. What software did you use or prefer?
4. What are the most significant project records for you? Why?
5. Are personal files separated from work files?
6. Are you solely responsible for creating these digital materials? If not, who are the other creators, and how are their files separated? Are there multiple user accounts on your computer?
7. What is the date range of the digital files?
8. Are there any files you would like to transfer to us in the future? Please provide details.

Digital Material Creation and Function
1. How are the digital materials organized?
2. Is there a folder and file naming system? Has it been used consistently?
3. Do file names incorporate some sort of version control for drafts of the same work?
4. Are any of the digital materials, including email, available in paper format?
5. Is there a backup routine for digital materials, and if so, what types of media are used?
6. Have you transferred or synchronized files between different computers, and if so, how was that done?
7. Have you ever had any problems transferring or backing up files or lost files in a hard drive crash?
8. Are all digital materials kept locally, on your hard drive or storage media (floppy disks, CD-ROMs, flash drives), or are some files kept centrally, such as on a shared server or in the cloud?

9. Do you use mobile devices such as smartphones or tablet computers?
10. Which email services and/or software do you use? Do you have more than one account?
11. How is your email organized? Is email stored on your computer, on a shared server, or in the cloud?
12. Do you use address books/contact lists or calendar software?
13. Do you post content to document/photo/video sharing web sites (e.g., Google Doc, Flickr, or YouTube)? If so, is this content duplicated elsewhere?
14. Do you maintain any web pages or blogs, or are any maintained on your behalf? If so, what software was used to create or maintain the webpage/blog? Are backups of previous versions kept? Is this content duplicated elsewhere?
15. Do you have accounts on social networking sites (e.g., Facebook, LinkedIn, Twitter, etc.)? If so, how often is the account information (e.g., profiles, photos, etc.) updated and by whom? Are backups of previous versions kept? Is this content duplicated elsewhere?

Digital Material Privacy and Security

1. Are any of the digital materials of a sensitive nature? If so, please specify which materials are sensitive, and whether they should be restricted or destroyed.
2. Are any of the digital files password-protected? If so, please provide usernames and passwords.
3. Do you have any alternative online persona/user names? If so, please provide details.

Digital Content Carriers

Please provide as much detail as you can about each type of digital material you are transferring to the Archives. Use an additional page, if necessary (for multiple accounts or for other types of carriers not listed here).

Downloadable Files

Material Type	Platform	Size	Address/ Username and Password
Email			
Website			
Video/Audio			
Other/Additional Email			
Twitter			
Facebook			
Other/Online Accounts			

Physical Media

Material Type	Quantity	Size	Serial Number and/or Manufacturer
Computer			
External Hard Drive			
Internal Hard Drive			
Flash/USB			
3.5" Floppy			
5.25" Floppy			
CD/CD-ROM/DVD			
Other			

Appendix B: Sample Deed of Gift

Courtesy of Georgia Institute of Technology's Archives, Records Management, and Digital Curation Department.

Description of Collection. A summary of the Collection is set forth below and described in further detail in Exhibit A, which is attached hereto and incorporated herein:

The Collection may include records and/or materials that lawfully belong to [insert organization name] and/or were created in the course of [organization] business, records and/or materials solely owned by and belonging to the Donor ("Donor Materials"), or both. The Collection specifically includes the following type of records and/or materials as indicated by the Donor below:

    _____   [Insert organization name] only

    _____   Donor Materials only

    _____   Both [Insert organization name] Records and Donor Materials

Donor Warranties and Representations. Donor warrants and represents, to the best of Donor's knowledge, that: (a) Donor is the sole lawful owner or an authorized representative of the sole lawful owner of the Collection, or if the Collection comprises only [insert organization name] Records, Donor is the lawful physical custodian of the Collection; (b) the Collection is fully free and clear of any liens, claims, judgments, or other encumbrances of any kind; (c) Donor has not and will not violate any laws, ordinances, rules, regulations, and/or policies pertaining to the Collection and the rights, donation, transfer, licenses, and releases granted to the Collection herein, including, but not limited to, customs laws, tax laws, inheritance laws, export laws, etc.; and (d) Donor has the legal right and authority to enter into this Agreement and grant the rights, donation, transfer, licenses, and releases set forth herein.

Regarding [Insert organization name] Records, Donor understands and expressly agrees that subject to any applicable third-party intellectual property or other rights in or to materials within [Insert organization name] Records, [Insert organization name] Records owns all right, title and interest in and to all [Insert organization name] Records, including, but not limited to, all copyright, trademark, and other intellectual property rights subsisting in the [insert organization name] Records and that this Agreement is transferring physical custody of the [insert organization name] Records to the [insert organization name] for preservation and access purposes. Donor shall not acquire and shall not claim any right, title, or interest in and to any [insert organization name] Records.

Transfer of Ownership of the Collection. Donor hereby transfers all title, right, interest, and other ownership rights to and in the Collection to [insert organization name] via [insert organization name] according to the terms and conditions set forth herein and the method described in Exhibit B.

Intellectual Property Rights in the Collection. Intellectual property rights in and to the Collection may owned by the Donor, [insert organization name] or a third party as indicated below by Donor to the best of Donor's knowledge:

__ Donor created the Collection or otherwise owns or controls all intellectual property rights in and to the entire Collection.

__ Donor created a portion of the Collection or otherwise owns or controls intellectual property rights in and to a portion of the Collection as indicated by the Donor in Exhibit A.

__ Donor does not own or control any intellectual property rights in and to the Collection, in whole or in part.

__ [insert organization name] created the Collection or otherwise owns or controls all intellectual property in and to the entire Collection.

__ [insert organization name] created a portion of the Collection or otherwise owns or controls intellectual property rights in and to a portion of the Collection as indicated by the Donor in Exhibit A.

To the extent Donor owns or controls intellectual property rights in and to the Collection, in whole or in part, Donor transfers intellectual property rights in and to the Collection as follows:

__ Donor hereby assigns and transfers to [insert organization name] and/[insert organization name] all title, right, and interest in and to the entire Collection or to the portion of the Collection that Donor owns or controls, including, but not limited to: (a) the right to reproduce, adapt, distribute, perform, display, communicate, and translate the Collection; (b) moral rights, publicity, and privacy rights pertaining to a person's image or likeness depicted in the Collection; (c) rights protecting against unfair competition pertaining to the Collection; (d) rights protecting against the extraction, dissemination, use, and reuse of data in the Collection; and (e) database rights and other similar, equivalent, or corresponding rights throughout the world based on applicable law or treaty, and any national implementations thereof, subject to the restrictions (if any) set forth below:

__ Restrictions:

List any restrictions:

__ Donor hereby grants to [insert organization name] an irrevocable, worldwide, perpetual, royalty-free, sublicensable, license to use, display, publish, post, reproduce, make derivative works, and allow others to use, display, publish, post, reproduce, and make derivative works of the Collection, in whole or in part, individually or in conjunction with other information or images, printed or electronic materials, in any media or format now or hereafter known, including, but not limited to, access via the World Wide Web, for any educational, scholarly, research, or noncommercial use or purpose, and to use Donor's name in connection therewith if [insert organization name] so chooses.

__ Donor also hereby grants [insert organization name] the right and permission to edit the media format used for Collection to the extent necessary to use, display, publish, post, reproduce, or make derivative works of the Collection, in whole or in part, in any media or format, now or hereafter known, including but not limited to, access via the World Wide Web.

___ Donor hereby waives any right to inspect or approve [insert organization name] use or any third-party use of the Collection or any finished version incorporating the same.

As indicated by the Donor below, the license granted by Donor herein to [insert organization name] v is:

___ Exclusive (i.e., no other individual or entity other than [insert organization name] can exercise the intellectual property rights granted herein)

___ Non-exclusive (i.e., others, including the Donor, [insert organization name] may exercise the same intellectual property rights granted herein)

___ Donor grants [insert organization name] and all other persons or entities an irrevocable, worldwide, royalty-free, non-sublicensable, non-exclusive, noncommercial license to exercise copyright and similar rights to the Collection according to the terms and conditions set forth in Creative Commons Attribution – Noncommercial 4.0 International Public License.

Donor overtly, fully, permanently, irrevocably, and unconditionally waives, abandons, and surrenders all of Donor's copyright and similar rights in and to the Collection and dedicates the Collection to the public domain according to the terms and conditions set forth in Creative Commons Universal CC0 1.0 – Public Domain Dedication License.

___ Donor grants specific, limited intellectual property rights in and to the Collection as set forth below:

___ Donor will retain all intellectual property rights in and to the Collection and provide [insert organization name] with the sufficient information for third parties to obtain permission from the Donor to use the Collection as set forth in Exhibit C. For each permission granted for use of the Collection, Donor will send [insert organization name] written notification of such permission, which shall include pertinent details and any restrictions regarding such use.

Preservation and Access to the Collection. Donor acknowledges and agrees that pursuant to this Agreement and the rights, transfer, licenses, and/or releases granted herein, the [insert organization name] has sole discretion to select the location of the Collection, to conduct retention, cataloging, preservation, and disposition of the Collection, and to provide access to the Collection, in whole or in part, through any means or medium, now or hereafter known, in accordance with applicable regulations, rules, policies, guidelines, standards, and practices of [insert organization name].

[insert organization name], within its sole discretion, may preserve and provide access to the Collection according to accepted professional standards and its mission and vision using various means and methods, including, but not limited to, preservation, exhibition, digitization for preservation and access purposes, or making works in the Collection available and full-text searchable, via the World Wide Web, digital or any other publicly accessible medium, now or hereafter known, for any educational, scholarly, research, or noncommercial use or purpose.

Donor acknowledges and agrees that the method and/or means by which [insert organization name] preserves or provides access to the Collection is within the sole discretion of the [insert organization name]. Notwithstanding anything herein or otherwise, Donor agrees that [insert organization name] is under no obligation to preserve or provide access to the Collection and Donor hereby waives any right to inspect or approve preservation of or access to the Collection by [insert organization name].

Time-Limited Access Restrictions and Sensitive Materials. In accordance with its mission as a public educational institution, [insert organization name] overarching goal is to provide broad access to the Collection and as such, [insert organization name] will not accept access restrictions to the Collection for indefinite or perpetual time periods. [insert organization name] may, however, within its sole discretion, accept the Collection with time-limited access restrictions and/or if it contains sensitive materials.

Prior to the donation or license hereunder, Donor shall inform [insert organization name] if the Collection contains any sensitive or private information, such as social security numbers, medical records, birthdates, etc. [insert organization name] will then determine if it wishes to accept the Collection. Should [insert organization name] decide to accept the Collection, [insert organization name] may request Donor's assistance with redaction, embargo, or restriction of such sensitive or private information. [insert organization name] will comply with all applicable privacy laws pertaining to the Collection, including the Family Educational Rights and Privacy Act of 1974 ("FERPA"), Health Insurance Portability and Accountability Act of 1996 ("HIPAA"), etc. Other than its obligation to comply with applicable privacy laws, [insert organization name] is under no obligation to determine whether materials in the Collection may require redaction, embargo, or restriction. Any restrictions will be applied fairly and equally to all persons accessing the Collection.

Donor shall list in as much detail as possible any materials in the Collection that may contain sensitive and/or private information and/or that requires time-limited access in Exhibit D, which is attached hereto and incorporated herein. Donor shall also indicate in Exhibit D all restrictions on such materials in the Collection, including access restrictions, during any time-limited restriction period, and when the restriction period ends.

Donor shall indicate below whether the Collection contains any sensitive and/or private information and/or materials that requires time-limited access:

- __ The Collection does not contain any sensitive or private information and restricted access to the Collection is not required.
- __ Some materials contained in the Collection contain sensitive or private information and access to such materials should be restricted as set forth in Exhibit D.
- __ Some materials contained in the Collection requires time-limited restrictions as set forth in Exhibit D.

___ The entire Collection contains sensitive or private information and access to the Collection should be restricted as set forth in Exhibit D.

Open Records Act. Notwithstanding anything herein or otherwise, [insert organization name] is subject to the [insert state] Open Records Act and Donor agrees that nothing herein or otherwise shall prevent [insert organization name] from fulfilling its obligations under the [insert state] Open Records Act.

Records Retention and Surplus Policy Compliance. Notwithstanding anything herein or otherwise, upon transfer of physical custody and ownership of the Collection or materials within the Collection to [insert organization name], Donor understands and acknowledges that the Collection becomes property of the State of [insert state] and subject to applicable records retention and surplus policies. Donor further understands and acknowledges that [insert organization name] shall retain and/or dispose of the Collection once [insert organization name], within its sole discretion, ceases use of the Collection in accordance with such records retention and surplus policies.

Access Credentials and Permissions. If the Collection contains digital materials that are protected by password(s), login, encryption, or other access credentials, Donor grants [insert organization name] permission to use such password(s), login, or other access credentials or keys as set forth in Exhibit E, which is attached hereto and incorporated herein.

If the Collection contains digital materials that require password(s), login, or other access credentials or keys to access such materials and Donor cannot or declines to provide such access credentials to [insert organization name], Donor shall indicate below whether [insert organization name] can access the materials via other means:

___ Donor declines to provide the access credentials or keys required to access the digital materials contained in the Collection. However, Donor expressly grants [insert organization name] permission to decrypt password(s) or use encryption systems, as applicable, to access the digital materials contained in the Collection.

___ Donor declines to provide the access credentials or keys required to access the digital materials contained in the Collection.

Disk Imaging. In accordance with archival best practices, the [insert organization name] may use digital forensic imaging* in connection with preserving and providing access to the Collection. Donor acknowledges that such digital forensic imaging may reveal information that was once deleted or overwritten, and Donor expressly grants [insert organization name] permission to use digital forensic imaging to preserve and provide access to the Collection.

In addition, Donor grants additional permissions to [insert organization name] as set forth below as to Donor's preferences regarding access to data recovered via digital forensic imaging:

Digital forensic imaging may recover deleted data, such as deleted computer files. Does [insert organization name] have your permission to provide access to such deleted data recovered via digital forensic imaging?

___ Yes

___ Yes, with the following conditions:

___ No

Digital forensic imaging may recover log files, system files, and other files that document use of computers or systems. Does [insert organization name] have your permission to provide access to such files if recovered?

___ Yes

___ Yes, with the following conditions:

___ No

Digital forensic imaging involves a sector-by sector copying of data that replicates the structure and content of the data.

Exhibit A

Description of Collection Materials

Description of Materials	Donor Owns the Materials as Indicated by Check Below

Exhibit B

Transfer of Collection Method

The Collection will be transferred via the following method(s) (please select all that apply):

__ Archivist will capture or collect the Collection with Donor's assistance onsite on the [insert organization name] campus or at another location agreed upon by Donor and Archivist.

__ Archivist will capture or collect the Collection from Donor's computer via remote desktop applications or similar software.

__ Donor will transmit the Collection to Archivist via an external storage medium or media (e.g., flash drive, external hard drive, optical media, etc.), supplied by the Donor. The external storage medium or media will be donated as part of the Collection.

__ Donor will transmit the Collection to Archivist via an external storage medium or media (e.g., flash drive, external hard drive, optical media, etc.), supplied by either the Donor or Archivist. If the external storage medium or media is supplied by the Donor, it will be temporarily loaned to the [insert organization name] during the time period of Collection data capture.

__ Donor will transmit the entire computer or other hardware device containing internal storage to Archivist. The computer or device will be donated as part of the Collection.

__ Donor will transmit the entire computer or other hardware device containing internal storage to Archivist. The computer or device will be temporarily loaned to the [insert organization name] during the time period of Collection data capture.

__ Donor will transmit the Collection to Archivist via a network transfer (e.g., Donor's web server, SFTP transfer to [insert organization name] Library server, Dropbox, Google Drive, direct digital repository submission, etc.).

__ Other method or means of Collection transfer as described below by Donor:

Additional Details of the Method of Collection Transfer

	Method Transfer Details
Planned Date(s) of Collection Transfer	
Location of Collection Transfer	
Devices Used for Transfer	
Additional Transfer Method Details	

Exhibit C

Donor Permission

Since Donor has elected to retain all intellectual property rights in and to the Collection, should [insert organization name] receive any requests to use the Collection, in whole or part, Donor request that [insert organization name] contact the Donor via the preferred method(s) of communications set forth below and forward such requests for permission to the Donor accordingly for handling:

_____ Home Telephone: _____

_____ Mobile Telephone: _____

_____ Email Address: _____

Exhibit D

Collection Materials That May Contain Sensitive Information and Require Access Restriction

Title/Description of Collection Materials *Be as specific as possible, e.g., Mary's Diary, John Doe's architectural course work, specific file, folder or document title, and so on.*	Type of Sensitive Information *Sensitive information examples: Social security numbers, medical records, student records, documents protected by attorney-client privilege, research data involving or related to human subjects, classified materials or information, and so on.*	Duration of Access Restriction and End Date of Restriction *Include the duration the Collection materials are to be embargoed or restricted from access and the end date of the restriction or embargo; please use this date format: (YYYY-MM-DD)*	Reason for Access Restriction *Be specific, e.g., FERPA, HIPAA, and so on.*	Individuals Permitted to Access Materials During Embargo or Restriction Period *These individuals may include None, Donor, heir(s) of Donor, Donor department, and so on.*

Exhibit E

Credentials and Permissions

Title/Description of Collection Materials to be Accessed via Password(s), Login or Other Access Credentials or Keys *(Be as specific as possible, e.g., social media account name, document, file or folder title, etc.)*	Type of Sensitive Information *(e.g., Username(s), password(s) login, and/or access key, etc.)*

Bibliography

Allen, Jennifer, Elvia Arroyo-Ramirez, Kelly Bolding, Faith Charlton, Patricia Ciccone, Yvonne Eadon, Matthew Farrell, Allison Hughes, Victoria Maches, Shira Peltzman, Alice Prael, Scott Reed, and Dorothy Waugh. "The Archivist's Guide to KryoFlux." GitHub. Last modified October 1, 2018. https://github.com/archivistsguidetokryoflux/archivists-guide-to-kryoflux.

Allen, Matthew. "Tell Me About a Rhino Command. Software and Architectural History." Exhibition at Harvard GSD, April 2016. Accessed October 1, 2019. www.academia.edu/24720335/Exhibition_Tell_me_about_a_Rhino_command._Software_and_Architectural_History_Harvard_GSD_April_2016.

Archive Team. "Rescuing Floppy Disks." www.archiveteam.org/index.php?title=Rescuing_Floppy_Disks.

Behrnd-Klodt, Menzi L. "Balancing Access and Privacy in Manuscript Collections." In *Rights in the Digital Era*. Edited by Menzi Behrnd and Christopher Prom. Chicago: Society of American Archivists, 2015.

Briston, Heather. "Understanding Copyright Law." In *Rights in the Digital Era*. Edited by Menzi Behrnd and Christopher Prom. Chicago: Society of American Archivists, 2015.

Caplan, Priscilla. *Understanding PREMIS*. Rev. ed. Washington, DC: Library of Congress Network Development and MARC Standards Office, 2017. www.loc.gov/standards/premis/understanding-premis-rev2017.pdf, captured at https://perma.cc/V2PA-SLU5.

Center for Research Libraries. "Digital Preservation Metrics." Accessed July 12, 2019. www.crl.edu/archiving-preservation/digital-archives/metrics.

Conway, Esther, Brian Matthews, Arif Shaon, Juan Bicarregui, Catherine Jones, and Jim Woodcock. "Towards a Methodology for Software Preservation." Paper presented at the 6th International Conference of the Preservation of Digital Objects, iPRES, San Francisco, California, 2009.

Dappert, Angela, and Adam Farquhar. "Significance Is in the Eye of the Stakeholder." In *Research and Advanced Technology for Digital Libraries*, 297–308. Berlin: Springer-Verlag, 2009.

De Stefano, Paula, Carl Fleischhauer, Andrea Goethals, Michael Kjörling, Nick Krabbenhoeft, Chris Lacinak, Jane Mandelbaum, Kevin McCarthy, Kate Murray, Vivek Navale, Dave rice, Robin Ruggaber, Trevor Owens, and Kate Zwaard. "What Is Fixity, and When Should I Be Checking It?" *Checking Your Digital Content*. National Digital Stewardship Alliance, 2014. http://hdl.loc.gov/loc.gdc/lcpub.2013655117.1.

Digital Curation Centre. "The BagIt Library." Last modified November 24, 2014. https://web.archive.org/web/20190405141208/https://www.dcc.ac.uk/resources/external/bagit-library.

Drucker, Peter F. "The Future That Has Already Happened." *Harvard Business Review* (September–October 1997).

"FAQ." *File Information Tool Set (FITS)*. Harvard University. https://projects.iq.harvard.edu/fits/fitsfaq, captured at https://perma.cc/2PLE-V7A4.

Heiss, Daniel, Morgane Stricot, and Matthieu Vlaminck. "Open the Museum's Gates to Pirates: Hacking for the Sake of Digital Art Preservation." Paper presented at the 15th International Conference on Digital Preservation, iPRES, Boston, Massachusetts, 2018.

Klaus Rechert, Dirk von Suchodoletz, and Isgandar Valizada. "Migration-by-Emulation Planets Web-Service." Poster presented at 8th International Conference on Digital Preservation, iPRES, Singapore, 2011. http://eprints.rclis.org/16263.

Lavoie, Brian. *The Open Archival Information System (OAIS) Reference Model: Introductory Guide*. 2nd ed. Digital Preservation Coalition, 2014. http://dx.doi.org/10.7207/twr14-02.

Leventhal, Aliza. "Architectural and Design Collections." In *The Digital Archives Handbook*. Edited by Aaron Purcell. Lanham, MD: Rowman and Littlefield, 2019.

Leventhal, Aliza. *Designing the Future Landscape: Digital Architecture, Design & Engineering Assets*. Washington, DC: Library of Congress, 2018.

Leventhal, Aliza, Jody Thompson, Alison Anderson, Sarah Schubert, and Andi Altenbach. "Design Records and Appraisal Tools." *American Archivist* 84, no. 2 (2021): 320–354. https://doi.org/10.17723/0360-9081-84.2.320.

Leventhal, Aliza, Laura Schroffel, and Jody Thompson. "Deeds of Gift as a Tool to Facilitate Born Digital Design File Processing and Preservation." Chicago: Society of American Archivists, 2019. https://www2.archivists.org/sites/all/files/Leventhal_Schroffel_Thompson_Deeds%20FINAL.pdf, captured at https://perma.cc/GHE6-F9FP.

Lowell, Waverly, and Tawny Ryan Nelb. *Architectural Records: Managing Design and Construction Records*. Chicago: Society of American Archivists, 2006.

McKay, Aprille. "Managing Rights and Permission." In *Rights in the Digital Era*. Edited by Menzi Behrnd and Christopher Prom. Chicago: Society of American Archivists, 2015.

National Institute for Standards and Technology. "Bit Stream Imaging." In Computer Security Resource Center Glossary. Accessed July 12, 2019, https://csrc.nist.gov/glossary/term/bit_stream_imaging, captured at https://perma.cc/KF3Q-EF6L.

Ngulube, Patrick. *Handbook of Research on Heritage Management and Preservation*. Hershey, PA: IGI Global, 2018.

O'Meara, Erin, and Kate Stratton. *Digital Preservation Essentials.* Edited by Christopher J. Prom. Chicago: Society of American Archivists, 2016.

Open Preservation Foundation. "Getting Started with jHove." 2015. http://jhove.openpreservation.org/getting-started, captured at https://perma.cc/LGS2-BBPB.

Phillips, Joanna, Deena Engel, Emma Dickson, and Jonathan Farbowitz. "Restoring Brandon, Shu Lea Cheang's Early Web Artwork." *Checklist* (blog). The Guggenheim Museums and Foundation, May 16, 2017. www.guggenheim.org/blogs/checklist/restoring-brandon-shu-lea-cheangs-early-web-artwork, captured at https://perma.cc/DS4B-YB48.

Phillips, Megan. "The NDSA Levels of Digital Preservation: An Explanation and Uses." Paper presented at the Archiving (IS&T) Conference, Washington, DC, April 2013.

Purcell, Aaron D. *Donors and Archives: A Guidebook for Successful Program.* Lanham, MD: Rowman and Littlefield, 2015.

Roeck, Claudia, Rafael Gieschke, Klaus Rechert, and Julia Noordegraaf. "Preservation Strategies for an Internet-Based Artwork Yesterday, Today and Tomorrow." Paper presented at the 16th International Conference on Digital Preservation, iPRES, Amsterdam, the Netherlands, 2019. https://ipres2019.org/static/pdf/iPres2019_paper_125.pdf, captured at https://perma.cc/6XTS-B59H.

Society of American Archivists. "Fair Use." In *Dictionary of Archives Terminology.* Chicago: Society of American Archivists, 2021. https://dictionary.archivists.org/entry/fair-use.html, captured at https://perma.cc/W9GA-673Y.

———. "A Guide to Deeds of Gift." 2021. www2.archivists.org/publications/brochures/deeds-of-gift, captured at https://perma.cc/C75G-WVDV.

———. "Open Archival Information System (OAIS)." 2021. www2.archivists.org/groups/standards-committee/open-archival-information-system-oais, captured at https://perma.cc/8W7W-E9V2.

Sustainable Heritage Network. "2018 POWRR Institute: Preservation Models and Packages." 2018. https://sustainableheritagenetwork.org/digital-heritage/2018-powrr-institute-preservation-models-and-packages.

University of California Systemwide Libraries. "The UC Guidelines for Born-Digital Archival Description." GitHub. Accessed August 12, 2019. https://github.com/uc-borndigital-ckg/uc-guidelines.

U.S. National Archives and Records Administration. "PII Considerations in Screening in Screening Archival Records." www.archives.gov/files/Before-Screening-Records.pdf, captured at https://perma.cc/S25S-LFPC.

MODULE 26
CASE STUDIES IN BORN-DIGITAL DESIGN RECORDS

ALIZA LEVENTHAL, STEFANA BREITWIESER,
ALEXANDRA JOKINEN, MIREILLE NAPPERT, AND ZACH VOWELL

Module 26 Contents

Introduction • 169

Design, Digital, and Born-Digital Design Records • 169
    Design Records: Niche and Ubiquitous • 169
    Born-Digital Records Specialization • 170
    Born-Digital Design Records: Merging Specialties • 171

Appraisal/Acquisition • 172
    Acquisition Strategies and Policies • 172
    Appraising Without Certainty • 174
        A Cal Poly Use Example • 175
        Using the Deed of Gift to Address Uncertainty • 178
        Minimizing Uncertainty • 179
    Initial Transfer from Donor to Organization • 179
    Accession Descriptions • 183

Arrangement and Description • 185
    Factors That Impact Arrangement • 185
    Transferring Records • 185
    State of Organization on Transfer • 186
    Scope of the Collection • 188
    Describing Born-Digital Material • 188
    Automation • 191
    Infrastructure Supporting Description • 191

Preservation and Storage • 195
    Preparing Files for a Digital Preservation System (OAIS) • 195
        SIP Structure and Additional Content • 196
        Transfer and Ingest into a Digital Preservation System • 198
        Understanding Characterization and File Format Identification • 201
        Further Processing with a Digital Preservation System • 204
    Digital Preservation Storage at the CCA • 205
    Digital Preservation Storage at the Cal Poly • 205

Access • 206
    Challenges to Access • 206
        Policy-Related Challenges to Access • 206
        Technology-Related Challenges to Access • 207
    Defining Users of Born-Digital Design Records • 208
    Access in the Reading Room: Software Dependence and Emulation • 210
    Need for Custom Development • 215

Conclusion • 218

Appendix A: CCA Format Policy Registry 2019 • 221

Appendix B: CCA Submission of Digital Files Questionnaire • 228

Bibliography • 234

ABOUT THE AUTHORS

Aliza Leventhal contributed to this module in her previous role as the corporate archivist and librarian for Sasaki, a Boston-based interdisciplinary design firm (2014–2019). She currently is the head of the Prints and Photographs Division's Technical Services Section at the Library of Congress. Leventhal is the co-founder and co-chair of the Society of American Archivists' (SAA) Design Records Section's Digital Design Records Task Force, and has written and presented extensively in a variety of forums including SAA, the Visual Resources Association, International Confederation of Architectural Museums, and the Library of Congress. She is the co-author of the Digital Preservation Coalition *Preserving Born-Digital Design and Construction Records* Technology Watch Report.s. She holds an MLIS and an MA in history from Simmons University's Archives Management Program.

Stefana Breitwieser is the digital archivist at the Arthur H. Aufses, Jr., MD Archives at the Icahn School of Medicine at Mount Sinai in New York, where she also provides reference for the Mount Sinai Beth Israel collections. She contributed to this module in her previous role as the digital archivist at the Canadian Centre for Architecture, where she focused broadly on digital preservation and access across the institution. She holds an MLIS from Simmons University's School of Library and Information Science.

Alexandra Jokinen is the digital archivist at the Canadian Centre for Architecture in Montréal, Canada, where she oversees the preservation of digital and audiovisual materials in the museum's collection. She has a master's degree from Ryerson University in film and photography preservation and collections management, as well as a bachelor's degree in art history, criticism, and conservation from the University of Guelph. Her areas of interest include architecture and design history, the preservation of time-based media, and the evolution of cinematic technologies.

Mireille Nappert is the digital archivist in the Institutional Information and Archives Management Service at HEC Montréal. She contributed to this module in her previous role as digital processing archivist at the Canadian Centre for Architecture. She holds an MLIS from McGill University.

Zach Vowell is a digital archivist at California Polytechnic State University's Robert E. Kennedy Library, where his responsibilities include preserving, describing, and providing access to born-digital design records. He also cofounded the Software Preservation Network (SPN) and co-led two SPN-affiliated IMLS-funded grant projects during his time at Cal Poly. Prior to moving to San Luis Obispo in 2013, Vowell worked as a digital archivist at the Briscoe Center for American History, University of Texas (UT) at Austin, as an archivist for the UT Videogame Archive, and as a digitization project archivist. Vowell also received his MS in information studies from UT–Austin in 2006.

Introduction

Institutions that are actively collecting born-digital design records range in collecting intention and organization type, from the active-use perspective of practicing firms and facilities management/maintenance to academic and private research institutions. The intention of each collecting space varies significantly from pursuing the earliest and notably outlier uses of design software, to capturing a representative sample of the design community's zeitgeist, to accepting digital files for maintaining newly constructed structures on a campus, to managing a firm's project records for future use. Each scenario comes with particular parameters and a learning curve to account for the variety of file types and information conveyed by creators in each file. Although some scenarios seem more challenging on the surface than others, each is comparatively complicated based on the archivists' available resources, access to the donor, technical skills, and the institution's expectations. This module walks through the activities and topics of consideration that every institution must take as staff members acquire, process, preserve, and provide access to born-digital design records. This discussion includes the lifecycle of collection materials from the perspective of archivists at an academic institution (California Polytechnic State University), an international research center and museum (Canadian Centre for Architecture), and an archives in a firm (Sasaki).

The authors of this module offer a diverse set of perspectives and experiences on how an archives can collect, preserve, and provide access to born-digital records. The following pages offer explanations of how each author has navigated the challenges of appraisal and acquisition of born-digital design records, arranging and describing collections, establishing preservation and storage plans, providing access to the collections, and, finally, providing a launching point for other collecting spaces that are facing similar challenges around born-digital design collections.

Design, Digital, and Born-Digital Design Records

Design Records: Niche and Ubiquitous

Design records document the built environment as it actually exists, as well as how it has been imagined. As such, these types of records often require that an archivist have specialized knowledge about the workflows of designers and have a level of visual literacy to be able to read drawings, sketches, and contextualizing data/information. This spectrum is represented in the collecting policies of repositories such as the Canadian Centre for Architecture (CCA), California Polytechnic State University (Cal Poly), and design firm Sasaki, as well as government departments of historic preservation, permits, and public works. The material collected by each office, institution, or department, is subject to numerous criteria to determine staff's capacity to process and provide access to collected materials. Key factors include the size of staff, technical capabilities, and designated community that can influence the type of access offered to collections.

Since 1973, the archival profession has categorized these records—produced and used by architects, landscape architects, planners, graphic designers, and the engineering professions—as a niche record set. It was at that time that the regional working groups Cooperative Preservation of Architectural Records (CoPAR) were established.[1] Today, the SAA's Design Records Section functions as a support for archivists who collect design records.[2] The special nature of these collections has presented a range of collecting spaces with concerns, frustrations, and questions. Academic institutions, research institutions, museum archives, government departments, and active design firms have all been collecting design records, to varying degrees, for decades, and as the prominence of born-digital records has continued to rise in the types of professions mentioned above, so has the presence of these records increased in archival collections.

Born-Digital Records Specialization

Similar to design record specialists, digital preservationists and stewards of born-digital collections also require a level of technical expertise that has been developing for decades, both formally and through experimentation. This professional space has continued to grow and diversify as record groups, software, and use cases have been defined

---

[1] "Cooperative Preservation of Architectural Records," https://www2.archivists.org/sites/all/files/copar-committees-2009.pdf, captured at https://perma.cc/M9RB-R6C8.
[2] Society of American Archivists, "Design Records Section," https://www2.archivists.org/groups/design-records-section.

and collaboratively solved through communities such as BitCurator[3] and the establishment of standards and guidelines. These include, for example, the Open Archival Information System (OAIS), which defines SIPs (Submission Information Packages, or pre-processed copies of digital archival material), AIPs (Archival Information Packages, or preservation copies), and DIPs (Dissemination Information Packages, or access copies), as well as an institution's responsibilities for its digital collection material.[4]

The majority of this work has addressed the needs of ubiquitous file types and media, and niche record groups have also focused attention on these records. Born-digital design records have only recently been elevated to the archival community's attention. It has been a gradual engagement—and mostly at the invitation of design records archivists, as many digital preservationists were not aware of the issues this community was facing. With design records archivists leading the conversation, it has taken longer to bridge the gap and appreciate the applicability of fundamental practices of digital preservation for this specialized record group. This module explores how the blending of design records expertise with digital preservation resources and skills has begun at institutions of varying sizes and capacities.

Born-Digital Design Records: Merging Specialties

Since the 1990s, design records archivists have been discussing the challenges and significance of born-digital design records.[5] It has only been since about 2010, more than fifteen years after SAA published topics covered in the 1994 Working Conference on Establishing Principles for the Appraisal and Selection of Architectural Records (held at the CCA), that digital preservationists began to be explicitly invited into the discourse around managing and supporting born-digital design records. This prolonged and unintentional barrier of practical and theoretical research has been a detriment to the development

---

3   "BitCurator Tools." Confluence. BitCurator. January 27, 2022. https://confluence.educopia.org/display/BC/Tools. All brand names, product names, or trademarks belong to their respective holders.

4   Consultative Committee for Space Data Systems, "Reference Model for an Open Archival Information System (OAIS): Recommended Practice, CCSDS 650.0-M-2" (Washington, DC: CCSDS Secretariat, June 2012), https://public.ccsds.org/pubs/650x0m2.pdf, captured at https://perma.cc/K5VR-S45E.

5   See *American Archivist*'s Special Issue on Architecture, 59, no. 2 (1996), https://meridian.allenpress.com/american-archivist/issue/59/2.

of best practices for preserving and providing long-term access to born-digital design records. The marrying and merging of these two specializations have only recently been explored as the broad spectrum of institutions collecting both design and born-digital materials has grown and the concerns around preserving and providing long-term access to born-digital design files has been more actively discussed since the mid-2000s.

Approaching the development of collections of born-digital design records does require both a level of familiarity with the design process and tools leveraged by those creators, as well as a foundation in best practices established around digital preservation. The combination of these skills is currently a rare commodity in a single archival practitioner. The perception is that design records are a niche record set and that digital records are a niche record set, which positions digital design records as a subset of both of those niche record types. As archives budgets are often limited, it may not be feasible to bring both sets of expertise into an institution as separate employees, leaving many archivists feeling intimidated or unable to master, or at least navigate, both the visual literacy and cultural nuances that design records require, as well as digital preservation principles and practices. Repositories with differing levels of staff and expertise around design and born-digital records have reconciled this anxiety to cover the breadth of understanding required to manage born-digital design record collections.

Appraisal/Acquisition

Acquisition Strategies and Policies

In ideal scenarios, appraisal and acquisition does not mark the beginning of a relationship with a design firm or office. Conversations with potential design record donors should be a part of a continuous relationship and open dialogue.

As part of such a relationship (or at least before the actual appraisal and acquisition activities), it is helpful for an organization's staff members to review their organizational mission, vision, and values statements, as well as any collection development policy that the organization has published or established. Doing so can bolster confidence while appraising potential collections and when confronted with the wide range of possible design records that may be offered.

It can also be helpful for an archivist to remain aware of their role in the appraisal and acquisition process. The following questions may help maintain perspective:
- Who makes the final appraisal decision?
- How will the recommendations of the archivist's appraisal be documented and communicated?
- Does the appraising archivist contribute information and appraisal analysis to a colleague or supervisor's appraisal decision?

The answers to these questions vary. This is due to the range of responsibilities each institution associates with the archivist and digital archivist positions. Each organization's context will be different, and knowing how to position oneself in such a process will help the archivist define the best practices appropriate at their level.

At Cal Poly, the archives are situated in the university's library. The library's current mission is clear: the library "helps every member of the Cal Poly community engage in open and informed inquiry, and contribute through creation, innovation, and collaboration to the quality of life of our community."[6] The archives are ultimately responsible to the Cal Poly community, an educational community like that of many other colleges and universities. Furthermore, Cal Poly has a state college mandate that focuses on undergraduate student teaching and success. When the Cal Poly Special Collections and Archives department appraises potential collections, and when it acquires collections it deems appropriate to its collecting scope, the relevance to student learning is paramount (although there are many other considerations). For example, if esoteric design file formats are identified as having little chance of being accessible in the near future, the department must seriously consider whether it is worth it to collect for bit-level preservation purposes alone.

At the CCA, the archives are part of the Collection division, alongside the Library, Prints and Drawings, and Photographs collections. As a museum and research institution, the archives follow a

---

6   Robert E. Kennedy Library, "Strategic Plan," 2018, https://lib.calpoly.edu/about-and-contact/strategic-plan, captured at https://perma.cc/XHS8-VD95. The quoted passage is found under "Mission."

primarily curatorial mandate related to exhibitions, publications, and other institutional activities. Generally, particular projects are selected for acquisition, though in certain instances the CCA will acquire a complete archival *fonds*. Users of the archives are both internal and external to the institution and include academics, architects, designers, students, art historians, and curators. The digital nature of archival records, though, brings up other possibilities of research, where the interest is focused on the data from the drawings or the use of software by the architects who created them. Although the leadership of the CCA had been reflecting on the impact of digital tools in architectural practices since the early 2000s, the push to formally develop a digital preservation program came with the twenty-five acquisitions, including a significant born-digital component, following the Archaeology of the Digital project (2013–2016). After receiving a significant grant from the City of Montréal and the Quebec Department of Culture and Communications, the CCA was able to hire three digital processing archivists to work on these *fonds*, begin to implement Archivematica,[7] and develop an access interface. The high level of technical expertise at the CCA also allows the organization to prioritize other, smaller development projects.

At an active design firm, a project's entire set of records is kept to support future work for that client and the opportunity to repurpose investments in design innovations, but the records are also kept for the length of the statute of limitations dictated by the state in which the project was completed. The mixture of uses, as well as the high level of familiarity with the types of records created, requires the access policy of the firm's archives to be significantly more open and facilitate unfettered access to the entire file directory. The use is almost entirely internal, with a super-user designated community that allows the archivist to focus on accession and preservation concerns, rather than access.

Appraising Without Certainty

It is not uncommon for uncertainty to be present when donors offer and archivists appraise born-digital collections. It seems especially common for uncertainty to cause frustration during the appraisal of

---

[7] Archivematica is an open-source digital preservation system developed and maintained by Artefactual Systems. See https://www.artefactual.com.

born-digital design records.[8] The donor may no longer be able to support the legacy media that they are donating, meaning that they can only make a best guess before media access by the archivist. When the material can be accessed, there can be uncertainty regarding folders (high-level directories being the most problematic). For example, folders representing different components of a project (i.e., an archival series) can be unclear, and it may be that the donor cannot clarify. It may be that the institutional memory in a design firm or architectural practice has been lost, or the donor may be several times removed from the original creator or record custodian. In either case, the result is that the archivist will need to make inferences and construct careful conjectures to make appraisal decisions.

It can be challenging for an archivist to make inferences about a collection that cannot be assessed at the file level. Here is where uncertainty may begin for the archivist, even if the donor has full knowledge at the folder/series level. File names can often be opaque or lack self-description (especially if the folder names are unclear), and near-total obfuscation emerges if the file itself cannot be easily opened.

The Cal Poly Use Example. The following example of how appraisal uncertainty can be addressed with a collection of design records transferred between two departments at Cal Poly in summer 2018, when Cal Poly's Facilities Management and Development unit transferred a collection of digital files (some digital surrogates of physical items, and others born-digital) to the Cal Poly Special Collections and Archives department (henceforth called "the primary Cal Poly use case"). The files were related to nearly every building constructed on the Cal Poly campus (which opened to students in 1903). The collection includes a series of files related to Building 192 (otherwise known as the Engineering IV building).

The following walks through the technical and analytical steps taken with this accession, includes notes of similar and varying practices at the CCA and Sasaki, and invites the reader to consider these practices in comparison to their institution's workflows and available infrastructure.

---

8   Terry Eastwood, "Digital Appraisal: Variations on a Theme," keynote address for the Conference on Appraisal in the Digital World. Rome Italy, November 15–16, 2007, www.interpares.org/display_file.cfm?doc=ip2_dissemination_cp_eastwood_delos_2007.pdf, captured at https://perma.cc/XW2R-CM79.

176 BORN-DIGITAL DESIGN RECORDS

Name	Size	Modified
192_0000_Gleeble_Electric	1 item	22 Oct 2015
192_2004_Bid_Set-all_pdf	2 items	22 Oct 2015
192_2004_Soils Report	1 item	22 Oct 2015
192_2005_Fire_Alarm_Plans	1 item	22 Oct 2015
192_2006_Engineering_Plaza_Concept_Plan	2 items	22 Oct 2015
192_2007_Engineering IV Landscape Plan	3 items	22 Oct 2015
192_2007_Engineering_Plaza_Record_Drawings	3 items	22 Oct 2015
192_2007_Fire_Sprinkler_Shop_Drawings	1 item	22 Oct 2015
192_2008_Original_Construction	12 items	22 Oct 2015
192_2008_Record_Set_CAD	9 items	22 Oct 2015
192_2010_PJ3246_Tile etching for Plaza 192	5 items	22 Oct 2015
192_2010_Third_Fl_North_Tis	2 items	22 Oct 2015
192_2012_Engineering Plaza Tiles	20 items	22 Oct 2015
192_2013_Cyber Lab	2 items	22 Oct 2015
192_2013_Lecture Hall	2 items	22 Oct 2015

Figure 1: A file browser view of folders associated with Building 192 at California Polytechnic State University

Figure 1 shows the file browser view of folders in the 192 collection.[9] Opening the "192_2008_Record_Set_CAD" folder in a browser and then opening the subdirectory "Arch" (see Figure 2) revealed file names which end in a .dwg extension, but do not explicitly describe the content of the files.[10]

How is an archivist supposed to appraise these files? In Figure 1, notice that the view of the top level for this Building 192 series shows another folder titled "192_2008_Original_Construction/Arch," which also has a corresponding "Arch" subdirectory. The ubiquitous .pdf file

---

9   Before proceeding with file browsing or opening any files to investigate, the archivist should make sure they are working in a read-only environment. Even something as simple as file browsing, if not done in a Linux environment, can cause complications later with processing. Default file browsers used by both Windows and Mac will write system files (typically files named Thumbs.db and DS_Store, respectively), inadvertently adding files to an accession.

10 Some organizations may have access to AutoCAD, which can open DWG files, and the prefix "cpu" might mean something to those versed in design or architectural terminology, but this module does not assume such resources or knowledge.

Case Studies in Born-Digital Design Records 177

192	192_2008_Record_Set_CAD	Arch					
Name		Size		Modified			
acad.err		184 bytes		27 May 2009			
BATCH PLOT.dst		85.5 kB		6 Sep 2007			
cpu-a001.dwg		396.7 kB		6 Sep 2007			
cpu-a002.dwg		2.2 MB		5 Sep 2007			
cpu-a003.dwg		1.3 MB		5 Sep 2007			
cpu-a004.dwg		141.9 kB		5 Sep 2007			
cpu-a005.dwg		224.5 kB		5 Sep 2007			
cpu-a101.dwg		837.1 kB		5 Sep 2007			

Figure 2: File browser view of DWG files in Cal Poly's Building 192's CAD record set

192	192_2008_Original_Construction	Arch					
Name		Size		Modified			
A-001.pdf		803.3 kB		8 Jan 2008			
A-002.pdf		555.0 kB		8 Jan 2008			
A-003.pdf		1.1 MB		8 Jan 2008			
A-004.pdf		683.2 kB		8 Jan 2008			
A-005.pdf		1.5 MB		8 Jan 2008			
A-101.pdf		473.5 kB		7 Jan 2008			

Figure 3: File browser view of PDF outputs of the DWG originals. Notice the similarity in file names between what is shown here and those seen in Figure 2.

extension found in this particular folder is likely to be a comforting sight for many archivists. On closer inspection, the file names bear a resemblance to the "cpu" files in the CAD set (see Figure 3). Both sets contain the letter *a* and a three-digit number (for example "005"). Furthermore, the patterns of letters and numbers in the file names generally correspond to the United States standard for drawing set organization.[11]

---

11 National Institute of Building Sciences buildingSMART alliance, "United States National CAD Standard – V6: Module 1 – Drawing Set Organization," 2014, www .nationalcadstandard.org/ncs6/pdfs/ncs6_uds1.pdf, captured at https://perma.cc/QH27 -UMK7.

Once an archivist determines that the file naming is intentional, it may suffice to open the file A-001.pdf to determine the content of the file cpu_a001.dwg. The PDF file will not give the archivist a complete idea of the DWG file (the PDF file is static, while the DWG file can be edited and modified with CAD software, for instance), but it will likely give the archivist an idea of what part of the building the DWG file describes, what kind of design it is, and how it might relate to the other DWG files in the folder. Such considerations are important for any appraisal analysis.

From this specific use case, general guidelines may be drawn out. Often, collections of born-digital design files have more than one iteration of a single design. There may be CAD drawings, digital 3D models, images, and presentation drawings all in the same set of digital files. Heterogeneous archival materials are common in predominantly paper-based collections, and this continues in the digital space today, where archivists can appraise iteratively, starting with the simpler files to become familiar with the collection.

Using the Deed of Gift to Address Uncertainty. Another strategy that archivists can employ during uncertain appraisal situations derives from a long-standing archival practice. Deeds of Gift are important documents, and they can also prove to be useful instruments. As shown in Appendix B of "Module 24: Navigating the Technical Landscape of Born-Digital Design Records," archivists can include language in their Deeds of Gift for born-digital design records that delays the full appraisal analysis and decision until the uncertainty is minimized. For instance, Cal Poly's short-form Deed of Gift includes the following: "Special Collections and Archives may dispose of the item(s) if they are determined to have no permanent value and/or historic or research interest."[12] The form further provides a place for donors to indicate that, if the final appraisal determines that some or all of the design files are not appropriate for the repository, the files in question will be offered back to the donor. For the CCA, Deeds of Gift have sometimes been revised to account for additional materials found in the records once archivists processed the collections. Projects of interest to the

---

12 Excerpted from the Robert E. Kennedy Library's short-form Deed of Gift, last updated September 2019. The library's Special Collections and Archives department uses this Deed of Gift to document collection donations from campus departments and units, as well as with collection donors who have previously signed a long-form Deed of Gift.

CCA (whether on their own or as context to previously targeted projects) are kept, and the Deed of Gift is reviewed in conversation with the donor to reflect the actual content of the donation. Some personal files, or records from unrelated projects are returned to donors.

Minimizing Uncertainty. How, then, can an archivist minimize the uncertainty around born-digital design files? The archivist can schedule more time to speak with people who have contributed to the creation of the donated collection. Or the archivist can seek out software emulation solutions that will allow a sampling of files to be rendered in an emulated environment. As shown in the Cal Poly use example, an archivist can dive deeper into the complex file directory structures to find similarities between different folders.

Another strategy involves video conferencing and group work. When the CCA formally acquired most of its digital archives during planning for the Archaeology of the Digital project (2013–2016), the curatorial team and an archivist met over video with someone who had knowledge of the records. Such calls were recorded, and the team would go through the various directories from the donation for which they needed more context. These were called "archival walkthroughs." Oral histories were also conducted with the architects for the series of publications.[13] All of these conversations were valuable to understanding the content of the archives. Most donors also provided additional feedback when needed.

Initial Transfer from Donor to Organization

Once the decision is made to accession a collection, the born-digital design files will be transferred to the archives. However, *transfer* has many meanings in the digital world. The first consideration is for the relatively straightforward case of a physical transfer of a portable digital storage device. In such situations, the primary issue to be aware of is the interaction between the portable device and any computers in the archives. General best practices for digital archives recommend only connecting such a portable device to a computer with, at minimum, software-based write protection enabled for external devices (for example, as is the default setting for BitCurator workstations). Ideally,

---

13 Canadian Centre for Architecture, *Archaeology of the Digital,* ePub Series, 2014–2018, https://www.cca.qc.ca/en/events/54966/archaeology-of-the-digital-epub-series.

software-based write protection would be accompanied by hardware-based write protection in the form of a write blocker. However write protection is ensured, archivists can then examine the contents of the portable device, verify that the contents match the collection description found in the Deed of Gift, and begin copying files from the device to a secure staging storage space in the archives.

At an active firm, this is often conducted by the information technology (IT) department, whose members facilitate the transfer of previously active project records to a read-only archives drive. A corporate archivist can work with the IT department to establish workflows to check the integrity of the files (e.g., checksums or fixity checks) during the transfer of files to ensure that all content has been successfully moved. Establishing the checksum aspect to the file transfer workflow may require some negotiating, but the argument for including this step to ensure the validity of the file transfer is often well received and accepted by both firm leadership and IT specialists.

The challenge in making this transfer possible within a firm is confirming that a project has officially closed out and that the project team will no longer need to continuously edit the project's records. It can be incredibly difficult to attempt milestone design data transfers from the active drive to an archives drive. A firm's archivist may find greater success supporting the development of a project closeout workflow to appropriately time the transfer of files out of an editable environment. This closeout workflow can be developed as part of the firm's records management policy and schedule, using specific monetary (e.g., XX percent paid or billed by client) or official certifications (e.g., certificate of occupancy). At Sasaki, several attempts were made to identify the best trigger to initiate the conversation with a project manager about their project's folder being shifted onto the archives drive. The most successful option used a percentage of the contract fee billed, a report provided by the accounting department, that allowed the archivist to begin the conversation with project managers. Much like a collecting repository, a corporate archivist must remain ever vigilant and proactive to ensure the project's files are accurately named, properly packaged, and organized before their transfer to the archives.

The corporate archivist has both formal and informal tools at their disposal to facilitate composed project folders. Formally, the records retention schedule, as part of their records management policy, provides clear guidance for how to start the clock for a built project's statute of limitations (the legal requirement for the creator to retain a building's records). Less formally, the firm has a self-interest in ensuring that its records are in good order for internal reference for future work for that client or for inspiration for similar projects in the future.

In the case of Cal Poly's Facilities collection, a 500GB Maxtor-brand external hard drive was given to Special Collections and Archives. The hard drive contained scans of physical photographic slides, as well as several backup copies of the Facilities' "Plan Room" digital storage space, which contained numerous born-digital design files. As the archivists analyzed the hard drive through a write-protected BitCurator workstation, the photographic scans and "Plan Room" backup files were treated separately, as different accessions. The archivists commenced creating a "Bag"—a type of packaging of a file or set of files—of the latest copy of the backup files ("PlanRoomBackup15-10") and attempted to save the Bag to the UnaccessionedCollections folder of the department's secure networked storage space (while the department worked out the details of the files' transfer).

However, the archivists' first two attempts to save the Bag to the network storage space failed, with a message from the application, Bagger, that read "Error-- Failed to save bag: Error trying to save bag due to: Negative time."[14] The save operation stalled at file 87,209 of 88,420! After some investigation, the archivists found that a KMZ file (Keyhole Markup language Zipped, a file extension for a placemark file used by Google Earth) with a directory path of PlanRoomBackup15-10/Utility-Atlas/Working/Power and Data Poles/doc.xml carried a Last-Modified date of November 19, 1601, and it was this impossible date that thwarted the Bag-saving operation.

During this early stage of the transfer process, when details had not been worked out yet and the accession was not completed, the archivists decided to find an alternative to Bagger. Instead, the archivists used Rsync (a tool available in BitCurator) and enabled the "Preserve Time" option during the copy/syncing process. Using this tool, the archivists could at least copy the files from the external drive with a log to document the transfer. When the Rsync operation was successful,

---

14 Bagger, an application used to create a Bag according to the BagIt specification, is available at https://github.com/LibraryOfCongress/bagger.

the log output was placed in the top directory of transferred files. At this point only one archivist had write access to the secure storage location, while everyone else in the department had read-only access. And a sample of the Last-Modified date and file checksums matched between the hard drive on the new copy on the department's network storage, although the Last-Accessed date was changed to the date of the Rsync copy operation. Once accessioning was finalized, the archivist was able to make (and document) any necessary changes to the files to successfully save a Bag of the accession.

The CCA has most often transferred materials on physical media (e.g., portable drives, floppy disks, CDs, DVDs, etc.) but at times has transferred through online platforms (such as WeTransfer or DropBox). For the latter case, donors have been encouraged to Bag or zip their material before transfer in an effort to reduce accidental changes. For physical media, accession of the content has sometimes been delayed for technical reasons. One *fonds* was made up of more than 900 CDs and DVDs; eventually, the team was able to acquire a disk-imaging robot, called Nimbie, and set it up to automate the disk imaging of all the optical media. The American Institute of Architects (AIA) Oliver Witte Software collection at the CCA contains hundreds of floppies that are being disk imaged with the help of the floppy controller KryoFlux. There were also a few SyQuest cartridges that were sent to a vendor for disk imaging.

The CCA's preferred method for transferring files from physical media has been disk imaging using write-blockers, creating a self-contained capture of the entire content of the media, to which one could go back, if necessary. This allows the archivist to standardize, and automate when possible, the accession processes for extensive media. Another advantage of disk images is that they ensure that file dependencies are not broken accidentally, as design records often rely on external files to render properly. Using Bagger or Rsync also maintains files' relationships, assuming that the files use a relative file path and enough of the directory structure is captured to reflect a complete relative file path.

At Sasaki, the majority of the born-digital design files are kept on the firm's networked server and transferred using a script developed by the IT department. About ten linear feet of CDs, floppy disks, Jaz drives, and Zip disks were slowly imaged as part of a backlog processing effort, using similar techniques as Cal Poly or the CCA (e.g., Nimbie CD readers), and the hashes[15] of each file imaged were compared with what existed on the firm's archives drive to determine whether the files were unique or not.

Various software programs have been used to create disk images, including GuyMager, IsoBuster, and FTK imager. Each of these tools have been found to have some limitations with some of the media in the CCA collection, so it has been worthwhile to use a combination of these tools, as needed.

At the CCA, a SIP of the disk image is created, using scripts on the BitCurator station, with one or more disk images, providing checksums and including contextual metadata about the accession. SIPs are then transferred to an Archivematica instance, awaiting further analysis by a processing archivist.

The main objectives behind such digital transfers, which tools like Bagger, Rsync, and GuyMager can facilitate, is to establish a means for verifying file integrity and documenting the structure of the collection's folders and directories. The latter objective can be especially important with architectural collections, where one file may reference and depend on other files in very specific folder locations.

Accession Descriptions

With the digital design records safely transferred to the collecting organization, the next step would typically be to accession the transferred records. While doing so, the accessioning archivist will take the opportunity to begin describing the accession as well, in an effort to apply "More Product, Less Process" (MPLP) methodologies to born-digital design records. First published by Mark Greene and Dennis Meissner

---

15 Hashing is "a technique to transform a string of characters into a unique, fixed-length code (a hash)," Society of American Archivists, *Dictionary of Archives Terminology*, s.v. "hashing," https://dictionary.archivists.org/entry/hashing.html, captured at https://perma.cc/QF3D-GFTE.
   The term "checksum" is also used to refer to such strings of characters and is described as "a unique alphanumeric value that represents the bitstream of an individual computer file or set of files." Society of American Archivists, *Dictionary of Archives Terminology*, s.v. "checksum," https://dictionary.archivists.org/entry/checksum.html, captured at https://perma.cc/NYD4-GYBC.

in 2005,[16] the MPLP framework has been developed since that time and typically proposes iterative, or "extensible processing," as Daniel Santamaria has more recently written.[17] In the present scenario, a description of the newly acquired records can be easily derived from all of the acquisition activity described in this section (and which should serve the collecting organization's description needs in the meantime between accessioning and more comprehensive processing).

At Cal Poly, the manifest-md5.txt file (a standard in the BagIt specification) in the initial Bag created during accessioning can provide a good overview of the accession's contents. Typically, the manifest-md5.txt file's contents are not arranged alphabetically, so it can be helpful to import the file's contents into a spreadsheet or OpenRefine,[18] which facilitates easier sorting. The bag-info.txt file in the Bag also articulates the extent of the accession, in number of files, and in the amount of digital storage the accession occupies. If one were to synthesize and summarize the information in the manifest-md5.txt file and the bag-info.txt file, the "Plan Room" backup files could be described at this early stage in this way:

> The files within PlanRoomBackup15-10 are comprised of scanned physical drawings (.pdf), CAD drawings (.dwg), photographic images, and other digital files documenting each building on the San Luis Obispo campus. Both original constructions and remodels are represented. In total, there are 122,195 files at 120.4 GB.[19]

Similarly, archivists at the CCA would use the metadata files from the SIPs to create this high-level type of accession description. Whether the files are packaged with Bagger or a script, enough information on files can be obtained to provide for a basic understanding in a short amount of time.

---

16 Mark A. Greene and Dennis Meissner, "More Product, Less Process: Revamping Traditional Archival Processing," *American Archivist*, 68, no. 2 (2005): 208–263, https://doi.org/10.17723/aarc.68.2.c741823776k65863.
17 Daniel A Santamaria, *Extensible Processing for Archives and Special Collections: Reducing Processing Backlogs* (Chicago: ALA Neal-Schuman, 2015).
18 OpenRefine, http://openrefine.org. Although typically used for "cleaning up" messy data, OpenRefine can also be helpful with simpler tasks such as sorting.
19 The *UC Guidelines for Born-Digital Archival Description* can provide more assistance on born-digital description. See Annalise Berdini, Charles Macquarie, Shira Peltzman, and Kate Tasker, *UC Guidelines for Born-Digital Archival Description, Version 1* (October 2017), GitHub, accessed February 5, 2022, https://github.com/uc-borndigital-ckg/uc-guidelines/blob/master/CompletePDF_UCGuidelinesForBorn-DigitalArchivalDescription_v1.pdf.

Arrangement and Description

Factors That Impact Arrangement

Generally speaking, the CCA aims to arrange born-digital records with related physical materials and avoids arranging individual files and instead focuses on arranging directories. While some legacy collections at the CCA silo digital material in their own series and subseries, co-arranging physical and digital material is meant to reflect the activities of the donor, where digital and physical record creation happen simultaneously, and often in conversation with one another. This practice has emerged out of concern expressed by donors, who note that the materials cannot be understood by being separated by format and that the arrangement must reflect the organic way that they were created.

Similarly, at Sasaki, maintaining the original folder structure and file organization has been critical for contextualizing the files, which in turn facilitates finding desired records in the future even if there are no longer any members of the original project team at the firm. Leveraging the project folder structure allows anyone familiar with that structure to make inferences and contextual deductions, such as those mentioned in the Cal Poly use example, more readily possible.

Cal Poly's Facilities Management and Development collection possesses a similar hybrid nature, where co-arranging physical and digital records would be desirable. However, processing for the 2018 accession has not yet integrated the physical with the digital. When they are integrated, the arrangement of digital records will be undertaken at the directory level, much like at CCA and Sasaki.

Transferring Records

Born-digital records arrive at the CCA either as large transfers or spread across a number of smaller storage media. The size of each transfer has a significant impact on the level of work involved in arrangement. When large amounts of records are transferred over a network connection (using services such as WeTransfer or DropBox) or entirely on a single hard drive, the ability to retain the original organizational structure of those records is possible and therefore preferred. There is also a greater chance that files in larger structures contain hidden dependencies that could break if they are moved, and so less manual arrangement and higher-level description becomes essential.

When born-digital material is contained on smaller individual carriers, more precise arrangement and description is often required. The limitations on storage capacity of legacy carriers (such as floppy disks or CDs) could reflect an order imposed out of technological necessity, not an organizational choice made by the creator, and its contents may benefit from re-arrangement. For example, a grouping of records might be too large to fit on one CD, and so the creator might spread them across four CDs; the archivist would then arrange the contents of the four CDs together and create one folder-level description, making a note of the original arrangement. Born-digital material stored this way is also more likely to have a specific relationship to physical material (for example, a floppy disk kept alongside correspondence) and therefore may require co-location or additional description to retain existing relationships.

State of Organization on Transfer

In rare instances, in preparing born-digital material for transfer to the CCA, the donor and/or creator of the records reviews and organizes the digital files. This can be helpful, as it provides a basis for understanding the records and usually results in weeding out material of lesser value. Most often, however, born-digital records are donated without consultation. To help bridge any gaps in knowledge, the CCA asks its donors to complete a questionnaire (see Figure 4 and Appendix B) that is intended to document details about the material such as file naming conventions, folder structures, software used during the development process in an architectural project, and so on. This contextual and technical information gathered from the donor informs the archivist about how records were created and used and which aids in arrangement and can also be useful when the archivist accesses and appraises the files.

Design Methodology

Please check the appropriate boxes if the software is used during the specific phase of design.

Conceptual Phase	Design Development
Schematic Diagrams, Research, Concept Sketches	Preliminary design of building system with consultation with engineers, Presentation of design development to Owner, Review of project cost estimate with Owner, Owner review and input, Design finalized.
SOFTWARE	**SOFTWARE**
☐ AutoDesk® 3Ds Max®	☐ AutoDesk® 3Ds Max®
☐ AutoCAD® (AutoCAD® For Mac, AutoCAD® Architecture) Autodesk®	☐ AutoCAD® (AutoCAD® For Mac, AutoCAD® Architecture) Autodesk®
☐ Revit®	☐ Revit®
☐ form•Z™	☐ form•Z™
☐ Maya®	☐ Maya®
☐ CATIA	☐ CATIA
☐ SolidWorks	☐ SolidWorks
☐ Graphiisoft® ArchiCAD®	☐ Graphiisoft® ArchiCAD®
☐ Digital Project	☐ Digital Project
☐ Rhino (Rhinoceros®)	☐ Rhino (Rhinoceros®)
☐ Sketch Up	☐ Sketch Up
☐ Adobe® illustrator®	☐ Adobe® illustrator®
☐ Microstation®	☐ Microstation®
☐ Adobe® Indesign®	☐ Adobe® Indesign®
☐ Adobe® Photoshop®	☐ Adobe® Photoshop®
☐ Non-Proprietary Software	☐ Non-Proprietary Software
☐ Other	☐ Other

Figure 4: Detail from the CCA Born-digital records donor questionnaire, which asks for information about software used during conception and design development

Scope of the Collection

The nature of an organization's archival collection can also have a significant impact on how born-digital records are arranged. The CCA collects a variety of material, from specific records pertaining to a single architectural project to the complete archives of an architect or firm. The born-digital material of those collections may constitute the entire contents or only part of a larger, hybrid archives. Depending on which is the case, file-level groups of born-digital material can be arranged together with physical formats or in a distinct born-digital series or subseries in the *fonds*. There are also instances when the physical material belonging to a hybrid *fonds* or collection has already been arranged by format, and the digital material is treated afterward. This often results in the born-digital material being arranged into a separate "born-digital" series. Documentation from the record creators and/or donation sources can greatly help in making these determinations.

Describing Born-Digital Material

Once arrangement has been finalized, archivists at CCA begin description. Both physical and digital material is described according to the archival standard ISAD(G)[20] and entered into The Museum System (TMS), the database used at CCA to manage its collections. High-level descriptions such as *fonds*-, series- and project-level, are written and reviewed before being entered into the database. File-level descriptions are entered into TMS after the automatic description is updated by archivists. Information about digital material in extent statements takes the following form: "x digital files (y KB/MB/GB)," or "760 digital files (18 GB)." The lowest level of description for born-digital material is file-level (Figure 5), and item-level metadata corresponding to individual computer files is generated by Archivematica and saved in the AIP METS[21] file for each digital file in a SIP.

---

20 The General International Standard Archival Description (ISAD(G)) was developed by the International Council on Archives. It is available at https://www.ica.org/en/isadg-general-international-standard-archival-description-second-edition.

21 METS stands for Metadata Encoding and Transmission Standard. The Library of Congress notes that "the METS schema is a standard for encoding descriptive, administrative, and structural metadata regarding objects within a digital library." Find more information at https://www.loc.gov/standards/mets.

Case Studies in Born-Digital Design Records 189

Archives AP168.S1.011			
☐ Hors service	☐ Acess public	☑ Responsabilité	☐ Objet virtuel

Classification

groupe

Période	**Date**	**Culture**
	1996	

Personne(s) et institution(s)	**Information de group**
archive creator, Neil M. Denari	Content aP168.S1, Neil M. Denari, Series: Project records from Neil Denari, 1994 – 2004 (AP168.S1)
	Est classé en tant que AR2014.0075, Neil M. Denari, versement AP168

Titre (1 Title)	**Nom de l'objet**
Softimage model dataases with full and section 3D models and animation, digital photographs, and renderings for interrupted Projections	File

| Fiche de couve | Citations | Documentation | Multimédias | Contexte |

Technique, médium et procédé photo	**Dimensions**

Description du contenu	**Ligne de credit**
Original directory name "DATA_Images." Most common file formats: Unidentified, Plain Text File, Tagged Image File Format, OLE2 Compound Document Format, Truevision TGA Bitmap.	Neil Denari interrupted Projections project records, Collection Centre Canadien d'Architecture Canadian Centre for Architecture, Montréal

Support premier	**Supports secondaires**	**Terme alternative, procédé photograph**

Inscriptions	**Emplacement actuel**
	AP168.S1.011, Centre canadien d'architectur (1920, rue Bale), Dark archive, [218-mai-30]

Fitgrane	**Description physique**
	The 3D models of the "interrupted Projects" installation were created

Figure 5: Example of a file-level record in TMS for born-digital material

> **Contents**
>
> **Series 1, Digital Audio Files, Transcripts, Supplementary Materials**
>
> **Bag bd-ms0185_bag001**
>
> Folder 1   Interview 000 John J. Miller, Meredith Rolfe, Bill Rolfe, Washburn Days, 1 November 2008
>
> Folder 2   Interview 001 Marilyn Elliot and Colleen Hayes, 19 January 2009
>
> Folder 3   Interview 002 Jerry and Susan Diefenderfer, Eleanor King Diefenderfer, 20 January 2009
>
> Folder 4   Interview 003 Susan Diefenderfer, 11 March 2009
>
> Folder 5   Interview 004 Chuck W. and Helen L. Kuhnle, Janelle (Jani) Kuhnle Kasfeldt, 18 March 2009 Includes genealogy, photograph scrapbook circa 1898 – 1960, manuscript of area history, interview responses, and other undated supplementary materials.
>
> Folder 6   Interview 006 Wayne Cooper, 25 March 2009. Includes genealogy, manuscript of family history and area history written circa 1984, and other undated supplementary materials.
>
> Folder 7   Interview 007 Thomas McCart, 18 April 2009
>
> Folder 8   Interview 008 Joseph William (Bill) Garcia, Jan Cooper, 22 April 2009. Includes photographs and family directory, 1918 – 1999, Tony Garcia's Family History circa 1984, history of Dan Garcia, other undated supplementary materials.

Figure 6: Example of directory-level inventory from a born-digital collection

Following the aforementioned extensible processing approach,[22] Cal Poly's initial processing goal is to create a collection-level description, accompanied by a directory-level inventory. This can be achieved efficiently using CCA Tools' Disk Image Processor or Folder Processor, which produces a spreadsheet and text file providing a listing of the disk image or folder's files and subfolders. The text file is displayed as a file tree. Either of these outputs are then manually converted into a traditional finding aid structure, with the Bag name serving as a box-level label and the directory names serving as the folder-level labels (see Figure 6 for an example).

---

22   Santamaria, *Extensible Processing for Archives and Special Collections*.

When Cal Poly Special Collections and Archives is ready to provide a more detailed description or conceptual arrangement (not so closely based on the received directory structure), the department will need to either (1) assemble an ad hoc (and possibly emulated) software environment to view the design files or (2) rely on presentation drawings embedded in PDF files to support such processing. Another alternative descriptive structure is the description of project files at Sasaki, which focuses on pulling multiple projects, by services and over time, for the same client together rather than on the arrangement of files. This allows the firm's staff members to understand and leverage their comprehensive portfolio of work for a client.

Automation

The main difference in practices used to describe born-digital archives compared to physical archives is that born-digital records typically require a combination of human- and computer-derived descriptive information. Digital forensics tools are capable of providing the majority of technical description, which allows archivists to focus on the descriptive information that only a human is able to add.

This is especially useful when dealing with large collections of digital material. For example, machine-actionable information such as extent, file formats, and file system metadata can be captured automatically with the use of digital forensics suite BitCurator, as well as the CCA Tools, Folder Processor, Disk Image Processor, and SIP creator. Each of the CCA Tools outputs a pre-populated spreadsheet (see Figure 7 for example) containing archival description for each SIP (which is assumed to be directory-level) for elements such as Dates, Extent and Medium, and preliminary information for the Scope and Content note, including original directory names and most common file formats. This leaves descriptive fields, such as Title and further description as needed in the Scope and Content note, to be updated by archivists.

Infrastructure Supporting Description

The accurate and meaningful description of born-digital design records also requires a more robust technological set-up than physical archives do. The digital archives lab at CCA is equipped with a series of workstations used exclusively for processing born-digital archival materials.

192 BORN-DIGITAL DESIGN RECORDS

Parent ID	Identifier	Title	Archive Creator	Date Expression	Date Start	Date End	Level of Description
AP179.S1	AP179.S1.001–AR2013.0045	Images of model and drawings, Casa La Roca, Caracas	Office dA	1996 - 2001	7/27/1996	2/27/2001	File
AP179.S2	AP179.S2.001–AR2013.0045	CAD drawings, correspondence, and images of model and drawings, Witte Arts Center, Green Bay	Office dA	1999 - 2001	11/29/99	7/30/01	File
AP179.S2	AP179.S2.002–AR2013.0045	CAD drawings, 3D models and renderings, images and other documents, Witte Arts Center, Green Bay	Office dA	1996 - 2002	8/5/96	2002	File
AP179.S3	AP179.S3.001–AR2013.0045	CAD drawings, photographs of site and other project files, Tongxian Art Center, Tongxian	Office dA	2001 - 2006	2/27/01	6/8/06	File
AP179.S3	AP179.S3.002–AR2013.0045	Digital photographs of Tongxian Art Center building, Tongxian	Office dA	2004	1/21/04	1/21/04	File
AP179.S3	AP179.S3.003–AR2013.0045	Digital photographs of Tongxian Art Center building and video of project team, Tongxian	Office dA	2003 - 2004	12/16/03	1/9/04	File
AP179.S3	AP179.S3.004–AR2013.0045	CAD drawings, photographs and other project files, Tongxian Art Center, Tongxian	Office dA	2000 - 2004	2/14/00		File
AP179.S3	AP179.S3.005–AR2013.0045	Email and CAD drawings, Tongxian Art Center, Tongxian	Office dA	A	4/9/02	2003	File
AP179.S3	AP179.S3.006–AR2013.0045	CAD drawings, digital renderings, email, and other project files, Tongxian Art Center, Tongxian	Office dA	A	2/19/01	6/7/03	File

Figure 7: Description spreadsheet produced by CCA Tools and updated by archivists at CCA

Extent and Medium	Scope and Content	Accession Number	Appraisal, Destruction, and Scheduling Information (Optional)
25 digital files (157 MB)	Original directory name: "Casa La Roca". Most common file formats: Tagged Image File Format, Adobe Illustrator, Adobe Photoshop	AR2013.0045	Four directories containing images related to projects other than Casa La Roca were removed.
389 digital files (1 GB)	Most common file formats: AutoCAD Drawing, JPEG File Interchange Format, Exchangeable Image File Format (Compressed), Tagged Image File Format, Adobe Photoshop	AR2013.0045	
592 digital files (4 GB)	File contains material submitted to the Progressive Architecture Awards, 2003 for Witte Arts Building. Most common file formats: Tagged Image File Format, JPEG File Interchange Format, Adobe Photoshop, OLE2 Compound Document Format, Windows Metafile Image	AR2013.0045	Duplicate directories, empty sources and files not created by Office dA were removed.
541 digital files (2 GB)	Original directory name: "0676_Tongxian_ GateKeeper". Most common file formats: AutoCAD Drawing, JPEG File Interchange Format, Unidentified, Truevision TGA Bitmap, 3DM	AR2013.0045	Directories related to projects other than Tongxian Art Center were removed.
1116 digital files (276 MB)	File contains digital photographs and related attribute files that are created when images are edited on a Mac. Original directory name: "2 of 2 CDs (Photos from Sack Tilton)". Most common file formats: Unidentified, JPEG File Interchange Format, Exchangeable Image File Format (Compressed), Raw JPEG Stream	AR2013.0045	Directory containing duplicate images named "1 of 2 CDs (NT Photos DEC 18)" was removed. Original images can be found in AP179.S3.00(012) in the directory named "NT trip images".
288 digital files (4 GB)	Most common file formats: Tagged Image File Format, Exchangeable Image File Format (Compressed), JPEG File Interchange Format, Audio/Video Interleaved Format	AR2013.0045	
4602 digital files (3 GB)	File contains all project folders for Tongxian Art Center including CAD drawings, images and scans, email, correspondence, proposals, invoices and other administrative records. Most common file formats: AutoCAD Drawing, JPEG File Interchange Format, Microsoft Word Document, Microsoft Excel 97 Workbook (xls), Exchangeable Image File Format (Compressed)	AR2013.0045	
273 digital files (900 MB)	File contains backup of project files and email on laptop used by an employee of Office dA in China during the Tongxian Art Center project. Most common file formats: Unidentified, MIME Email, AutoCAD Drawing, JPEG File Interchange Format, Plain Text File	AR2013.0045	Directory containing duplicate project files was merged with project files in AP179.S3.004
536 digital files (3 GB)	Most common file formats: AutoCAD Drawing, Unidentified, Tagged Image File Format, Adobe Photoshop, JPEG File Interchange Format	AR2013.0045	Directories containing duplicate material named "7 of 8 CDs (Tongxian Art 07)" and "8 of 8 CDs (Tongxian Art 08)" were removed

194 BORN-DIGITAL DESIGN RECORDS

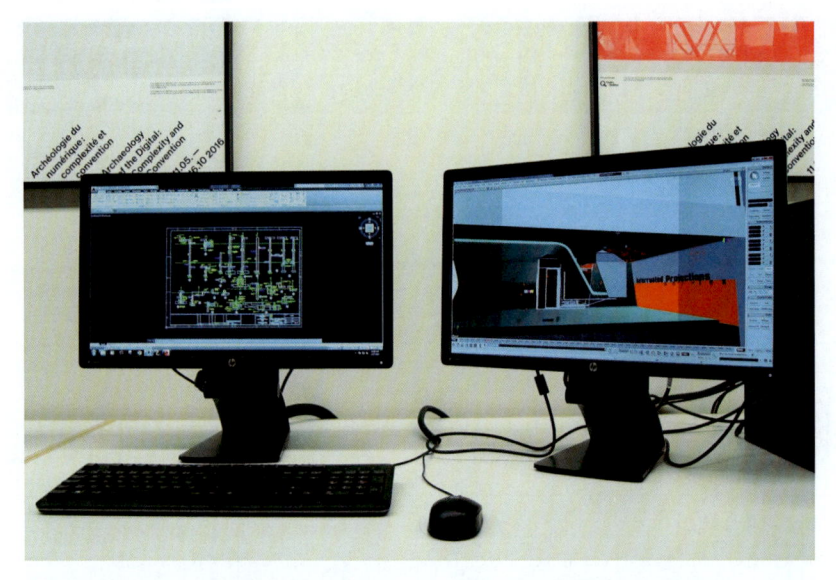

Figure 8: CAD workstation in the Digital Archives Lab at CCA displaying a CAD file in AutoCAD 2014 (left) and a SCN file in Softimage 2014 (right)

This includes three BitCurator machines that offer a host of digital forensics software programs, including CCA Tools, a CAD workstation that is loaded with a number of specialized CAD and design software used to access and describe different types and versions of architectural files, and a Mac environment used to open files extracted from Apple or HFS-formatted media. Examples of software include the Autodesk suite, Rhinoceros, the Adobe Suite, and form•Z, among many others.

In comparison, the born-digital processing infrastructure at Cal Poly is smaller. The workstation, situated in the same area as a flatbed scanning workstation and an audiovisual digitization workstation, comprises a Dell computer with a BitCurator operating system, a 3.25" floppy drive, an optical drive, and a Zip drive. No design software is installed on the born-digital processing workstation at this time, which can hinder detailed description efforts. However, like CCA, Cal Poly employs CCA Tools for generating automatic descriptions of its born-digital files, and creating SIPs according to the BagIt specification.

Sasaki's infrastructure, like that of many active design firms, is less comprehensive than that of either the CCA or Cal Poly, but it does have the distinct advantage of regularly acquiring new versions of core software (e.g., the Autodesk and Adobe Suites) while maintaining a few older generations of those programs. This is primarily due to the length of time it takes for a built design to be completed and for practitioners to recognize that it is unsafe to continuously upgrade their complex and highly detailed files under tight deadlines. As a result, myriad software programs are readily accessible either in the firm's software library or on an employee's personal machine, facilitating a legible rendering of older files when needed.

Preservation and Storage

Once the files have been arranged and described, they are ready to be prepared for preservation. Several choices have to be made as to which preservation software program to use, what metadata to capture along with the files, and the type of storage needed for long-term preservation. Over the years, the worldwide digital preservation community has developed many tools and standards that can also assist with the preservation of digital design records preservation.

Preparing files for digital preservation is a multi-step process that may be technically challenging for archivists who do not have digital records training. Adding to this challenge, there is a need to make sure a CAD file's context, in particular, is documented properly to ensure that it can be reopened in the long term. Automating this workflow as much as possible may lessen the technical burden on archivists in their day-to-day work, and, as such, organizations (particularly those with larger collections) may want to consider implementing a digital preservation system.

Preparing Files for a Digital Preservation System (OAIS)

Following the OAIS reference model, digital records must be packaged into a SIP before being ingested into a digital preservation repository for long-term storage and management. SIPs, which predetermine a formal structure for the organization of files, data, and metadata to be ingested, allow digital records, as well as their contextual information, to be interpreted and understood over time.

SIP Structure and Additional Content

The BagIt specification container format developed by the California Digital Library and the Library of Congress has been used to create SIPs, most often when other tools were unavailable. The information package defined by this specification is characterized by a hierarchical directory structure and data files referred to as a "Bag." Following are the basic elements in a Bag:

- /data: This is the directory that contains the records; it is also called *payload* in the BagIt documentation.

- bagit.txt: This file contains the BagIt version number and the Tag file character encoding.

- manifest-[algorithm].txt: This file contains a list of all the files in the /data directory and its subdirectories and their corresponding checksum. This will allow the archivist to validate the integrity of the files at later stages. The term *algorithm* in the file name must reflect the algorithm used for creating the checksums, such as MD5 or SHA256.

The BagIt specification allows practitioners to know what they have and enables them to validate the integrity of the files over time. Creating such SIPs can be done with open-source tools, which are usually available in the form of code to execute on a directory. It is also possible to use Bagger. At the CCA, archivists use Bagger to manage donor transfers by creating a Bag that can be stored until the born-digital material is ready to be processed.

After processing is complete, CCA Tools are used to package material into SIPs for ingest into Archivematica. The structure of SIPs created by CCA Tools differs from the BagIt specification. Typically, each SIP includes a top-level directory named after the material's unique identifier (usually a file-level group), plus a contextual identifier (usually an accession number), which contains an objects folder and a metadata folder. In the objects folder are the digital objects to be ingested, and in the metadata folder is a checksum file, which is a manifest containing checksums for each file in the objects folder, as well as a Submission Documentation folder containing any additional

Brunnhilde	Provenance	Statistics	File Formats	Versions	MIME	Types	Dates	Unidentified

Detailed reports

File Formats

Format	ID	Count
JPEG File Interchange Format	fmt/43	78
	UNKNOWN	61
Portable Network Graphics	fmt/11	55
Plain Text File	x-fmt/111	26
Acrobat PDF 1.3 - Portable Document Format	fmt/17	12
DS_store file (MAC)	fmt/394	7
Raw JPEG Stream	fmt/41	6
Microsoft Word for Windows	fmt/412	5
Acrobat PDF 1.5 - Portable Document Format	fmt/19	3
Exchangable Image File Format (Compressed)	fmt/645	2
Acrobat PDF 1.4 - Portable Document Format	fmt/18	1
Acrobat PDF 1.5 - Portable Document Format	fmt/20	1
Acrobat PDF 1.7 - Portable Document Format	fmt/276	1

Figure 9: Screenshot of sample Brunnhilde file format results. *Permission granted by Tessa Walsh.*

documentation related to the digital objects created by the processing archivist.

In the Submission Documentation directory are files generated by Brunnhilde,[23] a piece of software that is also part of the CCA Tools (Figure 9). Brunnhilde runs various analysis tools and aggregates information into reports that make it easier to assess the content of a set of files.

During the creation of SIPs, related groups of digital files typically amass extensive amounts of data. This becomes an issue at the CCA when the ingest of large individual SIPs of born-digital material into Archivematica becomes too great, outweighing local processing capacity. As a result, large SIPs are sometimes rearranged into multiple, smaller SIPs. In cases in which this occurs, the CCA preserves information about the original arrangement of files at time of transfer

---

23 Tessa Walsh, "Brunnhilde 2.0." GitHub, January 27, 2022, https://github.com/tw4l/brunnhilde-gui.

and makes it accessible to researchers via additional documentation, such as a textual document or spreadsheet that is attached to the *fonds*-level record. However, some technical considerations mean that very large SIPs are occasionally necessary.

These issues speak to challenges in accounting for outlier material in certain digital preservation workflows, particularly with regards to file size. Some organizations are able to set their server parameters to allow large ingests into their preservation systems, while other organizations are not. Because Artefactual has fixed this issue in recent releases, Archivematica continues to be an effective tool at the CCA.

Cal Poly has also encountered issues with large SIP transfers, although not with Archivematica. This will be discussed further below. The technical limitations of digital preservation tools and local IT capacities for many organizations will impact archival best practices and lead to workarounds. This will be increasingly true as archives begin collecting more contemporary materials and extremely large BIM files might be included. Though ideally digital preservation workflows and infrastructure will scale to the material, design records are always going to test the limits of any system as large, complex, multi-part objects.

Transfer and Ingest into a Digital Preservation System

Archivematica is a popular software program that will help with digital preservation workflows. It is used at the CCA because it is an open-source solution that has an energetic and widespread international community. Archivematica is actively maintained and developed, and it has proven over time to be an excellent fit for CCA's needs. It is used to ingest SIPs, manage the preservation storage of AIPs, and create DIPs. Because the CCA is the only use case represented that uses such digital preservation software, Archivematica is described in detail here; however, other digital preservation software, like Preservica, Rosetta, or RODA, will provide automated processes that are similar to the ones described below.

This type of digital preservation system is interesting because it automates a series of tools and scripts in a uniform way, rather than manually launching each individually, which is desirable, particularly for large-scale preservation programs in which the scale of this work makes it time- and labor-intensive.

Choices of tools in this area will depend on organizational context and resources. Open-source tools require more in-house expertise, while commercial software may provide more support to a less experienced user. Every option is valid as long as an organization's needs are met with respect to the digital preservation processes required by the collection.

On ingest, a set of files or SIP goes through a series of microservices that can be automated and set up according to an institution's requirements for its collection. All microservices are documented in the METS file, and preservation-specific steps are described through the Preservation Metadata: Implementation Strategies (PREMIS) Data Dictionary schema in the METS file.[24] The very first process is the Transfer, where it is verified that a set of files has been transferred successfully to Archivematica and some initial file characterization and clean-up is done. Microservices at the Transfer stage include:

- Assigning files with Universal Unique Identifiers (UUID) and checksums
- Generating a METS.xml file
- Scanning for viruses
- Cleaning file names of trailing spaces and special characters; changes are documented in the METS files
- Characterizing and extracting metadata for file format identification
- Extracting packaged files, such as zipped files
- Validating files' formats
- Creating SIPs ready for ingest

At the ingest stage, when SIPs become AIPs, microservices include the following:
- Verifying a SIP's compliance
- Normalizing file formats, based on rules
- Processing manually normalized files, if applicable
- Processing submission documentation
- Processing metadata
- Generating a METS file for the AIP
- Preparing the AIP
- Preparing the DIP

---

24   METS documentation and schema is available at www.loc.gov/standards/mets. PREMIS documentation and schema is available at www.loc.gov/standards/premis/index.html.

Systems Showcase Files

iPres 2014

File format corpos for the iPres 2014 (Melbourne)
Systems Showcase session.

Identifiers

pronoun

DROID_SignatreFile_v91 xml; container-signature-20170330.xml

tika

tika-mimetypes.xml

freedesktop.org

freedesktop.org.xml

loc

fddXML.zip (2017-06-10, DROID_SignatureFile_V91.xml, container-signature-20170330.xml

Details

Results path: ipres.yaml
Tool: Siegfried 1.7.5
Signature: default.sig
Signature created: 2017-08-11T20:39:46+10:00
Scan date: 2017-08-16T21:14:26+10:00

0 errors
598 warnings
250 unknowns
0 multiple IDs
0 duplicates

Reset (show all)

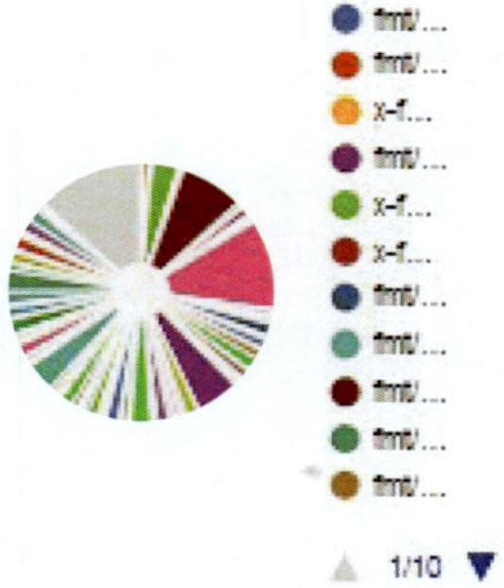

Format IDs | MIME-types

Copy | CVS

Search: .dwg

filename	filesize	modified	errors	id	format	version	mime	basis	warning
systems-showcase-files/3DPolygon.dwg	34282	2015-01-21T01:36:36+11:00		fmt/35	AutoCAD Drawing	2000-2002	image/vnd.dwg	extension match dwg; byte match at 0, 6	
systems-showcase-files/AIRPLACE.DWG	32219	2015-01-21T01:24:30+11:00		fmt/31	AutoCAD Drawing	R10	image/vnd.dwg	extension match dwg; byte match at 0, 6	
systems-showcase-files/ASHADE.DWG	5093	2015-01-21T01:23:16+11:00		fmt/30	AutoCAD Drawing	R9	image/vnd.dwg	extension match dwg; byte match at 0, 6	

Figure 10: An example of a Siegfried file format identification report. Richard Lehane, "Siegfried," IT for Archivists, www.itforarchivists.com/siegfried/results/ea1zaj

Case Studies in Born-Digital Design Records   201

- Uploading a DIP to an archival management system
- Storing AIPs and DIPs

Understanding Characterization and File Format Identification

Amongst the microservices listed above, characterization and file format identification have a particular value when dealing with design records. File characterization "[...] is the process of determining certain technical properties of a file, including format identification, validation, and metadata extraction."[25] Most common file characterization tools[26] targets files' metadata, while file formats identification tools[27] look into a files' bytes to identify its signature (more on this below). Capturing and maintaining this information about the records serves multiple purposes, which are important with any set of records but bear additional importance with design records.

Design records are associated with a wide variety of file formats. The 1990s were prolific for design experimentations with computers, meaning that not all design file formats are documented, and it is possible to encounter records that have not been documented yet.

This identification furthers the understanding of the records' context, including their creator's work process through embedded metadata. It provides the archivist with an understanding of the archives' holdings, which can inform decisions about material at risk, software needed for access, and need for file format normalization or migration.

The CCA uses Siegfried (Figure 10) as its main file format identification tool. Unlike other tools, Siegfried draws on a number of different signature databases to increase the likelihood of file formats being correctly identified. Siegfried is used iteratively during processing and is part of the SIP creation workflow. At the processing stage, when files bring back an "unknown format" message, the archivist will look for other clues to its file format, sometimes even looking for its file signature in a hex editor, such as Bless Hex or gHex. Samples can

---

25 Library of Congress, Digital Collections Management Program. *Glossary* "Characterization." https://www.loc.gov/programs/digital-collections-management/about-this-program/glossary.
26 Among others: FITS (https://projects.iq.harvard.edu/fits), MediaInfo (http://mediaarea.net/en/MediaInfo), and ExifTool (https://exiftool.org/index.html).
27 Among others: FIDO (https://github.com/openpreserve/fido), Siegfried (https://www.itforarchivists.com/siegfried), and DROID (www.nationalarchives.gov.uk/information-management/manage-information/preserving-digital-records/droid).

202 BORN-DIGITAL DESIGN RECORDS

```
                6X9X4.3dm - Ghex
00000000 33 44 20 47 65 6F 6D 65 74 72 79 20 46 69 6C 65  3D Geometry File
00000010 20 46 6F 72 6D 61 74 20 20 20 20 20 20 20 20 31   Format         1
00000020 01 00 00 00 D1 01 00 00 50 72 65 70 72 6F 63 65  ........Preproce
00000030 73 73 6F 72 3A 20 20 54 72 6F 75 74 20 4C 61 6B  ssor:  Trout Lak
00000040 65 20 47 65 6F 6D 65 74 72 79 20 66 69 6C 65 20  e Geometry file 
00000050 49 4F 20 28 63 6F 6D 70 69 6C 65 64 20 6F 6E 20  IO (compiled on 
00000060 4D 61 79 20 32 33 20 32 30 30 30 29 0A 49 6E 74  May 23 2000).Int
00000070 65 72 66 61 63 65 3A 20 20 20 20 20 52 68 69 6E  erface:     Rhin
00000080 6F 63 65 72 6F 73 20 31 2E 31 20 2D 20 52 68 69  oceros 1.1 - Rhi
00000090 6E 6F 63 65 72 6F 73 20 28 47 65 6E 69 75 5A 20  noceros (GeniuZ 
000000A0 47 6F 44 29 20 2D 20 32 30 30 30 2D 4D 61 79 2D  GoD) - 2000-May-
000000B0 33 31 20 20 2D 20 28 63 6F 6D 70 69 6C 65 64 20  31  - (compiled 
000000C0 4D 61 79 20 32 33 20 32 30 30 30 29 20 4F 70 65  May 23 2000) Ope
000000D0 72 61 74 69 6E 67 20 53 79 73 74 65 6D 3A 20 57  rating System: W
000000E0 69 6E 64 6F 77 73 20 39 38 20 28 34 2E 39 30 29  indows 98 (4.90)
000000F0 20 76 65 72 73 69 6F 6E 20 31 31 31 34 20 62 75   version 1114 bu
00000100 69 6C 64 20 33 30 30 30 20 20 20 0A 46 69 6C 65  ild 3000   .File
00000110 20 57 72 69 74 65 20 4D 6F 64 65 3A 20 46 41 53   Write Mode: FAS
00000120 54 0A 0A 20 20 52 6F 62 65 72 74 20 4D 63 4E 65  T..  Robert McNe

Signed 8 bit:   51            Signed 32 bit: 1193296947    Hexadecimal: 33
Unsigned 8 bit: 51            Unsigned 32 bit: 1193296947  Octal: 063
Signed 16 bit:  17459         Signed 64 bit: 1193296947    Binary: 00110011
Unsigned 16 bit: 17459        Unsigned 64 bit: 1193296947  Stream Length: 8
Float 32 bit:   4.102820e+04  Float 64 bit: 3.816924e+180

● Show little endian decoding     ○ Show unsigned and float as hexadecimal

Offset: 0x0
```

Figure 11: A screenshot of a 3DM file opened in gHex on a BitCurator machine

then be sent to PRONOM, a file format signature database,[28] for future additions. Though the level of detail seen in Figure 11 is unusual, note that the text in the right column provides helpful data, not only about the file and its format, but about the context in which it was created. Because design records are often software dependent, understanding and capturing information on files' formats becomes crucial to ensuring future access.

As part of sound preservation planning, a file format policy registry (FPR) should be created to document choices made in a particular institution for its collection (see Appendix A: CCA Format Policy

---

28   Available through https://www.nationalarchives.gov.uk/PRONOM/Default.aspx.

Registry 2019 for an example). Creating an FPR entails determining the preferred format for preservation and for access files in the future, as well as the level of support an institution can provide toward the digital preservation and long-term access of a given file format (Table 1). In a preservation system, the implementation of this process is called *file normalization*, and resulting files are kept alongside the original file in the AIP, and may be included in the DIP.

Table 1. An example of an FPR entry for email.

Email	Extension	Preservation Format	Access Format	Level of Support
Preferred Format	MBOX	MBOX	MBOX	Full
Accepted Format	MAILDIR	MBOX	MBOX	Full
	PST	PST	PST	Bit-level

Simon Fraser University Archives and Records Management Department, "Format Policy Registry (FPR)," July 18, 2017, www.sfu.ca/content/dam/sfu/archives/PDFs/DigitalPreservation/LinksResources/FormatPolicyRegistry.pdf, captured at https://perma.cc/8JM3-MK4U.

The MBOX format is a fully documented open format and retains the characteristics of emails, although there is no satisfying automated way to transfer a PST file into an MBOX file using open-source tools—hence the choice to not normalize into the preferred format.[29] The integrity of PST files would be closely monitored through fixity checking based on the files' checksums, to make sure it is maintained, but no other steps would be taken at this time.

At the CCA, CAD files are not normalized and are only supported for bit-level preservation. There is no method to automatically normalize CAD, and, even for manually normalized files, there is no way to ascertain that they retain all the characteristics and data of the original file.[30] Another prominent issue with CAD files is that they often rely on sets of external references (data libraries, images, etc.) to be rendered

---

29 The command line tool readpst can convert some PST files to the MBOX format; however, fidelity to the original varies greatly. Some paid email conversion tools, like Emailchemy, exist, but, as proprietary options, they cannot be easily embedded into an open-source automated tool workflow like the Archivematica microservices can.
30 Manually normalized files would be the exception and are added to the SIP only if they had already been created for exhibition or publication purposes.

properly. By changing the nature of the file through normalization, the archivist breaks these dependencies, making the new version of the file incomplete or inaccurate, and it may not open. Even when migrating a file from an early version of a format to a more recent one, it can be difficult to validate that all data is still there.

Further Processing with a Digital Preservation System

Many formats can be automatically normalized through the microservices available in Archivematica. If so, the AIP includes the original file and the normalized file. Retaining the original file allows the organization to reassess its preservation strategy in the future. For example, if, in fifteen years, it is determined that there is a better format than MBOX for preservation, a different rule for normalization could be created and the AIP could be re-ingested according to that new rule. It also reduces the risk of updating the formats, because the original is always maintained. Storing both formats means that preservation of the original will be ensured, but a copy more suitable for long-term storage and access will also be available.

An AIP is managed to maintain digital archival records over time. The data it contains ensures that records' authenticity and integrity can be monitored and that they may remain accessible, technology permitting.

Metadata that is extracted or captured at various stages of the process needs to be formatted according to standards such as METS, PREMIS, Digital Forensics XML (DFXML), or Dublin Core.[31] This ensures the accessibility of the data for the long term, across platforms, either the ones used to manage the records' preservation or the ones to access them.

In the context of the work done at the CCA, DFXML files were generated and included in the SIPs made with CCA Tools. DFXML files document provenance, and the technical context of creation includes a file's operating system of origin. This data enables potential reuse of files on the long term through emulation.

As mentioned above, the CCA's METS files are generated in Archivematica. They are used to document the content of the package as well as any changes made to its content during ingest. Other

---

31 DFXML schema is available at https://github.com/dfxml-working-group/dfxml_schema, and Dublin Core schema documentation is available through https://www.dublincore.org.

metadata schemas can be embedded in the METS file to document more specific materials. In the CCA's context, a crosswalk was defined to capture certain fields from TMS, where the CCA's archival description is stored. The data is pulled from TMS to Archivematica, using a custom-built TMS API, and is included in the METS formatted as Dublin Core elements to ensure that the AIP is self-describing.

Digital Preservation Storage at the CCA

The CCA uses the Archivematica Storage Service to manage AIP and DIP storage. Fixity checks are done quarterly to validate that no accidental changes or bit-rot has occurred. Three copies of the AIPs are maintained: one copy is kept on local servers by the CCA's IT department; one copy is kept on a server offsite at a third-party data management facility, which has a different environmental risk profile to that at the CCA; and a final copy is written to linear tape open (LTO) biannually and stored offsite. Having these different backup versions allows the CCA to restore a corrupted file, or even retrieve a complete copy of the entire digital archives, if necessary. These measures are sufficient for the size and scope of the CCA born-digital collections, as well as its long-term access mandate.

Digital Preservation Storage at the Cal Poly

Like the CCA, Cal Poly has experienced problems when copying large SIPs (packaged as Bags) to a secure local network server, because both the transfer of files, and the creation of checksums that BagIt enables, can result in long network processes that are more liable to cause disruption and error. In one case, a SIP transfer failed from one workstation but was successful from another. Only through a post-transfer verification process (built into the Bagger interface) did the archivist discover that the first transfer had been unsuccessful.

In either case, transfers to local network servers have become a common step in Cal Poly's digital preservation workflow. To ensure that this step, and others, are performed reliably, Cal Poly has incorporated many digital preservation standards and tools into its preservation ecosystem. As described above, the BagIt specification and CCA Tools provide a baseline documentation of file extensions and file formats found in its digital design records. Furthermore, the checksums documented in the Bags provide a benchmark for future fixity checks. After acquisition, accessioning, and description, digital design records like the Plan Room Backup are copied (as Bags) to a local network drive location to which only two people have write access. This networked Bag becomes the local master and is regularly backed up to an Amazon Web Services (AWS) "bucket."

For more long-term preservation and disaster planning, Cal Poly participates in the MetaArchive Cooperative, a distributed digital preservation network governed by its cultural heritage membership. Digital design records that are ingested into this network are exact copies of the Bags stored locally and are monitored on a scheduled basis for any fixity issues. The network's LOCKSS[32] implementation also produces information on each file's MIME type as part of the ingest process, providing more file-level technical documentation. Should a regional disaster disrupt the library's local network drive or access to its AWS account, Cal Poly can be confident that seven copies of all of its born-digital collections exist on other servers across the country.

In the future, Cal Poly plans to implement more automated methods for compiling, monitoring, analyzing, and developing solutions for certain file formats. Digital design records will be a high priority in those plans. It may be implementing a tool or service such as Archivematica, as described above, or through a flexible, lightweight home-grown solution. In either case, the goal will be to add a layer of ongoing, periodic, and at least partially automated preservation to Cal Poly's baseline bit-level preservation program.

Access

Access to born-digital archives is a pervasive challenge, regardless of an institution's particular collection material. More generalized access challenges to the collection of born-digital records fall into two categories: policy-related and technology-related.

Challenges to Access

Policy-Related Challenges. Though many institutions have existing access policies, those policies will often need to be revisited to make

---

[32] LOCKSS stands for Lots Of Copies Keep Stuff Safe, and the acronym can refer to the principle of LOCKSS, the LOCKSS Program operating at Stanford University, the community of LOCKSS users, or the LOCKSS software. See The LOCKSS Program, "What Is LOCKSS?," Stanford University, 2022. https://www.lockss.org/about/what-lockss. In the context of MetaArchive, LOCKSS refers primarily to the principle and the software.

certain that considerations for born-digital material are taken into account: How should born-digital files be accessed internally and externally? Is online access possible or desirable? Should access be password-protected or on-demand? Do existing donor agreements cover this usage of the material, and if not, can donors consent to the broad dissemination made possible by the internet? What is an acceptable level of reproduction for high-resolution, interactive, or time-based material within the limits of fair use/fair dealing and donor's wishes? To answer these types of questions, a common understanding, if not consensus, is needed between organizational management, archives staff, donors, and users. Answers to these questions will vary at every organization and will depend on the organization's user group and mandate.

Technology-Related Challenges. Technical challenges can also provide a significant barrier to access. Access copies of born-digital material need to be discoverable to users, readily understandable, and, ideally, regenerated with each new user to preserve the authenticity of the files over time. This often results in a demanding access workflow for archives staff members, from description through providing users with the material. Though digital asset management systems (DAMS) and institutional repositories are able to manage item-level description and access for simple formats like text documents and still images, there are few solutions that can maintain archival context in file-level description and handle more challenging formats.

The technical challenges also have obvious implications for digital design records, particularly CAD and BIM formats, which, as technically complex software-dependent multi-part files, need additional description and technical support to remain usable and understandable over time. In particular, problems of software dependency are exacerbated by the mandate of long-term access. In addition, there are unique challenges involved in providing access to born-digital design records. User groups vary widely between institutions, both in their capabilities, research questions, and expectations, which means that ongoing conversations between archivists and users are necessary to archivists providing appropriate levels of access. Thus, long-term access to digital design records becomes a complex proposition informed by local priorities.

Defining Users of Born-Digital Design Records

Navigating born-digital design records is a two-fold problem: it requires a certain comfort level and subject expertise, not only with architectural and design records, but also with digital preservation, computer history, and the use of legacy software. How can digital preservationists prepare themselves and their research community and reference colleagues for these challenges?

Defining user groups may be a helpful exercise for all organizations providing access to born-digital design records. Research institutions, universities, and firms will necessarily have different sets of users who have different levels of comfort with design technology, different expectations, and different research questions.

In September 2016, Tessa Walsh, the former Digital Archivist at the CCA, undertook a survey of the institution's internal and external researchers to gauge their expectations around discoverability, accessibility, and use. The survey indicated that "CCA staff and researchers ... self-identify as having high levels of expertise as users of archives, legacy/obsolete digital files, and design (CAD/BIM) software." Internal users working at the CCA overwhelmingly cited curatorial and publication activities as their reason for consulting born-digital archives, while external researchers typically focused on scholarly output. Research topics largely fell into three groups: the impact of software on design itself, the impact of software on design workflows, and the best way to represent or publish digital design records. Users were split regarding how much technical support the CCA needed to provide in terms of dealing with legacy formats and software environments, and while they understood the donor concerns about making collection material available online, some users suggested having a virtual private network (VPN) or virtual reading room option.[33]

It is worth noting that the survey's respondents constituted only a small sample of users who were all early adopters of born-digital design records and digital archives. As the use of CCA's digital archives grows, the range of users—particularly their technical comfort level and areas of research—is expected to broaden. Research into architectural records is increasingly informed by other humanities and social

---

33 Tessa Walsh, "CCA Access to Born-Digital Archives User Survey," May 4, 2017, www.bitarchivist.net/blog/2017-05-04-usersurvey/, captured at https://perma.cc/3F8Q-AQ8A.

science research, and, while it is possible to define certain research trends, the CCA has identified an ongoing need to converse with researchers to understand their changing needs. As such, the CCA has committed to providing and developing certain resources for both users and reference staff members to lower the barrier to access. This includes providing training, developing guides on common design formats, and, most significantly, developing a digital archives access interface called SCOPE[34] (described shortly).

In an architectural or design firm, these older files are used for reference when returning to a project years later, such as a renovation, or designers will borrow elements from previous models. In both cases the work is most likely performed by an expert user of the tools who has some knowledge of the workflows the firm used to create the older files. This technical proficiency and contextual awareness alleviates a significant amount of the access and mediation the archivist has to provide to the user. The institutional knowledge, and ability to speak directly with the original file creators (or members of the project team), is a privileged position that is not attainable for most archival researchers. This is part of the explanation for why design record creators have not felt the same levels of urgency in preparing their files for long-term access, because they are able to navigate the nuanced layers and potential technological barriers with far greater dexterity than an archivist can.[35]

The users of Cal Poly's digital design records have not been documented as thoroughly. Indeed, the demand for such records has been minimal to date. Anecdotally, design records in general (including both physical and digital) have been used by faculty and students for class instruction, course assignments, and projects as part of the architecture, art, and engineering curriculum; researchers analyzing some aspect of a building or particular designer; residents, occupants, operators, or developers of buildings that are documented in the library's

---

34   As of writing, SCOPE is the name for CCA's digital archives access interface, though it is expected to change in the coming year(s) pending copyright.
35   For further reading on this topic, see Daniel Cardaso-Llach, Eric Kaltman, Emek Erdolu, and Zachary Furste, "An Archive of Interfaces: Exploring the Potential of Emulation for Software Research, Pedagogy, and Design," *Proceedings of the ACM on Human-Computer Interaction* 5 (2021): 1–22, https://doi.org/10.1145/3476035; and Aliza Leventhal, Julie Collins, and Tessa Walsh, "Of Grasshoppers and Rhinos: A Visual Literacy Approach to Born-Digital Design Records," *American Archivist* 84 no. 2 (2021): 281–319, https://doi.org/10.17723/0360-9081-84.2.281.

collections; and internal Special Collections and Archives staff members using the records for exhibits, tours, and public presentations.

Regardless of the organizational context, it is clear that stakeholders, including firms, records creators, donors, archivists, and researchers, all need to be in an ongoing conversation to continue providing meaningful access to these challenging formats. The 2017 meeting at the Library of Congress, "Designing the Future Landscape: Digital Architecture, Design and Engineering Assets," assembled many of these stakeholders and suggested that preservation and access levels need to be appropriate in relation to current and future scholarship, concluding that

> Archivists, even with subject expertise, will most likely not be familiar with the majority of the digital file types their future collections will contain, and thus the archival community must begin to develop partnerships with practitioners and scholars for ongoing awareness and familiarity with the various design software and file formats in use.[36]

Especially given the challenging and often niche quality of digital design records, it is crucial that archival practice and digital preservation in this area is informed by record creators and scholars who are already familiar with the material.

Access in the Reading Room: Software Dependence and Emulation

Software dependency is arguably one of the largest hurdles to providing long-term access to digital design records. The issues of software dependence and processing remain and are often compounded by the demands of long-term access, whether that involves a ten-year retention schedule or an indefinite research mandate. What might be simply outdated software that still runs on contemporary computers at the moment of processing will often be genuine legacy software at the moment of access. Issues to consider include that many pieces of software will only run on certain operating systems, many different file formats will only render successfully in one type of software, and backward compatibility should not be taken as a given between versions of the same software. With all that in mind, how can an institution

---

36 Aliza Leventhal, *Designing the Future Landscape: Digital Architecture, Design & Engineering Assets* (Washington, DC: Library of Congress, March 12, 2018), 16–17, www.loc.gov/preservation/digital/meetings/DesigningTheFutureLandscapeReport.pdf, captured at https://perma.cc/GC8Y-LLVF.

provide long-term access to its software-dependent collection material, particularly digital design records?

At the CCA, access to born-digital archives is provided through two PC workstations running in Windows 10. Notably, the workstations, which are located in the study room, are closed network computers. Just as internal researchers are not allowed to take physical drawings to their desks and external researchers can't check out archival material, use of born-digital archives is strictly limited to the study room workstations. This means that the internet (beyond the cca.qc.ca domain) and CCA server access is blocked, and the optical disk drive and USB ports are set to read-only.

One workstation is loaded with a broad but incomplete range of CAD software, including Bentley View V8i, QuickView Plus, Rhinoceros 5, form•Z versions 6.7.3 and 8.5, VectorWorks 2015, as well as complete software suites from Adobe, Autodesk, and Microsoft Office. This software is generally contemporary and the CCA holds a license to them; however, this also includes a number of pieces of legacy software (namely form•Z) donated by vendors. The majority of CCA's born-digital collection material is at least partially accessible through this environment. However, accessing born-digital archives through a contemporary machine running largely contemporary software has drawbacks. Although much of the material will at least open, it is not uncommon to see files that are obviously a low-fidelity version of the original, with broken external references, atypical formatting, and missing data. For the files that do "look right," it's still often impossible to validate that the data is authentic or complete, as data validation is not possible for many file types, particularly those created in vendor-specific design software (e.g., form•Z).

For these reasons, some researchers prefer to open digital design files directly in the files' original software environment. The second workstation at the CCA is outfitted with VMWare, virtualization software that runs two stock virtual machines (VMs): Windows NT and Windows XP.

The reading room environment at Cal Poly's Special Collections and Archives provides access to born-digital records in much the same way as CCA. However, instead of two desktop computers, Cal Poly has one Macintosh laptop dedicated to born-digital collection access. Internet access and USB ports are disabled on the laptop, so records cannot be copied without acknowledgment to a location outside of the reading room. Reference copies are made available on a case-by-case basis, such as for records that have no sensitive, private, or rights-restricted information, or for copy requests that identify a specific set of records; by default, indiscriminate or wholesale copying of born-digital collections is restricted. At this time, no specialized software has been loaded on the laptop, but Cal Poly does currently have educational licenses for software titles such as AutoCAD, Revit, ArcGIS, InDesign, Photoshop, and Illustrator. In addition to these licensed titles, Cal Poly plans to install free readers. The digital design records must be requested one to two days before the researcher's visit (much like physical records stored offsite must be requested in advance). Staff members must download the records from the local network drive to the reading room laptop and then examine the records to note any access requirements or challenges.

Having VMs does allow the CCA to provide a broader range of access to its collection material, especially software. Born-digital design records are complex digital objects; they are often software-dependent and rely on various external references, such as data libraries and images, to be rendered properly. Therefore, the software used to open the file needs to interpret all the related data in a specific way to ensure that the rendering is accurate. For some born-digital design records, this means that the only way to make sure that all the data is being interpreted properly is to access the record with its original software version. However, creating these emulation environments has a significant technological overhead, and it's presently not possible for the majority of individual institutions to provide the broad range of emulation environments necessary for complete access to their collections.[37]

The technology for doing so is rapidly advancing, as demonstrated by the recent development of the Emulation-as-a-Service Infrastructure (EaaSI) program of work.[38] The makers of EaaSI aim to improve access to legacy software and collection material by creating an infrastructure

---

37 Aliza Leventhal, *Designing the Future Landscape*.
38 EaaSI is described in greater detail in "Module 25: Emerging Best Practices in the Accession, Preservation, and Emulation of Born-Digital Design Materials." Additional information can be found at "Emulation-as-a-Service Infrastructure," Software Preservation Network, https://www.softwarepreservationnetwork.org/emulation-as-a-service-infrastructure.

to provide networked access to shared emulation environments, using software contributed by a variety of organizations and individuals. At the time of writing, EaaSI is being rolled out, and some organizations are actively preparing to implement and contribute to the project.

For example, as part of a larger digital design preservation effort, the CCA is currently stabilizing its Oliver Witte American Institute of Architects (AIA) software collection. The AIA received a large range of software to review throughout the 1980s and 1990s. The collection contains approximately 400 titles stored on approximately 800 disks, largely 3.5" and 5.25" floppy disks, that the CCA received on loan to stabilize contents. The project is to disk image the media and to capture some contextual information, such as the technical requirements. With this collection, it will be possible to render a CAD file in an emulation of the environment in which it was created. By disk imaging each piece of software, the CCA hopes to provide access to this material via EaaSI in the next few years. As such, efforts to collect and preserve software support the larger goal of maintaining long-term collection access. Even a software collection of that scale represents only a fraction of the design software on the market in recent decades, and acquiring older software (the first hurdle to overcome in the journey to build emulation environments) will continue to be a challenge in and of itself.[39]

Unfortunately, it can be difficult to rely on software companies to preserve their old software and to expect them to give access to old versions.[40] An important number of CAD software companies from the 1990s have either closed or been bought. For records that are currently being created, the subscription and browser-based model for design software will add another layer of complexity to future reuse of contemporary design records, as institutions no longer have ongoing access to software outside of the subscription model.

---

39 Other initiatives toward maintaining access to older software include projects and collections from the computer gaming community; the Internet Archive's software collection; the advocacy work from the Software Preservation Network (SPN); the harvesting of publicly available software by the Software Heritage Network; and the National Institute of Standards and Technology's (NIST) National Software Reference Library.
40 Documentation on software releases may be found online and is helpful to identifying which version of the software should be retrieved for emulation. For example, Shaan Hurley has listed all AutoCAD releases at https://autodesk.blogs.com/between_the_lines/autocad-release-history.html.

If software dependencies prevent access to a series of files at Cal Poly, it is possible that staff could overcome such obstacles through emulation, because Cal Poly staff members have gained some experience with the EaaSI service through participation in the Fostering Communities of Practice (FCoP) project.[41] However, given the small size of the Special Collections and Archives staff and the needs of the department's users, initial interactions with researchers would focus on providing access to design files in archival formats or original files in backward-compatible environments.

Emulation as a strategy can bring users closer to the original experience of interacting with a digital design record. However, it is worth noting that it may not always be preferred universally by researchers in an access environment. The CCA user survey found that users prefer working with legacy files on contemporary software and machines, and they rated emulators and VMs as the second-best option. Similarly, Julia Kim, the former National Digital Stewardship Member at New York University's Fales Library and Special Collections, conducted a similar user survey and found that users "all found the emulation's authentically slow-processing speed and instability impediment enough to prefer contemporary computing system access." She notes that "access by any means, and ease of access were stressed by the majority," suggesting that overcoming the high technological barrier required by emulation for both users and staff is less important than simple, user-friendly, and timely access to materials.[42] In the CCA user study, Walsh suggests that contemporary access environments and emulation "should be pursued in parallel."[43]

In most design firms, older files are opened in contemporary software. Firms rarely maintain more than a few versions of a software program at any given time, due to the significant drain on computing power and to comply with the immediate needs of the practitioner. The possibility of data loss or issues around file integrity are accepted

---

41 Software Preservation Network, "FCoP," 2021, accessed August 22, 2019, https://www.softwarepreservationnetwork.org/fcop.

42 Julia Kim, "Researcher Interactions with Born-Digital: Out of the Frying Pan and into the Reading Room," *bloggERS* (blog), Society of American Archivists Electronic Records Section, January 28, 2016, https://saaers.wordpress.com/2016/01/28/researcher-interactions-with-born-digital-out-of-the-frying-pan-and-into-the-reading-room, captured at https://perma.cc/3F6J-9LXV.

43 Walsh, "CCA Access to Born-Digital Archives User Survey."

as part of the workflow for using older design files. The strength of the current practitioner's ability to navigate in the current and recent versions of design software often allow them to overcome the confusion or frustration of losing some information when reading older files in newer versions of software. With almost unfettered access to project records, the critical role of the archivist and IT staff in a firm is to ensure read-only copies of older project files and that the project folders are well kept to facilitate reasonable findability by future employees.

In a corporate setting, having an understanding of the software used by the employees can help in identifying whether specific assets are at risk of becoming inaccessible. If software stored on media is available, it could be useful to disk image the media and to document its technical specifications, which would be the baseline requirements to ensure potential future reuse.

Need for Custom Development

Best practices in digital preservation and access have been rapidly formalizing. However, it is increasingly clear that niche formats, including born-digital design records, require special considerations. Institutions should consider looking for or developing specialized tools and workflows as needed to overcome these hurdles.

At the CCA, it was clear that special development to its digital preservation system, Archivematica, was necessary. Archivematica is configurable so that DIPs can be created at the moment of ingest. However, the out-of-the-box DIP creation script restructured the files in a way that broke many of the external references between files. External references are common in CAD formats. They occur when one file uses the content of another file, often a still image (e.g., a JPEG or TIFF file) to add texture, images, color, and so on, to a design file. For the CAD file to be able to find its external reference, the file path and file name both need to remain the same as the original. However, Archivematica changes the file path and file name by default during DIP creation.

The CCA sponsored development with Artefactual to build a custom "CCA-style" DIP creation workflow that preserves external references with a relative file path. (Absolute file paths will always be broken and are often broken at the moment of transfer from the

Table 2. Comparison of CCA DIP structure to the default Archivematica DIP structure

Default Archivematica DIP Structure	Current CCA DIP Structure
/dip-name	/dip-name
/dip-name	/objects
/objects	DIP.zip
uuid-file1.jpg	/objects
uuid-file2.jpg	/files
uuid-file3.jpg	file1.jpg
mets.xml	file2.jpg
/ocr	file3.jpg
/thumbnails	/diskimage
	disk.img
	mets.xml

donor.) Time stamps and original file names are also restored, so that the access copy is as close to the original SIP as possible (Table 2).[44]

In addition, the CCA user survey revealed that users would prefer higher levels of access and discoverability:

> CCA staff and researchers want to be able to search, sort, and browse through extensive item-level metadata for the individual digital files in the digital archives. They want to be able to do this within archives as a whole and within particular projects, while seeing the archival context for each individual digital file.

The survey found that "100% of respondents . . . would want an access interface to provide detailed item-level records for each individual digital file."[45] Meanwhile, providing access copies required the digital archivist to query the Archivematica Storage Service to produce DIPs on demand. This involved coordinating reference staff, archives staff, IT staff, and the researcher in what was a time-consuming and labor-intensive workflow.

---

44   The CCA-style DIP creation script can be used freely and is available at https://github.com/artefactual/automation-tools.
45   Walsh, "CCA Access to Born-Digital Archives User Survey."

As a result, the CCA, in collaboration with Artefactual Systems, developed SCOPE.[46] SCOPE is a free and open-source born-digital archives access interface. It provides users with direct access to the entire body of CCA's born-digital archives. Users can search for individual files in and across records using keywords and filters. This allows users to do more traditional, top-down archival research in individual collections or search across the entire born-digital archives. The latter is especially powerful in facilitating more digital humanities or software-driven research questions, where users are often less interested in the work of a particular architect and more interested in a timeframe or file format, regardless of its creator. Once the user has selected materials of interest, they can download an access copy of the files directly from the Archivematica DIP Storage Server to CCA's locked-down workstations. The adoption of SCOPE has greatly reduced reference workflows and improved discoverability and responds to current research trends in digital design records.

In a firm, the "researcher" often has access to all unclassified project records on the firm's server. This allows for unfettered searchability and emphasizes the need for intuitive and consistently implemented project folder structures for organizing project files. This is an area in which many firms struggle, as individual idiosyncratic practices appear throughout the highly iterative and often stressful timelines punctuated by many deadlines. Understanding a firm's organizational practices for its project records, including how employees package project files for milestones and deliverables, is critical context for understanding the workflows and significance of particular files created during a project.

As discussed at the 2017 "Designing the Future Landscape: Digital Architecture, Design & Engineering Assets" summit at the Library of Congress, several firms have experienced some level of loss of information in a file or the inability to re-open a file years later. During the second panel of this summit, practitioners Noémie Lafaurie-Debany from Balmori Associates and Greg Schleusner from HOK (formerly

---

46 SCOPE can be downloaded and used freely. The CCA welcomes comments, questions, and contributions. It is available at https://github.com/CCA-Public/scope. Additional information about the collaborative development process and contributing to open-source projects can be found here: Kelly Stewart and Stefana Breitwieser, "SCOPE: A Digital Archives Access Interface," *Code4Lib Journal,* February 14, 2019, https://journal.code4lib.org/articles/14283.

Hellmuth, Obata + Kassabaum) explained that even with the best of intentions, the pressure of a deadline might result in the lapse in the project team's maintaining a file formatting standard when there are no immediate ramifications or consequences for this delinquency.[47] This offers a window into the prioritization of a design firm's attention and resources and is a strong indicator that without a time or cost-saving business case for developing archival workflows, they will not be created. Sasaki experienced some success through an in-house search tool that crawled the firm's active and archives project servers to produce search results of indexed project files. In addition to this search tool, Sasaki implemented a formalized project folder structure across all projects to establish better control and a shared practice for organizing project files. The value of finding and controlling project files has become a higher priority for many firms, especially those with multiple offices, and has been taken up by several firms under Knowledge Management initiatives.

Discussions in the digital preservation and design records communities also suggest that there are a number of additional advancements that would greatly improve access. This includes, for example, the suggestion by both Julia Kim and Tessa Walsh of multiple arrangements of born-digital objects to allow users to discover and make sense of a group of records in multiple ways.[48] The various points of inquiry around born-digital design records may mean that archives staff members will want to provide additional access points and navigation functionality. Archivists will continue to need to learn from the worlds of software studies and digital humanities to better prepare and future-proof digital design collections for preservation and access workflows.

Conclusion

Organizations dedicated to collecting and providing access to design records, no matter their collecting scope and researcher expectations, are experiencing additional challenges, but also opportunities,

---

47 Kristine Fallon, Greg Schleusner, and Rick Zurray, "'How We Create and Save': An Insider's Look at Lifecycle Management." Presentation, "Designing the Future Landscape: Digital Architecture, Design and Engineering Assets," Washington, DC, November 16, 2017.
48 Kim, "Researcher Interactions with Born-Digital"; Walsh, "CCA Access to Born-Digital Archives User Survey."

as their collections begin to include born-digital design records. The entire process of collecting design records will need to change as organizations begin conversations earlier and much more frequently with record creators and potential donors. With earlier intervention and engagement between archivists and born-digital design file creators, critical information about the functionality of software and intention of design through using the wide variety of programs will allow organizations to better plan the technological infrastructure required to ingest, preserve, and provide access to current and future born-digital design collections.

Understanding who users are and how their research might be best supported is a good first step in defining local access best practices. Access is the fundamental reason for doing work in digital preservation and archives. The access challenges particular to born-digital design records are clear and include issues of software dependency and high technological barriers that are exacerbated by a long-term access mandate. In many organizations, contemporary access to legacy files is a sufficient level of playback. Other organizations, particularly those with an academic research mandate, might be more interested in serving files using an emulated environment to ensure higher levels of authenticity and fidelity. Overall, by remaining flexible and responsive to users' needs and expectations, organizations can provide sustained access to their digital design records. And by understanding the design record creator's workflow and the technological tools they use throughout their process, archivists can facilitate more effective conversations with potential donors and researchers and develop creative technological solutions to researcher requests.

Furthermore, it is critical that any archivist working with design collections become more familiar and comfortable with the fundamentals of digital preservation. Through this expanded scope and skill development, archivists with subject expertise will be able to better connect and engage with born-digital design files, as well as with the creators of those files. Regardless of an organization's collecting scope, anticipated designated community, and resource levels for technological investment, establishing connections with record creators and opening a dialogue with potential donors will support a more sustainable collecting, preserving, and access-providing practice. Remembering that all archival collections, from *fonds* to selective donations, are not entirely complete is useful context when considering the potential loss of data and capabilities in collecting born-digital design files. Rather than fixating on keeping *everything* for fear it will one day have a research purpose, archivists must continue to embrace the institution's collection scope and policy and leverage discussions with donors to ensure that the design intent and development are captured in one form or another.

Appendix A: CCA Format Policy Registry

Introduction

General Introduction

The CCA Format Policy Registry[49] (FPR) defines the file format policies implemented by CCA's digital preservation program. CCA always keeps each digital object accessioned into the Collection in its original file format. For files in some formats, derivative versions in **Preservation Formats** are also created and stored alongside original files in the Dark Archive. The FPR defines which file formats receive this type of treatment.

  Preservation Formats have qualities that increase their likelihood of being usable over a longer period of time. These qualities include:
- Wide use and support
- Stable and preferably open specifications
- Uncompressed or lossless compression

When Preservation Formats are created, they are stored alongside the original files in the Dark Archive in Archival Information Packages (AIPs).

  For consultation by users, files are delivered in Dissemination Information Packages (DIPs), which by default contain copies of files with their original filenames, last modified dates, and file formats preserved. This is an intentional choice to ensure that complex digital objects with links between files (CAD files, HTML/CSS/JS web assets, source code, et al) continue to work in the packages we provide for end-user access. When original formats prove difficult for researchers, CCA can provide normalized preservation files on demand.

Levels of Support

Levels of support indicate CCA's ability to maintain the usability of a digital object over time. These assessments are made on the basis of file formats. CCA has three levels of support: Bit-level, Watch, and Full.
All files in the CCA Dark Archive are stored on secure and backed-up servers and are regularly audited using checksums to ensure that no files have corrupted or changed in any way.

---

49 This is version 3, approved August 21, 2019.

Bit-level

The minimum level of treatment that all digital objects accessioned into the CCA Collection receive.

At this level, CCA preserves the bitstream (i.e., the 1s and 0s that comprise the code) of a file exactly as-is. No format migration is performed. This practice ensures that CCA is able to provide an exact copy of original files over time. It does not necessarily ensure that files will be usable by software available at a future point in time.

Any formats not explicitly mentioned in the Format Policy Registry are preserved by CCA at the Bit-level.

Watch

File formats at this level of support are those for which CCA is currently only able to offer Bit-level support, but for which we hope to provide Full support in the future. This may be because the formats are common or highly valued at CCA (such as computer-aided design models) or because there is reason to believe that developments in the software industry and digital preservation community will make it easier to perform high-quality batch file format migrations or other means of access (e.g. emulation) in the future.

Full

File formats at this level of support are those for which CCA has high confidence in their long-term usability, either because the original format is already a preferred Preservation Format, or because CCA consistently and reliably normalizes files in this format to a documented Preservation Format.

Format Policy Registry

Text and Word Processing

Type	File Formats	Preservation Format	Level of Support	Notes
Plain text	txt, csv, tsv	Original	Full	Preferred format
Rich text	rtf	Original	Full	
Microsoft Office Open XML Word	docx, docm	Original	Full	Preferred format
Microsoft Word and Works (legacy)	doc, wps	docx	Full	
OpenDocument Text Document	odt	Original	Full	Preferred format
Clarisworks Word Processor	cwk	odt	Full	
WordPerfect	wpd	odt	Full	
Markup languages and scripts	py, sh, rb, md, xml, et al.	Original	Full	
WordStar	ws	Original	Watch	J

Presentation

Type	File Formats	Preservation Format	Level of Support	Notes
Microsoft Office Open XML Word	pptx	Original	Full	Preferred format
Microsoft Powerpoint (legacy)	ppt	pptx	Full	
OpenDocument Presentation Document	odp	Original	Full	Preferred format
Keynote	key	Original	Watch	

Portable Document Format (PDF)

Type	File Formats	Preservation Format	Level of Support	Notes
PDF/A	pdf/a	Original	Full	Preferred format
Standard PDF	pdf	pdf/a	Full	

Desktop Publishing

Type	File Formats	Preservation Format	Level of Support	Notes
Quark XPress	qxd, qxp, qxl, qxt	Original	Watch	Files may be selectively manually normalized to PDF/A during processing on a case-by-case basis.
Adobe InDesign	indd	Original	Watch	Files may be selectively manually normalized to PDF/A during processing on a case-by-case basis.
Adobe Pagemaker	dmd, pmt	Original	Watch	Files may be selectively manually normalized to PDF/A during processing on a case-by-case basis.

Data Sets

Spreadsheets

Type	File Formats	Preservation Format	Level of Support	Notes
Microsoft Office Open XML Excel	xlsx	Original	Full	Preferred format
Microsoft Excel (legacy)	xls	xlsx	Full	
OpenDocument Spreadsheet	ods	Original	Full	Preferred format
Clarisworks Spreadsheet	cwkx	ods	Full	
Lotus 1-2-3	wk1, wks	Original	Watch	

Databases

Type	File Formats	Preservation Format	Level of Support	Notes
SQL-based	various	Original	Watch	Preferred format
NoSQL	various	Original	Watch	

Architecture and Design Models/Drawings

Type	File Formats	Preservation Format	Level of Support	Notes
Computer-aided design (CAD) and 3D modeling	dwg, dxf, dwf, 3ds, max, 3dm, dgn, ma, mb, wire, fmz, stl, igs, step	Original	Watch	
Building Information Modeling (BIM)	rvt, ifc	Original	Watch	IFC is ideal format, though scalable migration pathways remain unclear.

Images

Raster Images

Type	File Formats	Preservation Format	Level of Support	Notes
TIF	tif	Original	Full	Preferred format
GIF (animated or still)	gif	Original	Full	Preferred format
Windows Bitmap	bmp, jpg, jp2, pct, png, psd, tga	uncompressed tif	Full	
JPEG	jpg	uncompressed tif	Full	
JP2 (JPEG 2000 part 1)	jp2	uncompressed tif	Full	
PICT	pct	uncompressed tif	Full	
PNG	png	uncompressed tif	Full	
Adobe Photoshop	psd	uncompressed tif	Full	
Truevision TGA Bitmap	tga	uncompressed tif	Full	
Silicon Graphics Image	sgi	uncompressed tif	Full	

Vector Images

Type	File Formats	Preservation Format	Level of Support	Notes
Scalable Vector Graphics	svg	Original	Full	Preferred format
Illustrator files	ai, eps	svg	Full	

Camera Raw

Type	File Formats	Preservation Format	Level of Support	Notes
Digital Negative	dng	Original	Full	Preferred format
Camera raw formats	3frm, arw, cr2, crw, dcr, dng, erf, kdc, mrw, nef, orf, pef, raf, raw, x3f, ari, bay, cap, data, dcs, drf, eip, fff, iiq, k25, mdc, mef, mos, nrw, obm, ptx, pxn, r3d, rwl, rw2, rwz, sr2, srf, srw	Original	Watch	Camera raw files may be normalized to Adobe DNG prior to ingest if they belong to the Photography collection or are particularly important to the work of an archives' creator and CCA does not have corresponding raster images.

Video

Type	File Formats	Preservation Format	Level of Support	Notes
Matroska	mkv	Original	Full	Preferred format (ffv1 encoding)
MOV	mov	ffv1/matroska	Full	
AVI	avi	ffv1/matroska	Full	
MPEG-1	mpg, mpeg	ffv1/matroska	Full	
MPEG-2	mpg, mpeg, mp2	ffv1/matroska	Full	
MPEG-4	mp4	ffv1/matroska	Full	
Macromedia FLV	flv	ffv1/matroska	Full	
Material Exchange Format	mxf	ffv1/matroska	Full	
Windows Media Video	wmv	ffv1/matroska	Full	
Digital video from tape-based media such as MiniDV, DVCAM, DVCPro, Digital-8, D1, D2, D3, D5, D9, HDCAM, and HDCAM SR	DV, HDV	Original/avi	Full	Wrapped in AVI container. Digital video contains metadata about the original recording that would be lost in transcoding to other formats such as ffv1/matroska.
Digital betacam (Digibeta)	DV	ffv1/matroska		Digital Betacam doesn't allow you to keep the original encoding as stored on tape, and should be captured using the same codec as for analogue tapes (10-bit uncompressed files wrapped in AVI container).

Note: CCA's preferred lightweight access format for streaming and internal use is H264 (video)/AAC (audio)/MPEG-4 (container).

Presentation

Type	File Formats	Preservation Format	Level of Support	Notes
Microsoft Office Open XML Word	pptx	Original	Full	Preferred format
Microsoft Powerpoint (legacy)	ppt	pptx	Full	
OpenDocument Presentation Document	odp	Original	Full	Preferred format
Keynote	key	Original	Watch	

Note: CCA's preferred lightweight access format for audio streaming and internal use is MP3.

E-publications

Type	File Formats	Preservation Format	Level of Support	Notes
EPUB	Epub	Original	Full	Preferred format

Geospatial (GIS) data

Type	File Formats	Preservation Format	Level of Support	Notes
ArcGIS geodatabase file	gdb	Original	Watch	
Shapefile	shp	Original	Watch	

Video games

Type	File Formats	Preservation Format	Level of Support	Notes
All formats		Original	Bit-level	

Executables, installation files, and binaries

Type	File Formats	Preservation Format	Level of Support	Notes
All formats		Original	Bit-level	

Appendix B: CCA Submission of Digital Files Questionnaire

Please complete the following form and submit it along with the digital files requested.

In the instance where a question might be answered better through an existing document, please include it in the email and specify which question it is assigned to.

The series of questions that follow are designed to serve several functions for both the CCA and also for the donor. The information sheet is designed to facilitate: email and specify which question it is assigned to.

- An understanding of individual files, their interrelation to each other, and their relationship to specific projects
- Sorting and organization of files
- The selection of files for archival ingest
- Access to the files
- Long-term preservation of the files
- Monetary appraisal and evaluation (if applicable)

It is advised to use a sufficient amount of time to allow the donor to:

- Consider who within your organization can best answer the questions
- Allow these individuals to create thorough responses

In order to be most useful, responses to these questions should be carefully considered and sufficiently thorough. It may be helpful to note that the questions can be generally described as being either computing/information technology oriented or organization/project management oriented.

1. GENERAL QUESTIONS

1.1 ORGANIZATION AND PROJECTS

- Please describe your firm (i.e., number of employees, principals, year of foundation)
  _____

- Please list the projects that you are submitting
  _____

- Are some of the submitted files unrelated to a specific project? (i.e., website, database, etc.)
  _____

- What is the time period that is covered by all of the donations collectively? (This will be the start date of the earliest project and the finish date of the most recent project.)
  _____

1.2 DIGITAL FILES RELATED PROCEDURES

- What is your file naming protocol and can you provide us with a document describing this?
  _____

- Do you have a naming protocol in place for layers contained within files, i.e., CAD, Adobe Suite, etc.?
  _____

- If some of your files have dependencies, i.e., linked files or associated files that are essential, do you have systems in place for preserving those links? If yes, please describe.
  _____

- Do you use versioning software? If 'yes,' please name this software. If 'no,' are there specific instructions given to staff for how to assign versions to files (i.e., putting certain files in specific directory, naming, etc.)?
  _____

- Do you backup your files? If 'yes,' please describe the software and/or hardware that you have used to do this over time.
  _____

- Indicate any known limitations to accessing your backups.
  _____

- Is a password required to access the software? If 'yes,' please provide.
  _____

- In creating files, did you rely on 'share folders' or libraries for certain resources like fonts, surface textures, etc.? If these 'share folders' become dissociated with files, the files can lose information. If you used these 'share folders', please:

    Specify the topology _____

    Indicate if these libraries are included with the submitted files _____

    Provide these files with the submitted files _____

1.3 COMPUTING AND NETWORK ENVIRONMENT

- Were the files kept on a network or local drive?

  _____

- Do you have a records management system or document management system used internally (i.e., Microsoft Sharepoint or other)? If 'yes':
  What operating system (OS) do your server and workstations exist on?

  _____

- Please name the records management software that you use.

  _____

- Before submitting a file to the system, do you add any metadata to the file (i.e., keywords)? If 'yes,' please name the fields that are regularly filled.

  _____

- Do you rely on a specific vocabulary for entering metadata? If 'yes,' please describe the vocabulary used. Please provide a document describing the vocabulary, if possible.

  _____

2.1 PROJECT HISTORY

- Please describe the project.

  _____

- Do you have an updated document containing the project schedule?

  _____

- Can you provide us with a list of the names and titles of personnel that worked on the project(s)? This will be useful in determining what role various people may have played in creating and/or modifying electronic documents.

  _____

2.2 PROJECT: DIGITAL FILES

Understanding what software was used to create a file is essential for its access and preservation. Also, understanding the information associated with a file, such as its name, date, or modification history, can facilitate several things, including a sense of how a project was executed. This same information can also be essential in all stages of compiling a digital archive, from accessing files to arranging and selecting them.

- Describe the design process in relation to the various software used. In particular, we are interested in knowing a typical software workflow leading to the files that we are receiving.

  _____

- What is the logic of the file structure, and how does it relate to the evolution of the project?

  _____

- Are passwords needed to access certain files or software? If 'yes,' please provide.

  _____

- Was any custom software (non-proprietary software) used to create any of these files? If 'yes,' do you still have this software?

    _____

    Please provide this software on CD with any installation instructions.
- What software did you use to create CAD/BIM files?

    _____

- If files were created by the use of several software packages, please describe the work process that involved these software packages. (Please give details of workflow.)

    _____

- Knowing how files may have changed since their creation is useful information. Should we be aware of any particular file migrations (conversions) that may have affected groups of files? Please consider and describe.

    _____

- Do you use parametric scripting during your design process? If yes, please provide the coded script if it is still accessible.

    _____

2.2 QUESTIONS REGARDING INTELLECTUAL PROPERTY

- I am familiar with the digital files included in the proposed donation and I can comment on the status of the intellectual property.

    ☐ YES
    ☐ NO

    If the answer is NO, who at your firm is familiar with the intellectual property of this material?

    _____

- Do you or your firm own copyright to all the work produced by employees or other contracted workers (i.e., they are "work for hire") in relation to the donated digital files?

    ☐ YES
    ☐ NO

- Do any employees, interns, consultants, or other collaborators own any intellectual property to any part of the digital files that you are donating?

    ☐ YES
    ☐ NO

- Have you written any original software or code in relation to the digital files that you are donating?

    ☐ YES
    ☐ NO

Design Methodology

Please check the appropriate boxes if the software is used during the specific phase of design.

Conceptual Phase	Design Development	Construction Documents
Schematic Diagrams, Research, Concept Sketches	Preliminary design of building system with consultation with engineers, Presentation of design development to Owner, Review of project cost estimate with Owner, Owner review and input, Design finalized.	Working drawings and specifications production, Owner review

Conceptual Phase

SOFTWARE

- ☐ AutoDesk® 3Ds Max®
- ☐ AutoCAD® (AutoCAD® For Mac, AutoCAD® Architecture) Autodesk®
- ☐ Revit®
- ☐ form•Z™
- ☐ Maya®
- ☐ CATIA
- ☐ SolidWorks
- ☐ Graphisoft® ArchiCAD®
- ☐ Digital Project
- ☐ Rhino (Rhinoceros®)
- ☐ Sketch Up
- ☐ Adobe® illustrator®
- ☐ Microstation®
- ☐ Adobe® Indesign®
- ☐ Adobe® Photoshop®
- ☐ Non-Proprietary Software
- ☐ Other _____

PLUG-INS

Name: _____
Associated Software: _____
Name: _____
Associated Software: _____

Design Development

SOFTWARE

- ☐ AutoDesk® 3Ds Max®
- ☐ AutoCAD® (AutoCAD® For Mac, AutoCAD® Architecture) Autodesk®
- ☐ Revit®
- ☐ form•Z™
- ☐ Maya®
- ☐ CATIA
- ☐ SolidWorks
- ☐ Graphisoft® ArchiCAD®
- ☐ Digital Project
- ☐ Rhino (Rhinoceros®)
- ☐ Sketch Up
- ☐ Adobe® illustrator®
- ☐ Microstation®
- ☐ Adobe® Indesign®
- ☐ Adobe® Photoshop®
- ☐ Non-Proprietary Software
- ☐ Other _____

PLUG-INS

Name: _____
Associated Software: _____
Name: _____
Associated Software: _____

Construction Documents

SOFTWARE

- ☐ AutoDesk® 3Ds Max®
- ☐ AutoCAD® (AutoCAD® For Mac, AutoCAD® Architecture) Autodesk®
- ☐ Revit®
- ☐ form•Z™
- ☐ Maya®
- ☐ CATIA
- ☐ SolidWorks
- ☐ Graphisoft® ArchiCAD®
- ☐ Digital Project
- ☐ Rhino (Rhinoceros®)
- ☐ Sketch Up
- ☐ Adobe® illustrator®
- ☐ Microstation®
- ☐ Adobe® Indesign®
- ☐ Adobe® Photoshop®
- ☐ Non-Proprietary Software
- ☐ Other _____

PLUG-INS

Name: _____
Associated Software: _____
Name: _____
Associated Software: _____

- Have any employees, interns, consultants, or other collaborators written any codes or software which they claim as being their intellectual property in any of the digital files that you are donating?
    - ☐ YES
    - ☐ NO

- Have you or anyone in your office incorporated any works protected by copyright, trademarks, or patents belonging to third parties that are part of the donated digital files?
    - ☐ YES
    - ☐ NO

- Have you cleared any copyrights or obtained permissions to works that have been incorporated in the donated digital files for which there may be restrictions?
    - ☐ YES
    - ☐ NO

- Are there any legal requirements in regard to the crediting of any of the donated materials (e.g., do any employees, collaborators, or consultants need to be credited when the work is presented)?
    - ☐ YES
    - ☐ NO

Bibliography

Berdini, Annalise, Charles Macquarie, Shira Peltzman, and Kate Tasker. *UC Guidelines for Born-Digital Archival Description, Version 1.* October 2017. GitHub. https://github.com/uc-borndigital-ckg/uc-guidelines/blob/master/CompletePDF_UCGuidelinesForBorn-DigitalArchivalDescription_v1.pdf .

Consultative Committee for Space Data Systems. "Reference Model for an Open Archival Information System (OAIS): Recommended Practice, CCSDS 650.0-M-2." Washington, DC: CCSDS Secretariat, June 2012. https://public.ccsds.org/pubs/650x0m2.pdf, captured at https://perma.cc/K5VR-S45E.

DFXML Working Group. "DFXML Schema 1.2.0." GitHub, December 12, 2017. https://github.com/dfxml-working-group/dfxml_schema.

Eastwood, Terry. "Digital Appraisal: Variations on a Theme." Keynote address for the Conference on Appraisal in the Digital World, Rome, Italy, November 15–16, 2007. www.interpares.org/display_file.cfm?doc=ip2_dissemination_cp_eastwood_delos_2007.pdf, captured at https://perma.cc/XW2R-CM79.

Kristine Fallon, Greg Schleusner, and Rick Zurray, "'How We Create and Save': An Insider's Look at Lifecycle Management." Presentation at "Designing the Future Landscape: Digital Architecture, Design and Engineering Assets," Washington, DC, November 16, 2017. https://youtu.be/8XMko7E49E4?t=4853.

Greene, Mark A., and Dennis Meissner. "More Product, Less Process: Revamping Traditional Archival Processing." *American Archivist* 68, no. 2 (2005): 208–263. https://doi.org/10.17723/aarc.68.2.c741823776k65863.

Kim, Julia. "Researcher Interactions with Born-Digital: Out of the Frying Pan and into the Reading Room." *bloggERS* (blog). Society of American Archivists Electronic Records Section, January 28, 2016. https://saaers.wordpress.com/2016/01/28/researcher-interactions-with-born-digital-out-of-the-frying-pan-and-into-the-reading-room, captured at https://perma.cc/3F6J-9LXV.

Kunze, J., J. Littman, E. Madden, J. Scancella, and C. Adams. "The BagIt File Packaging Format (V1.0)." IETF Tools, September 17,

2018. Accessed August 27, 2019. https://tools.ietf.org/html/draft-kunze-bagit-17.

Leventhal, Aliza. *Designing the Future Landscape: Digital Architecture, Design & Engineering Assets.* Washington, DC: Library of Congress, 2018. www.loc.gov/preservation/digital/meetings/DesigningTheFutureLandscapeReport.pdf, captured at https://perma.cc/GC8Y-LLVF.

Library of Congress. "Sustainability of Digital Formats: Planning for Library of Congress Collections." 2021. www.loc.gov/preservation/digital/formats/fdd/descriptions.shtml.

National Institute of Building Sciences buildingSMART alliance. "United States National CAD Standard – V6: Module 1 – Drawing Set Organization." 2014. www.nationalcadstandard.org/ncs6/pdfs/ncs6_uds1.pdf, captured at https://perma.cc/QH27-UMK7.

"PREMIS: Preservation Metadata Maintenance Activity." Library of Congress. Accessed August 30, 2019. https://www.loc.gov/standards/premis/index.html.

Santamaria, Daniel A. *Extensible Processing for Archives and Special Collections: Reducing Processing Backlogs.* Chicago: ALA Neal-Schuman, 2015.

Simon Fraser University Archives and Records Management Department. "Format Policy Registry (FPR)." July 18, 2017. https://www.sfu.ca/content/dam/sfu/archives/PDFs/DigitalPreservation/LinksResources/FormatPolicyRegistry.pdf, captured at https://perma.cc/8JM3-MK4U.

Software Preservation Network. "FCoP." 2021. www.softwarepreservationnetwork.org/fcop.

Tessa Walsh. "CCA Access to Born-Digital Archives User Survey." *BitArchivist* (blog). May 4, 2017. www.bitarchivist.net/blog/2017-05-04-usersurvey, captured at https://perma.cc/3F8Q-AQ8A.